D0370194

The Modern
Numerology

The Modern Numerology

A Practical Guide to the Meaning and Influence of Numbers

JOHN KING

BLANDFORD

133.335

KIN

For my father, Frederick Ypres King

First published in the UK 1996 by Blandford

A Cassell Imprint

Cassell Plc, Wellington House
125 Strand, London WC2R 0BB

Copyright © 1996 John King

The right of John King to be identified as author of this work has been
asserted by him in accordance with the provisions of the UK Copyright,
Designs and Patents Act 1988

All rights reserved. No part of this book may be reproduced or
transmitted in any form or by any means, electronic or mechanical,
including photocopying, recording or any information storage and
retrieval system, without permission in writing from the copyright holder
and publisher.

Distributed in the United States by Sterling Publishing Co., Inc.
387 Park Avenue South, New York, NY 10016–8810

Distributed in Australia by Capricorn Link (Australia) Pty Ltd
2/13 Carrington Road, Castle Hill, NSW 2154

**British Library Cataloguing-in-Publication Data
A Catalogue entry for this title is available from
the British Library**

ISBN 0-7137-2560-5

Design and Typesetting Ben Cracknell

Printed and bound in Great Britain by Hartnolls Ltd, Bodmin, Cornwall

CONTENTS

1·2·3·4·5·6·7·8·9·10·11·12·13·14·15·16·17·18·19·20·21·22·23·24·25·26

ACKNOWLEDGMENTS

I am grateful to my wife Mary Jane, to my daughter Emmeline, and to my good friend and colleague Doug Hutton, for their comments and suggestions on the first draft of this text. Some of my students contributed helpful ideas in discussion; they are: Dhapher Ajmi, Peter Becker, Peter Boynton, Jess Brannock, Dan Brucker, Mike Cady, Tess Carney, Priscilla Carson-Lindberg, Sayu Ichikawa, Jamie Kaufman, Jason Abdul Ridgley, Josh Sessoms and Go Yoshida.

FOREWORD

Picasso once said, 'In this age of grief, there is nothing more important than to excite enthusiasm.' The first purpose of this book is to try to excite in the reader an abiding enthusiasm for the beauty and poetry to be found in numbers. A second, directly related purpose is to reveal to the reader some of the fascinating ways in which ancient cultures have used the magical power inherent in numbers for esoteric and practical purposes. The final objective is to modernize traditional numerological techniques by applying to them more recent mathematical ideas, so that the interested reader may actually attempt some practical numerology and number magic.

Numerology has a bad press – mostly well deserved. An ancient and venerable mystery science, deeply rooted in the philosophical traditions of both East and West, numerology has been progressively bowdlerized into a bunch of nonsensical prognostication tricks. This book is not about winning jackpots or lotteries: it is a serious and sincere attempt to describe the mystery of number, and the mystery of the magic associated with number. It is based on two premises: first, that there is a discernible relationship between numbers and the sacred mysteries at the heart of creation; second, that a deep understanding of that relationship, properly applied, makes possible the transformations in events and experiences commonly called magic.

This book has no proselytizing intent. If you believe that numbers are just numbers and that there is nothing sacred or mysterious about them (or the universe they describe), by all means rest content in your conviction. That many cultures do believe in the efficacy of number magic is, however, a historical fact.

Numbers are concepts, not concrete objects. They are simple enough for a small child to understand, yet, simultaneously, complex enough to keep philosophers busy for millennia. Consider the number 5 for a moment. Five apples, five orang-utans and five Martian spaceships have only one element in common: their fiveness. We can illustrate fiveness very easily; so easily that a toddler can soon recognize five fingers, five toes, five balloons, and so on. Yet defining fiveness without recourse to any example or illustration is extremely difficult. We can say that it is a quality exactly equidistant from and centred between fourness and

7

sixness; but that is not helpful, because we cannot define fourness or sixness either. The same is true with other abstract concepts, such as love or fear, but the paradox peculiar to numbers is that in essence they are as abstract as anything imaginable, yet in application they are considered the very foundation of our observation and measurement of the real and the concrete.

Few things seem more purposefully designed to induce panic in some people than mathematics. Countless students have worried themselves thin trying to work out how long it takes three and a half men to dig a ditch four feet by seven and one-eighth inches while water is filling a bath at the rate of two gallons a minute, but the bath has a hole in it. This book assumes only a minimal mathematical competence in the reader; to be more specific, an understanding of the four basic operations: addition, subtraction, multiplication and division. The first time anything else appears – even if it is a common topic like powers and roots – it will be explained slowly and patiently. There will be no sudden squiggly Greek characters or peculiar symbols. These explanations may be laborious or redundant for the more mathematically adept reader, but they are intended to make reading the book a comfortable experience for a wide range of people. Some mathematical explanations requiring a little more time or thought have been banished to appendices at the end of the book, where more ambitious or competent mathematicians may study them at their leisure. In any case, the reader should be reassured that there is very little higher mathematics in this book; we deal mostly with common arithmetic, geometry and basic algebra, with a few cautious sniffs around calculus here and there.

Numbers have been part of our thinking since before we lived in caves. There is not a single religion, past or present, which fails to attribute a special significance to some number or group of numbers. Our most fundamental visualizations of the human soul, or psyche, are rooted in numerical concepts, like unity and dualism. We make machines to crunch numbers; we measure the universe and plot our courses through time and space using numbers; we live in numbered houses, with numbered telephones and fax machines; we have numbers allocated to us for health-care and social-security provisions; we have numbered tags on wrists or ankles after we are born and sometimes again before we are buried or cremated.

Numerologists believe that numbers not only recur throughout our daily lives, but that they influence our lives more or less directly, since they are the representations of real and eternal truths beyond space and time, and of a purposeful pattern to the universe.

Consider for a moment these numerical 'coincidences' between two well-known historical events. Abraham Lincoln was elected American president in 1860. His surname has 7 letters. He was assassinated on a Friday, the sixth day of the week. His secretary, whose name was

Kennedy, had advised him not to go to the theatre. His assassin was John Wilkes Booth, whose name has 15 letters. Booth was born in 1839. He was assassinated before he could be brought to trial. Lincoln was succeeded by his vice-president, Andrew Johnson, whose name has 13 letters. Andrew Johnson was born in 1808.

American president John F. Kennedy was elected president in 1960. His surname has 7 letters. He was assassinated on a Friday. His secretary, whose name was Lincoln, had advised him not to go to Dallas. His assassin was Lee Harvey Oswald, whose name has 15 letters. Oswald was born in 1939. He was assassinated before he could be brought to trial. Kennedy was succeeded by his vice-president, Lyndon Johnson, whose name has 13 letters. Lyndon Johnson was born in 1908.

To the modern, scientific mind, such numerical correspondences must be entirely coincidental, despite the remarkable apparent similarities. To the numerologist, such correspondences are not at all surprising. The numerologist believes that similar correspondences and synchronicities occur with great frequency, as do abundant and often beautiful numerical patterns in nature. Put simply, numbers appear to 'want' to generate patterns, and patterns represent relationships, some of which cannot be explained by rational, scientific means.

The last chapters of this book offer practical suggestions for the reader who would like to attempt some numerological analysis or some number magic. A word of caution: magic of any kind is not an enterprise to be undertaken flippantly.

one

THE HISTORY OF NUMBERS

I·II·III·IV·V·VI·VII·VIII·IX·X·XI·XII·XIII·XIV·XV·XVI·XVII·XVIII·XIX·XX·XXI·XXII·XXIII·XXIV

'Ug.'

'Ug–ug.'

'Ug–ug–ug.'

Is that how it went in the beginning? And if that is how human counting started, is there anything unique about that? We have abundant evidence that some other animals appear to be able to recognize number. The psychologist B.F. Skinner trained pigeons to peck a fixed number of times in order to earn a food reward. In *The Natural History of Selborne* (1786), Gilbert White records how he secretly removed one egg each day from a plover's nest, and each day the mother laid a new egg to restore the original total. Chimpanzees have been trained to indicate numbers, even doing simple addition and subtraction, using sign language.

In the early 1900s there was a famous vaudeville act featuring Hans the Educated Horse, who would supply the answer to 9 + 14 by tapping his left hoof twice and his right hoof three times. Hans was responding to almost imperceptible signals from his trainer, of course – nobody seriously believes horses can do arithmetic. Yet, the topic of recognizing numbers is filled with curiosities. There are still, for example, peoples who have what Westerners would call a very limited numerical vocabulary: they count one, two, many. We laugh at such simplicity, but then are baffled by some autistic persons – sometimes called idiot savants – who can look at a pile of spilled straws and immediately 'see' that there are exactly 173 straws there. We pick the straws up, count them carefully, and the answer is correct. When thousands of fish swim tightly packed in a school and move as if they were one being, do they know how many they are? How is it that a Tibetan shepherd knows immediately if one of his flock is missing, without having to count them? What do we actually see, when we see 5 trees, 11 houses, 52 playing cards, 3,000 stars?

There is no simple answer to these questions, which is paradoxical, since many people believe that mathematics is all about simple answers and absolute rights and wrongs. Early humans seem to have had an understanding of number and of mathematical relationships millennia before recorded history. In the 1950s, the English biochemist Joseph Needham began a monumental study of early Chinese civilization (see note 1), in which he points out that the Chinese devised a magnetic compass (pointing south) in the first century AD, a seismograph in the same century, a toy helicopter in the fourth century, and a flame thrower ('Fierce Fire Oil Projector') in 1044. Earlier than the Chinese were Pythagoras and other Greeks. We find geometric patterns tattooed on the leathery skin of a mummified corpse of a woman belonging to the Pazyryk culture in ancient Siberia, as old as Pythagoras if not older (see note 2). Earlier than the Greeks were the Egyptians, Chaldeans and Babylonians. Earlier than them were countless generations who must have had at least some basic concept of number. Somewhere along that faint line to way back when, there is a human ancestor with a stone axe in his hand counting one animal, two animals, three animals, perhaps deciding which one to chase for dinner.

The most fundamental numerical concept, the concept of one and two, 'I' and everything 'not-I', throws itself off history's launchpad into the outer space of metaphysics, psychology and philosophy. It is possible that the very ideas of oneness, twoness and threeness even predate language. One could argue that any pair of animals producing at least one offspring must have at least some innate understanding of the numbers one, two and three.

At some stage, however, human beings began recording numbers systematically. The first systems were based on concrete correspondences: fingers, tally sticks, pebbles and so on. The Latin word *digitus* – from which the word digit is derived – means finger. The ancient Aztec word *matlactli* meant two hands as well as ten (see note 3). Ten and twenty are the counting bases most widely noted in different cultures, for the obvious reason that humans have ten toes and ten fingers. In all the major language families of the world, counting systems are recursive; in other words, higher numbers are built on elements found in lower numbers. In English, we combine four and ten to make fourteen. Japanese (which actually uses both native and Chinese words for numbers) writes 21 as *ni ju ichi* (two ten one). For reasons we shall discuss in later chapters, the numbers 12, 20 and 60 have also been important bases in number systems.

The early development of mathematical thinking was not confined to one race, one continent, or even one hemisphere. China and Egypt made major contributions to the advancement of mathematical knowledge, but so also did India, Greece and Arabia. Within the general narrative account of mathematical development, certain individuals stand out like giants: Pythagoras, Plato, Euclid, Newton, Einstein. But mathematical discoveries have also emerged frequently from practical application as much as from pure theory: the classical archetype of the applied mathematician is Archimedes. Attempts to improve astronomy have generated many new mathematical ideas. Agriculture, commerce, architecture and engineering are all dependent to varying degrees on mathematics, and in turn have generated new mathematical thinking.

Most histories of mathematics are organized by civilizations: Chapter One for the Egyptians, Chapter Two the Babylonians, and so on. Here, we are more concerned with a brief overview of the development of mathematical ideas throughout the world, so we shall be doing some geographical leaping around in order to follow a reasonably consecutive chronological sequence.

Nevertheless, this method does create some problems. Take, for example, the interesting number 0, or zero. The Babylonians used two small wedges to show that a place was unoccupied, and so they were able to distinguish between, say, 305 and 35. But this was not a true zero. That number was first discussed by Hindu philosophers in the second century BC. However, it did not appear regularly in manuscripts until the third century AD. In Sanskrit, the number was called *sunya*. The Egyptians and the Greeks did not recognize the number at all. Only centuries later did the Arabs pick up the idea from earlier Indian texts. They called the number *sifr*, which came into Latin as *zephirum*, from which are derived our words zero and cipher. As late as the Middle Ages, however, zero was still not widely accepted or used as a number in Europe, even though the original concept had been discussed well over a thousand years earlier in India.

Homo sapiens emerged somewhere around 30,000 BC. The cave paintings at Lascaux in France date from around 25,000 BC, and flint tools were used from about 20,000 BC. We have no idea what understanding of number these early humans had. The Neolithic or New Stone Age is usually dated from about 7000 BC, and the first recorded settlements in Iraq and Anatolia (in modern-day Turkey) date from about 5500 BC. Ancient historians use phrases like 'cradle of civilization' to describe this period of expansion in the fertile crescent of Asia Minor, and it is reasonable to suppose that new patterns of settlement and agriculture may have coincided with new thinking about numbers, and, in particular, about the pattern of the annual cycle or calendar.

The first exactly dated year in history is 4241 BC. That was the year in which the Egyptians promulgated a calendar of 365 days, consisting of 12 months of 30 days each, followed by 5 feast days. Egyptian mythology describes the event as follows. Nut, goddess of the sky, was married to Re, god of the Sun and creator of all, but she also slept with her brother, Geb, god of the Earth, and with Thoth, lord of magic. Re discovered that his wife had been sleeping with her brother and placed a curse upon her: that she would not give birth to the child within her in any month of the year. Nut approached Thoth for help, since one of the children inside her was his. Thoth went to the Moon and made a bargain with her: every time he beat her in a game, she would give him a little of her light. Finally, Thoth gathered enough fragments of light to create five complete days to add to the solar year of 360 days. When the year came to its end, Nut gave birth to five children, one on each of the days which Thoth had created. Thus it was that Nut became the Mother of the Gods.

The first known numerals are also Egyptian. They date from about 3400 BC, approximately the same time that the Sumerians were developing cuneiform, the earliest form of writing known. By 2900 BC, the Sumerians had condensed cuneiform (which was not an alphabetic language) to 550 symbolic characters, and the Egyptians had introduced standard measurements of length based on the length from the elbow to the tip of the middle finger – now known as a cubit from the Latin word *cubitum*.

The Egyptians built their pyramids, from the Great Pyramid and the Great Sphinx of Gizeh erected by Khufu (Cheops) in 2900 BC or thereabouts, to the late pyramids of the Fourth Dynasty in about 2600 BC, using design and measurement systems which are studied to this day. About 2800 BC, the Chinese determined equinoxes and solstices, although this information took a very long time to reach the Western hemisphere. Some time around 2500 BC, new systems of measurement were introduced in northern India, which later passed into Asia Minor and Europe.

The first organized astronomers of any significance were the Chaldeans and the Babylonians. The Babylonian calendar was lunar, based on the full lunation cycle of 29.5 days. A year consisted of twelve months (i.e., 354 days) and the 'missing' ten and three-quarter days at the end of each year were reconciled by the addition of a thirteenth month every three years. It was an inaccurate calendar, complicated by ill-informed observations of the five bright planets and some of the brighter stars, which were associated with good and evil consequences. It was the Babylonians who first attached significance to the constellations which lay along the apparent pathway of the sun through the sky – now referred to as the 'ecliptic'. They divided the ecliptic into three regions, each assigned to a divinity. This division was later increased to 12, and because 11 of the 12 regions or constellations were associated with animals, the division was later called the *zoidiakos* by the Greeks, related to *zoion* (meaning animal) and *kukos* (circle), from which is derived our term zodiac. The 12 signs of the zodiac as we now know them were actually named by the Greek astronomer and mathematician, Anaximander in 560 BC.

One of the earliest mathematical documents is the Rhind papyrus, an Egyptian document dating from about 1650 BC. It was named after a Scottish antiquary, Alexander Rhind, who bought it while on holiday in

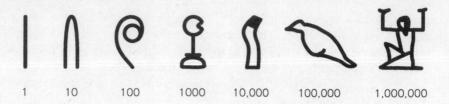

| 1 | 10 | 100 | 1000 | 10,000 | 100,000 | 1,000,000 |

Figure 1 Hieroglyphs from the Rhind papyrus

Egypt in 1858. (The original is now in the British Museum.) The papyrus is signed by the scribe who copied it – a nice personal touch across many centuries – and his name was Ahmes or Amos. Amos wrote numbers very differently from the way we would write them now. There were different signs for units, tens, hundreds, and so on, so the relative position of numbers was not significant. For us, 103 and 301 are different numbers simply because the 3 and the 1 are in different places: their position is significant. For Amos, there was a symbol for 300 and there was a symbol for 1, and it made no difference which way round they were written. The hieroglyphs for numbers are shown in figure 1. Amos also had no zero, or decimal places. He did use fractions, however, and it is clear that many of the algorithms (step-by-step problem-solving procedures) in the Rhind papyrus concern fractions principally because dividing and apportioning accurately was a commercial necessity. At the time Amos was writing, the Egyptians did not have metal coinage, so fine division of loaves of bread or barrels of beer would have been an important part of general skill in barter.

The Chinese were making great advances in astronomy and cartography during this period. They completed the first map of the entire country about 1122 BC. They calculated the obliquity of the ecliptic around 1100. These are very sophisticated mathematical achievements for such ancient times.

For broadly political reasons, Greek mathematics and astronomy developed along different lines from the Chaldean, Babylonian and Egyptian. Divination and augury had been the chief concerns of the Babylonian priesthood, and the astronomers' first duty was to the emperor. The Greeks were also concerned with fate, but in a less monolithic fashion: they were more concerned with the individual, and with the general intellectual and philosophical adventure epitomized by the study of pure number and geometry. The greatest of the early Greek astronomers were Eudoxus, Theophrastus the disciple of Aristotle, and Hipparchus. All of them were indebted to the genius of Pythagoras. Most readers will be familiar with the famous Theorem of Pythagoras: namely, that in a right triangle the square of the hypotenuse equals the sum of the squares of the other two sides. If you were taught this in

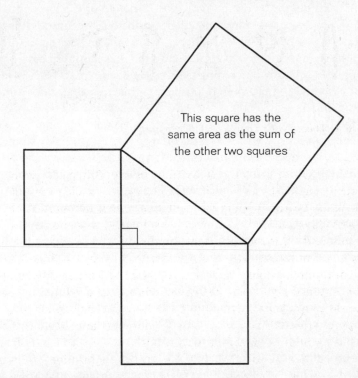

This square has the
same area as the sum of
the other two squares

Figure 2 Pythagoras's Theorem

school, can remember it perfectly and love Pythagoras for having
thought of it, by all means skip the next paragraph.

Pythagoras demonstrated that in a right triangle – that is a triangle
with one angle of 90° (right angle) in it – there is a consistent relationship between the side opposite the right angle (the hypotenuse) and the
other two sides, no matter what lengths they may be in any given
triangle. The value of the hypotenuse multiplied by itself (squared) is
always equal to the sum of the other two sides squared. Even those who
have fully mastered this topic in school find it hard to see the point: so
what? The point is in the eternal truth of the relationship. For
Pythagoreans, numbers represented far more than just a correspondence
with rows of objects: in numbers was to be found the very mystery of life
itself.

Pythagoras was born on the Greek island of Samos, probably about
581 BC. He seems to have travelled widely, certainly to Egypt, quite
possibly to India, and perhaps even to Britain. Between 540 and 530 BC
he settled at Crotona in southern Italy, a powerful and influential Greek
settlement in the region which is now known as Calabria. He was
worshipped as a semi-deity, in part because he had undergone a severe
ritual initiation at the sacred Orphic temple on Crete, and also because

he had been taught by the Daktyls, five Phrygian or Cretan deities. The name Daktyl means finger or digit, and one of the Pythagorean mysteries was a secret finger-alphabet, which underwent several revivals and restorations in medieval alchemy and has counterparts in other cultures and religions, including Celtic Druidism.

The essential Pythagorean doctrine was this: all things are assimilated to numbers. It was Pythagoras who first used the word *harmonia* to describe the relationship between the notes created by lengthening and shortening a plucked string. But harmony came very quickly to mean far more than just a musical relationship. Pythagoras's observation was that if the length of the string was halved, the note produced was exactly one octave higher than the original note. The ratio 3 to 2 produced a note which we would call a perfect fifth in modern terminology; 4 to 3 produces a perfect fourth. The significance of this discovery is that the harmonious relationship is not created by humans, or by the action of performing the experiment, but it is eternally and inherently present in the universe, waiting only to be discovered or realized. There is a cosmic harmony, which is founded in the eternal perfection of number. So, for Pythagoras and his followers, human illness is caused by a disruption of the complex harmony of the body. Evil is the chaos produced by the *apeiron* (unlimited), when *peperas-menon* (limitation) is required. All the notes possible, sounded together without limit, produce nothing but noise, the exemplar of evil for Pythagoreans. Notes limited by mathematical relationships produce harmony. Therefore, the harmony of the universe is maintained by numbers.

It is fashionable for modern mathematicians and scientists to deride Pythagorean mysticism. John McLeish, Emeritus Professor at the University of Victoria in British Columbia, talks of the 'baneful influence' of Pythagoras and Plato on Western mathematics (see note 4), and most modern academics agree with him. Needless to say, this book takes a completely opposite view, and for reasons stronger than mere wishful thinking and New Age optimism. There is a real and undeniable aspect to mathematics which goes beyond the material and temporal. If five, or the concept represented by the number five, has any meaning at all, then the meaning is eternal, immutable, beyond time and space, ineffable, mysterious. Even the most hardened materialist has to admit that these are qualities associated with religious thought, even if he does not accept them himself. Bertrand Russell, a very eminent mathematician and philosopher, and by no means a mystic, expresses the point eloquently:

Mathematics is, I believe, the chief source of the belief in eternal and exact truth, as well as in a super-sensible intelligible world. Geometry deals with exact circles, but no sensible object is exactly circular; however carefully we may use our compasses, there will be some imperfections and irregularities. This suggests the view that all exact reasoning applies to ideal as opposed to sensible objects; it is natural to go further, and argue that thought is nobler than sense, and the objects of thought more real than those of sense perception. Mystical doctrines as to the relation of time to eternity are also reinforced by pure mathematics, for mathematical objects, such as numbers, if real at all, are eternal and not in time. Such eternal objects can be conceived as God's thoughts. Hence Plato's doctrine that God is a geometer, and Sir James Jeans' belief that He is addicted to arithmetic. Rationalistic as opposed to apocalyptic religion has been, ever since Pythagoras, and notably ever since Plato, very completely dominated by mathematics and mathematical method (see note 5).

Russell says specifically of Pythagoras:

I do not know of any other man who has been as influential as he was in the sphere of thought. I say this because what appears as Platonism is, when analysed, found to be in essence Pythagoreanism. The whole conception of an eternal world, revealed to the intellect but not to the senses, is derived from him. But for him, Christians would not have thought of Christ as the Word (see note 6).

Pythagoras is particularly important to numerology because many of the assumptions upon which numerology is based are essentially Pythagorean: there is an infinite and ordered truth in the universe, which is metaphysical and metatemporal; number, divinity and harmony are related; action, cause and effect, which are physical and temporal phenomena, can be observed, measured and recorded using numbers; numbers can influence action, cause and effect. In other words, numbers can be used for magic (this term will be discussed more fully later).

The Pythagoreans hit a devastating setback during their deliberations, however. They found some numbers which defied expression and which seemed to defy the whole concept of an infinite and ordered truth in the universe. Today we call those numbers irrational numbers. They are important both in mathematics generally, and in numerology specifically. These numbers are not called 'irrational' numbers because they behave in crazy and irrational ways, although perhaps Pythagoras thought they did. They are numbers which cannot be expressed as a fractional ratio; here, irrational means 'without ratio'. The Pythagoreans handled complex fractions very easily, but these numbers could not be written as fractions. Suppose we apply Pythagoras's Theorem to a right triangle which has the two sides forming the right angle both 1 unit long. The theorem tells us that the area of the square on the hypotenuse must

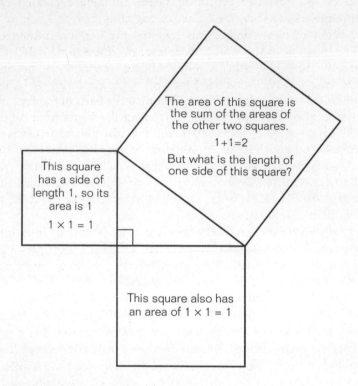

The area of this square is the sum of the areas of the other two squares.

1+1=2

But what is the length of one side of this square?

This square has a side of length 1, so its area is 1

1 × 1 = 1

This square also has an area of 1 × 1 = 1

Figure 3   The discovery of irrational numbers

be 2 square units (1 times itself, or 1 squared, or 1^2, equals 1, and $1^2 + 1^2 = 2$). But the number which we multiply by itself to obtain 2 (i.e., the square root of 2, written $\sqrt{2}$) cannot be expressed as a fraction. (See Appendix One for Euclid's demonstration.) The Pythagoreans never resolved this problem, and arithmetic and geometry began separate journeys from this point onward.

The same Anaximander, mentioned earlier, who named the 12 signs of the zodiac, also produced the first Greek map of the world in 580 BC. He described the world as hanging in space, but he gave it a rectangular shape. Thales, like Pythagoras, developed the idea that mathematics should be a logical, deductive process, as opposed to the earlier Babylonian and Egyptian notions that mathematics was all about empirical observation and practical applications. Thales was the first astronomer to predict correctly an eclipse of the sun, a feat he achieved in 585 BC. At about the same time, the Chinese were beginning to use the abacus, but they also still used small bamboo rods for computation – like the Babylonians and Egyptians, they were locked into an empiricist view of mathematics. In 517 BC, Hecateus produced the first map which depicted the world as a disc.

Over the next two centuries, Greek thinking expanded rapidly in mathematics, science, medicine, cartography and philosophy, and this explosion of new thinking has had the profoundest influence on our understanding of the world. Anaximenes (*c*.590 to 525 BC) described the universe as consisting of four elements – earth, water, fire and air – a taxonomy which has survived for millennia. Hippocrates – after whom the Hippocratic Oath is named – founded the basis of modern medicine. Alemaeon, a Greek physician, discovered the Eustachian tubes in 500 BC. Zeno of Alea formulated eight mathematical paradoxes which remained unanswered for 2,000 years. Anaxagoras established reason as the conceptual basis of the universe. Melissus described reality as infinite in 440 BC. Democritus (*c*.460 to 370 BC) advanced the theory that matter consists of very small and indestructible particles, the basis of modern atomic theory.

The two greatest figures emerging from this period of Greek intellectual hegemony are Plato and Aristotle. They knew each other personally, were teacher and student, later colleagues, and their combined influence on the intellectual history of the world is incalculable.

'Plato' is a nickname meaning 'broad-shouldered.' His original name was Aristocles. He was born about 429 BC. In 387 he founded the Academy in Athens. At the door was this inscription: 'Let no one who knows no geometry come under my roof.' Aristotle joined Plato at the Academy twenty years later – presumably he passed the admission test. In Plato's idealized republic, only four subjects were worthy of study: arithmetic, astronomy, geometry and music. Plato studied in Egypt for some time before founding the Academy, and he was very impressed by the mathematical games and puzzles the Egyptians used for teaching children. They made great use of what we would call 'manipulatives': piles of apples, blocks of wood, geometric tiles, and so on. Plato's most important contribution to mathematical thinking was that he went beyond the physical reality of objects and proposed an eternal, unchanging reality beyond time and space in which all that is true resides. There are countless chairs, all different shapes and sizes, but in eternity there is the eternal archetype of chairness, the chair without form or dimension which represents all chairs, just as in eternity there is a perfect circle, without dimension, which is the perfect paradigm of all the approximations to circles ever drawn or imagined. The idea is essentially Pythagorean, but it finds its fullest and clearest expression in Plato.

Expressing numbers clearly was, however, no easy task for Plato, because the world had not yet created the sophisticated mathematical vocabulary and conventions which we now take for granted. For example, Plato in his *Republic* attempts to describe the unusual number 216; unusual because it is the smallest cube number (a number multiplied by itself, then multiplied by itself again) that is the sum

19

of three cubes, which themselves are the cubes of the significant progression 3, 4, 5:

$$3^3 + 4^3 + 5^3 = 6^3$$
$$27 + 64 + 125 = 216$$

Plato's description of this relationship begins:

> But the number of a human creature is the first number in which root and square increases, having received three distances and four limits, of elements that make both like and unlike and wax and wane, render all things conversable and rational with one another (see note 7).

The language of this passage, which has received a great deal of attention from mathematicians and mystics alike, is not deliberately obscure. As David Wells points out: 'It illustrates perfectly both the intimate relationship that Plato, as a Pythagorean, perceived between numbers and the real world, and the difficulty that he had in using the then available language to express himself' (see note 8).

Socrates, Plato and Aristotle all held reason to be higher than observation – in that sense, their thinking is very much at odds with contemporary scientific thought. Democritus, Heraclitus and the other pre-Platonic Greek thinkers were derided for their sense-perception and practical experience-bound observations; according to Platonists, all they could generate was opinions, not knowledge.

The Greek who comes closest to the modern scientific archetype is Archimedes. He was born in 287 BC at Syracuse in Sicily, and died there 75 years later when the city was captured by the Roman general Marcellus and a soldier ignored the general order that the great sage was not to be killed. The legend is that Archimedes was so preoccupied with drawing mathematical figures in the sand that he hardly noticed the soldier's lance pass through him. He was a very practical mathematician, devising the water-screw, screw-pump, laws of leverage, as well as mighty engines of war, including a deadly fire-throwing catapult. He is most famous in dusty school texts for leaping out of his bath and shouting 'Eureka!' ('I have found it!') while puzzling over how to measure the specific gravity of coins of pure gold as opposed to gold coins adulterated with baser metal. He is reputed to have run home naked, too excited by his discovery to notice the stares of passers-by. It was also Archimedes who said, 'Give me a place to stand and I will move the Earth', to illustrate the principle of leverage across a fulcrum.

Around 250 BC, Eratosthenes mapped the course of the Nile, suggested that the Earth moves around the Sun, and made a very accurate estimation of the Earth's circumference. In 225 BC, Appolonius first calculated the value of π (pronounced 'pi'), that mysterious number which relates the radius of a circle to its area and circumference. In the first century BC, Hipparchus invented trigonometry, which has been of immense importance to astronomy, architecture, engineering and general mathematics ever since.

The Greek passion for numbers and astrology found its way in time to Rome, where it became a semi-religion. Augustus and Tiberius were both keen proponents of astrology and maintained retinues of soothsayers and numerologists, some of them Greek or Persian, to assist them in their divine imperial duties. The Greek for 'to learn' was *manthanein*, from which came the noun *mathema*, or 'learning'. This new sect of soothsayers and numerologists called themselves *mathematekoi* (in Greek) or *mathematici* (Romanized), meaning 'men of learning', and this is, of course, the origin of our term mathematics.

Greek thought, Latinized and revised, dominated Europe for sixteen centuries. Julius Caesar introduced our present calendar, with its 365.25 days and one additional day every leap year, in 46 BC, but the idea was not his: it had been suggested by Eudoxus, a pupil of Plato's, 350 years earlier. Pliny the Elder produced his books on mathematics and natural history about 80 AD, and they remained greatly influential until the twelfth century. In 85 AD, Nicomachus produced *Introductio Arithmetica*, one of the earliest works on arithmetic dealing with ordinary numbers.

About 250 AD, Diophantus of Alexandria introduced the first book of algebra (although that name had not been invented yet). He devised a form of indeterminate equations, now known as diophantine equations, which have played an important role in modern mathematics.

Ptolemy wrote in Greek and is usually thought of as a Greek, but in fact he was an Egyptian. He was born about 100 AD at Ptolemais Hermii, a Greek settlement in Egypt, and lived and worked in Alexandria, where he died in 178 AD. As early as 130, he observed the persistence of vision, the principle on which modern cinematography is based. As well as studying optics, he produced works on mathematics, astronomy and geography. Hipparchus had begun the study of what we now call spherical trigonometry, which is applicable to astronomy, for which purpose it was devised. Ptolemy extended trigonometry so successfully that later Arab mathematicians called his work by a superlative *al mejest* ('the great'), from which the name Almagest is derived. Ptolemy is most famous for his description of the solar system, based on the geocentric model suggested by Hipparchus, which places the Earth at the centre of the universe. Most readers will already know that it was several centuries before this notion was seriously challenged. One incidental but interesting fact about Ptolemy is that his work inspired one of the first female mathematicians of note. Theon of Alexandria, who flourished about 400 AD, spent a lifetime studying Ptolemy's works. His studies were continued by his daughter Hypatia (370–415) who is recognized as one of the earliest women to achieve fame as a mathematician.

When Alexandria was captured by the Arab leader Omar in 614, a new era in mathematical history began. In the so-called Dark Ages of Europe, it was in Islam and the work of Arab mathematicians that the growth of mathematical thinking continued most strongly. They translated into Arabic the works of earlier Babylonian, Egyptian, Greek, Indian and Chinese mathematicians, so that many of these earliest works eventually came into the West via Arab translations. Without this important Arabian contribution, the Western scientific revolution of the fifteenth and sixteenth centuries could never have taken place. It has been fashionable for historians to denigrate the Arabic contribution, on the grounds that little of the work is original, or that the chief Arabian mathematical thinkers were not Arabs at all: for example, Moses Ben Maimon was a Jew, and Omar Khayyam a Persian. The truth is that all mathematical thinking – even the most radically innovative – is related to earlier work by somebody, and the dominant thinkers of the Islamic period, whatever their origins, thought, spoke and wrote in Arabic.

The Arabs developed whole new branches of mathematics, including algebra and analytical geometry. They laid the foundation for the discovery of logarithms by Napier 600 years later. They devised the system of using place to denote value, from which the decimal system stemmed. This, in turn, led to the notion that fractions and integers (whole numbers) can be treated similarly, since in a decimal system fractions can be rewritten so that a digit's position indicates value: for example, one-quarter can be written as 0.25. They opened up the treasure store of ideas associated with powers (a number multiplied by itself a number of times: such as 3 times 3 times 3, now called 3 cubed or 3 to the third power or 3^3) and roots (the same process in reverse, by which we identify the number which has been multiplied by itself – a square root finds a number multiplied by itself once: for example, the square root of 64, usually written as $\sqrt{64}$, is 8, because 8 times 8 equals 64; a cube root is a number which has been multiplied by itself twice: for example, the cube root of 64, usually written as $^3\sqrt{64}$, is 4, since 4 times 4 times 4 equals 64; the fourth root of 16, or $^4\sqrt{16}$, is 2, since 2 times 2 times 2 times 2 equals 16; and so on). They showed the relationships between systems of counting established on different bases: for example, the decimal (based on 10), sexagesimal (based on 60) and binary (based on 2). Apart from these general achievements, there are European individuals, like Leonardo of Pisa – whom we shall discuss in more detail shortly – whose discoveries sprang directly from their studies at Arab institutes of learning.

The scale of ten, now virtually taken for granted by all of us, was probably devised in India about 175 AD. About 815, the Arabs resurrected the idea, introducing zero (which has had profound consequences for all mathematical thinking ever since) to indicate multiplication by ten. We have become so accustomed to the idea that 4 and 40 and 400 are different numbers, it is difficult for us to imagine the enormous impact of this very simple idea of indicating value by place; the Egyptians and the Greeks, brilliant as they were, had no conception of it.

The Indians had written the *Surya* – a work on astronomy using sexagesimal fractions and introducing what we would now call tables of trigonometrical sines – in about 350 AD. The Arabs discovered this ancient text and translated it into Arabic, adding much new commentary and interpretation of their own. In fact, Indian mathematicians generated new ideas for a period of about 700 years until 1100, and most of these ideas have come down to us from Arabic translations. Decimal notation, for example, discussed in the previous paragraph, is first noted in a Hindu text dating from as early as 595, but it was the Arab mathematicians who brought it into the West.

In particular, we are indebted to the Arabs for these now commonly accepted symbols: 1 2 3 4 5 6 7 8 9 0. These are Arabic numerals. They originated in India and reached the Baghdad region around 760 AD. They are now accepted throughout the world as standard notation for numbers, even in cultures which have had their own numeral symbols for many centuries.

Baghdad, founded by Al-Mansur in 763, became the centre of the Muslim world. Euclid's *Elements* was translated there about ten years after the founding of the city. Jabir, born in 722, was a great Arab chemist who developed knowledge of chemical reactions and compounds, and who helped to establish chemistry as a science distinct from alchemy. For 400 years from its foundation, Baghdad was the centre of Arab learning.

In 822, or thereabouts, a mathematician in Baghdad produced an interesting new work. Neither his name nor the title of his book are well known now, but from his book title is derived a very common mathematical word. The mathematician was Mohammed ibn Musa al-Khowarizmi, and his book *Al-jabr w'al-muqabala*. The word *al-jabr*, from which algebra is derived, literally means 'transformations'.

Most readers are probably already familiar with what the term algebra means, but it is worth clarifying one simple, basic element of it. In algebra, we distinguish two types of number. The first are constants: these are numbers whose value is always constant, as the name suggests; numbers like 5 or 73 or 471. The second are variables: these are numbers whose value we do not yet know, so we use a letter to represent them. The convention is to use a lower-case letter (capitals are used to denote points in geometry), such as x or y or n. The chief advantage of this simple idea is that we can represent patterns even when the actual value of the patterns is not known. For example, we can take a series of equations, as follows:

$$2 + 2 = 4 \qquad 5 + 5 = 10 \qquad 100 + 100 = 200$$

The pattern for all these equations is 'something plus itself is twice itself', which can be far more neatly expressed using an algebraic equation:

$$x + x = 2x$$

Using this system, we can now write rules which apply to all real numbers without having to give actual values. For example, the commutative property of addition states that 'for every real number a and real number b, a plus b equals b plus a', or in simpler notation:

$$a + b = b + a$$

This rule describes a pattern which holds true for all real numbers; whatever actual values you ascribe to a and b, the equation will always hold true. This seems a very simple observation, but before the invention of algebra, describing universal rules and patterns was extremely difficult, as we saw earlier in Plato's efforts to describe the properties of the number 216.

Through the European Dark Ages, Arab discoveries continued. Around 960, Abul-l-Wafa discovered the sine formula for a spherical triangle. As early as 850, the Arabs refined the astrolabe, an important astronomical and navigational device (later replaced by the sextant) which did not reach Europe until about 1050.

The decline in Islamic science began about 1100. There had been a constant tension between scientific progress and fundamental religious doctrine in the Arab world, just as there was centuries later in the Christian world, and this tension eventually stifled further development of mathematical and scientific ideas. The most powerful leader of the religious opposition to scientific progress was Al-Ghazali, who died in 1111.

Now, very slowly, began the resurgence of mathematical thinking in the West. Al-Khowarizmi, the originator of the term *al-jabr*, had also produced astronomical tables in the ninth century. These were translated into Latin in 1126, and there followed a long succession of Latin translations of Arabic works, which themselves may have been translations of earlier Syriac or Sanskrit texts. In 1144, Robert de Chester's translation of Arabic writing on chemistry appeared as *Liber de Compositione Alchemiae*. Earlier Greek writers now appeared in Latin translation for the first time: Aristotle's *Posterior Analytics* in about 1155, Ptolemy's *Almagest* in about 1160. One of the most prolific translators from Arabic into Latin was Gerard de Cromona, who translated works by Aristotle (copied in Arabic) and Al-Khowarizmi, among others;

Western science owes a great debt of gratitude to this relatively obscure scholar.

In 1202 *Liber Abaci* (The Book of the Abacus) was published by Leonardo of Pisa, also known as Fibonacci. His work has had a very great influence on Western mathematics, and his famous numerical series – usually called simply the Fibonacci series – is of the greatest importance in numerology, as will be explained in more detail in later chapters. It was in *Liber Abaci* that Fibonacci first described and explained Arabic numerals, and we have used them ever since. Fibonacci also published *Practica Geometriae*, a collection of geometric and trigonometric knowledge, in 1220.

The first independent Western 'scientist' of note is Roger Bacon, whose work dominates the second half of the thirteenth century. He was given the nickname Doctor Mirabilis in recognition of his extraordinary accomplishments. He was born about 1214 near Ilchester in Somerset, England. He died in 1292, having written works on optics, linguistics, natural science and mathematics. He spent the last fifteen years of his life imprisoned for his attacks on the corruptions and inadequacies in translations of the Bible. To some extent, the condemnation of his works explains why his influence is not seen very clearly in the work of his immediate successors.

Nicolas Copernicus was born about 1473 and died in 1543. He was a mathematician, physicist and classics scholar. He was the first Western scientist to propose that the Earth revolves once every 24 hours and that, rather than being at the centre of the universe, it actually revolves around the Sun. This was an unthinkable heresy in the view of the Church, and the Copernican revolution took a long time to become established in Western thought.

Leonardo da Vinci (1452–1519) also belongs to this period. Not only did he paint *La Gioconda*, known also as the *Mona Lisa*, but he was also an engineer, architect, sculptor and musician – the paradigm of the Renaissance man.

Some time during the 1400s – the date is not known exactly – two new signs or symbols were introduced into mathematical writing. The first was the symbol + , which was originally called 'surplus' but became shortened with use to 'plus'. The second was – , which was called 'minus', the Latin comparative of *minor*, meaning less.

In 1542, with the lively and intellectually accomplished Henry VIII on the throne of England, another significant advance took place, although it, too, has tended to disappear into historical obscurity. The event was the publication of Robert Recorde's *Ground of Artes*, the first of a series of mathematical works in English. Before 1542, all mathematical and most scientific work had appeared only in Latin. Henry VIII is reputed to have admired the book greatly. In the same year, he increased the amount of base alloy in coins, thus effecting a great saving for the royal Treasury. It is possible that he thought of the idea after reading Recorde's book.

Another of Recorde's mathematical books, *The Whetstone of Witte* – a treatise on algebra – was published in 1557. In this book appears for the first time a mathematical symbol which most readers will probably have assumed to be of much greater antiquity: it is the equality sign, or = . It is curious to think that before about 1400 a simple equation like $2 + 2 = 4$ would have had to be written as '2 surplus 2 gives the sum 4'.

As the sixteenth century came to a close, and the great expansions and colonizations of the Elizabethan period were under way, a series of new discoveries and ideas contributed to the expansion of mathematical and scientific knowledge. Galileo Galilei (1564–1642) confirmed the Copernican revolution by observing through a telescope the movements of Jupiter's four largest moons, although he was forced to recant his support for Copernicus before his death. In 1582, Pope Gregory introduced the modern, Gregorian calendar into Italy and other Catholic countries, although it was many years before it was universally adopted in the West. At about the same time – perhaps from around 1585 – the decimal point began to be used widely. Decimal notation, or at least the place-value system and the decimal counting base, had been introduced much earlier, but it was only at the end of the sixteenth century that the decimal point began to appear frequently in mathematical manuscripts and texts. The idea of using letters for algebraic quantities, described above, was popularized by the French mathematician François Vieta. He published (in Latin) his important work *In Artem Analyticam Isagoge* in 1591. The first complete trigonometric tables were published by G.J. Rheticus in 1596, and in 1600 William Gilbert's great work *De Magnete* introduced the words electricity and magnetism to the English language. Pierre Fermat, whose famous Last Theorem has been mentioned and will be discussed more fully later, was born in 1601; he is considered by many to have laid the foundations of modern number theory. Other important figures of the seventeenth century are Napier, who introduced the foundation of logarithms in 1617; Kepler, whose works explained planetary motion; Cassini, the first of four generations of scientists of the same name, which was subsequently given to the divisions in the rings of Saturn; and Blaise Pascal, the French mathematician and philosopher, born in 1623, who, among other achievements, laid the foundations for modern calculus.

In this very brief summary of the history of numbers, two towering figures dominate the modern age: Newton and Einstein. Both had an almost incalculable impact on the development of human knowledge, yet it would be difficult to imagine two more dissimilar personality types.

Sir Isaac Newton was born in England on Christmas Day 1642. In adulthood, he was a cold, distant and arrogant figure, which many attribute to his unhappy childhood: his father died two months before he was born, and his mother married Barnabas Smith, Rector of North Welham in Leicestershire, when Newton was still only three, the new parents neglecting the child severely from that time onwards. Newton and Einstein share the ironic distinction that both were considered dullards at school. Newton was eventually admitted to Trinity College, Cambridge, in 1661. By 1665, he had produced what is now known as the binomial theorem (see Appendix Two). Shortly afterwards appeared Newton's first explanation of what he called 'Fluxions', but which we now refer to as differential calculus. (The basic elements of calculus are briefly described in Appendix Three.) In May 1666, Newton wrote of further work in what he called 'the inverse method of Fluxions', which we now call integral calculus. In the same year, Newton began to consider gravity, in his own words 'having thereby compared the force requisite to keep the Moon in her orb with the force of gravity at the surface of the Earth and found them to answer pretty nearly.' There is no historical evidence to support the folk tale of Newton being struck on the head by a falling apple. It was another 21 years before his theories on gravity and motion were published in *Philosophiae Naturalis Principia Mathematica*.

Although theoretical physics has advanced greatly since Newton – in particular because of Einstein's theories – for almost all practical purposes, human endeavours, great and small, are predicated on a Newtonian model of the laws of nature. Relativity played no part in landing a man on the Moon in 1969 – that was all done by Newtonian physics.

The challenge which Albert Einstein presented to this model is not easy to describe in just a few sentences. The mathematics of relativity are well beyond the scope of this book. Einstein was born of Jewish parents in Ulm, in Baden-Württemberg, south Germany, in 1879. His first work on relativity was published in 1905, with the full generalized theory appearing in 1915. Quantum theory, the foundation for much of this century's theoretical science, was first proposed by Max Planck in 1900, but it was Einstein who verified the essential points of the theory and therefore made it available to the scientific community. Einstein's most famous equation is $E = mc^2$, or energy equals mass times the speed of light squared, which led us to Hiroshima and the new nuclear world which was born in 1945.

Time line of main events and personalities

BC

30,000	emergence of *Homo sapiens*
25,000	Lascaux cave paintings
7000	Neolithic or New Stone Age begins
5500	first recorded settlements in Iraq and Anatolia
4241	first calendar (Egyptian)
3400	first known numerals (Egyptian) and earliest writing (cuneiform)
2900	Great Pyramid of Cheops and Sphinx of Gizeh
2800	Chinese determine equinoxes and solstices
2500	systems of measurement in India
2500	Babylonian calendar
1650	Rhind papyrus: Ahmes or Amos, Egyptian mathematician, describes circles and fractions
1122	first map of China
1100	Chinese calculate obliquity of the ecliptic
590–525	Anaximenes describes elements of fire, air, earth and water
585	Thales correctly predicts eclipse of the sun
581–507	Pythagoras of Samos, founder of Pythagorean school
580	Anaximander names 12 signs of the zodiac and produces first map of the world
580	Chinese develop the abacus
517	Hecateus depicts the world as a disc
440	Democritus describes particles
429–347	Plato, founder of Platonic school of philosophy, work on polyhedra
384–322	Aristotle, geometry, infinity, logic
365–300	Euclid, founder of geometry, Elements published in 13 volumes
287–212	Archimedes of Syracuse, angles, circles, polyhedra, applied mathematics
250	Eratosthenes maps course of Nile, suggests Earth moves around Sun
225	Apollonius, first detailed calculation of π, conic sections
180–125	Hipparchus of Alexandria, introduces trigonometry
46	Julius Caesar introduces 365.25-day calendar

AD

85	Nicomachus publishes *Introductio Arithmetica*
100–178	Ptolemy, mathematician and astronomer, declares Earth centre of the universe
250	Diophantus of Alexandria introduces indeterminate equations; foundation of algebra
370–415	Hypatia of Alexandria, work on conic sections, one of earliest female mathematicians
614	Arabs capture Alexandria
760	Arabic numerals first introduced
763	founding of Baghdad by Al-Mansur

815	decimal scale and zero (both Indian in origin) introduced by Arab mathematicians
822	Mohammed ibn Musa al-Khowarizmi introduces *Al-jabr w'al-muqabala*, source of word 'algebra'
960	Abul-l-Wafa discovers sine formula for a spherical triangle
1100	Hindu and Arabic mathematical works translated into Latin and spread throughout western Europe
1126	Al-Khowarizmi's astronomical tables published in Latin
1144	Robert de Chester, *Liber de Compositione Alchemiae*
1202	Leonardo of Pisa (Fibonacci) publishes *Liber Abaci*, introduces Arabic numerals to West
1214–92	Roger Bacon, optics, natural science
1452–1519	Leonardo da Vinci, engineer, architect, painter, sculptor
1473–1543	Nicolas Copernicus, mathematician, physicist, first Western scientist to suggest the Earth revolves around the Sun
1542	Robert Recorde's *Ground of Artes*, first mathematical text in English
1557	Robert Recorde's *Whetstone of Witte*, equality sign or = introduced
1582	Gregorian calendar adopted in Catholic countries
1585	decimal point begins to appear widely
1591	François Vieta popularizes lower-case letters for algebraic quantities
1596	first trigonometric tables
1596–1650	René Descartes, philosopher and mathematician, inventor of Cartesian plane, coordinate geometry
1600	William Gilbert's *De Magnete* introduces theories of electricity and magnetism
1601–65	Pierre de Fermat, coordinates, introduces famous Last Theorem
1617	John Napier, Scottish mathematician, introduces foundation of logarithms
1623–62	Blaise Pascal, algebra, computers, probability, number theory, inventor of first adding machine
1642–1727	Sir Isaac Newton, father of modern physics, founder of differential and integral calculus
1665	Newton introduces binomial theorem
1680	Leibniz, German philosopher, works on calculus, functions and infinity
1686–1736	Gabriel Fahrenheit, inventor of Fahrenheit scale
1701–44	Anders Celsius, inventor of Celsius scale
1707–83	Leonhard Euler, functions, sets, topology, number theory
1792–1871	Charles Babbage, foundation work on computers
1799	metric system of measurement introduced
1815–64	George Boole, algebra, set theory, mathematical logic
1824–1907	William Thomson, Lord Kelvin, inventor of Kelvin scale
1870	George Cantor describes infinite sets
1900	work of Max Planck foundation of quantum theory
1905	Einstein introduces theory of relativity
1912–54	Alan Mathison Turing, development of computers
1915	Einstein publishes full generalized theory of relativity
1945	first construction of modern computers
1945	first atomic bombs used at Hiroshima and Nagasaki

two

NUMBERS AND NATURE

1·1·2·3·5·8·13·21·34·55·89·144·233·377·610·987·1597·2548·4145·6693·10838

The Pythagorean view is that 'All things are assimilated to number.' Some natural phenomena have very obvious number properties, like snow flakes, crystals and the cells in a honeycomb. Certain minerals have regular geometric shapes: for example, tourmaline is triangular, salt is cubic, diamond is made of octahedrons, quartz of hexagons, and sulphur crystals are rhombic prisms. In all animals, including humans, and in all plants, symmetry is far more common than asymmetry. With such observations, it is easy to assume an underlying correspondence between number and nature. However, not all of creation yields such instant comparisons, for two main reasons – both of which are to do with perspective and human perception.

The first reason is that our perception of the universe is extremely limited. Science has achieved a great deal, but there are many aspects of nature which are still far beyond our comprehension. At one end of the spectrum, astronomers are investigating what appear to be the furthest reaches of the universe at virtually unimaginable distances; while at the other, physicists are investigating sub-atomic particles so small that their size is not actually quantifiable. We conceptualize the creation of the universe in a period of time so short that new language is necessary to describe it; while at the same time we study a solar system about 6,000,000,000 years old, and a universe considerably older than that. Even given the enormous range of these investigations, human perception still remains very limited. We have only vague under-standing, if that, of universal phenomena like gravity. We perceive certain information much less efficiently than many other species: dogs have better senses of smell and hearing than we have; many birds see further and more clearly than we do; certain fish are vastly more sensitive to vibration and movement, and so on. But beyond these simple limitations to our perception – which to some extent we manage to overcome by technological means – there is the greater limitation of human experience in general. We only know this tiny pocket of a fairly undistinguished part of the spiral arm of a very ordinary galaxy, and, by comparison with the length of the time during which we estimate the universe has been in existence, our presence as thinking beings here has been ludicrously brief.

The second reason is that, as yet, the universe as we know it empirically, or by observation, is far more severely delimited than the universe described by pure mathematics. In number theory, for example, it is now accepted that there is an infinite number of sizes of infinity. That concept is mindbogglingly more vast than our observation of the 'real' universe. Consider the following simple illustrations.

Imagine the first few real positive numbers indicated on a number line, thus:

```
|   |   |   |   |   |
0   1   2   3   4   5
```

If we were to extend this line to the right, its length would be infinite. But now consider the interval between the numbers 2 and 3. We could divide this into tenths, to give the following:

```
|   |    |    |    |    |    |    |    |    |    |
2  2.1  2.2  2.3  2.4  2.5  2.6  2.7  2.8  2.9  3
```

Now, consider the interval between 2.6 and 2.7. We could divide this into tenths, to give:

```
|    |     |     |     |     |     |     |     |     |    |
2.6  2.61  2.62  2.63  2.64  2.65  2.66  2.67  2.68  2.69  2.7
```

Now, consider the interval between 2.61 and 2.62. We could divide this into tenths ... and so on, *ad infinitum*. In other words, the total number of numbers between 2 and 3 is also infinite. Instinctive logic tells us that this infinity ought to be smaller than the infinity which describes the whole set of positive numbers, but in fact, in mathematical terms they are the same size.

These different infinities were investigated in depth by Georg Ferdinand Ludwig Philipp Cantor (they obviously favoured almost infinite name length in his day), a German mathematician who was born in Russia in 1845, but who was educated at Zurich, Berlin and Göttingen. Between 1895 and 1897, Cantor published *Bergrundung der transfiniten Mengenlehre*, in which he set out radically innovative new ideas in what was to become a completely new branch of mathematics, of very great importance to modern mathematics and theoretical physics alike: set theory.

As with many profound mathematical ideas, the basic description is very simple. A set is defined as a collection of mathematical objects. The usual convention is to write the objects between braces, thus:

{2, 3, 4}

In mathematics, these are braces { }; these are brackets [ ]; and these are parentheses ( ).

The set {2, 3, 4} is the set of positive integers (whole numbers) greater than 1 and smaller than 5. The size of a set is determined by the number of objects in it. These two sets have nothing in common except their number of entries:

{apple, peach, orange, plum, pear} {trawler, ketch, sloop, dinghy, catamaran}

Sometimes, a consistent relationship connects two different sets. We call this relationship a *function*. The first set is called the *domain* of the function and the second set is called the *range*. Consider these two sets:

{1, 2, 3, 4, 5} {3, 4, 5, 6, 7}

The consistent function in the relationship between these two sets is that each term in the first set relates, or *maps*, to one term in the second set which is two units higher: 1 maps to 3, 2 maps to 4, 3 maps to 5, 4 maps to 6 and 5 maps to 7. The function, which would be written as $f(x)$ if we were to apply it to a larger domain, is to add 2 to whatever the value of x is. As a functional equation, this would be written: $f(x) = x + 2$.

When there are more objects in a set than can be conveniently listed, we use a standard notation to describe the property (P) which validates, or explains, the inclusion of the set members. In full, this looks like this: $\{x \mid P(x)\}$ and would be read as 'the set of all those objects x for which the property $P(x)$ is valid.' In the first set above, the property, or $P(x)$, is existence as a piece of fruit, so the full set (larger than the set of five fruits given) would be 'all those objects which are pieces of fruit.'

The two sets {all objects which are pieces of fruit} and {2, 3, 4} are different in size, but they are both finite. We do not know the size of the first set, but theoretically we could discover it by exhaustive enquiry. We do know the size of the second set.

Cantor used the Hebrew letter ℵ or aleph, to denote the size of a set with an infinite number of members. He called the 'smallest' infinity $\aleph_0$, which is read as 'aleph-null'. The set of all positive numbers has this size. So, too, does the set of all positive and all negative numbers, which one might think would be twice as large, but it is not. So, too, does the set of all even numbers, which one might think would be half the size, but it is not. Infinities are very curious objects. However, the set of all real numbers (the term 'real' will be explained later) is actually larger than ℵ. At first, Cantor was not able to decide what the size of this set was; he just knew that it was larger than aleph-null. Eventually, this problem – known as Cantor's continuum problem – was resolved and a whole infinity of set sizes emerged: after $\aleph_0$, or aleph-null, comes $\aleph_1$, or aleph-one, followed by $\aleph_2$, or aleph-two, in an infinite series. This is perfectly logical and mathematically consistent with itself, yet extremely difficult to understand in everyday terms.

Most of our conclusions about the structure of nature and the universe have been achieved through what is commonly called the scientific method, which is empiricist in character. Put crudely, empiricism says that you only deal with realities which you can observe. We work out that the acceleration caused by the force of gravity is 9.75 m (32 ft) per second per second by repeated observations.

Pure mathematics does not operate in the same way. We do not assert that the internal angles of a triangle add up to 180° because we have empirically observed millions of different triangles; we assert it because it follows by inexorable mathematical logic from certain very simple axioms and postulates (general statements intended to encapsulate elemental truths about all numbers and number properties) which were first established thousands of years ago.

Numbers are not real objects. We treat them according to rules which are not empirical at all, but entirely abstract. Numbers do not exist in space or in time. If there is such a quality as fiveness, it would continue to be a real quality even if the entire universe consisted of objects grouped in any combination except a group of five. The quality of fiveness (and of every other number, including infinity) existed before the universe came into being. It will continue to exist after the universe has ended.

When we think of numbers in these terms, it is easy to see why various traditions of numerology have asserted that a deep understanding of number is synonymous with a deep understanding of the eternal and divine. God, or The Goddess, or the gods and goddesses, and all that is eternal and divine in humans – in other words, the eternal soul – all belong to the same realm as number, a realm which is beyond time and space.

Imagine for a moment that you are a dot on a line. You have infinite size, because a dot (or at least the concept of what a dot is) has no dimension. The line, or at least the imaginary concept of the line, has just one dimension. (As soon as we physically draw a line, no matter how thin the pencil, we actually create a certain measure of width as well as length, thus creating two dimensions.) You exist in one dimension. You would not even be able to conceptualize left and right: they would be meaningless.

Now, imagine yourself as a dot on the surface of a sheet of paper. Your size is still infinite, but you exist in two dimensions: forwards and backwards, and left and right.

Next, think of yourself as being a dot hanging in the solar system, say somewhere between Mars and the asteroids. You exist in three dimensions, the space we normally think of as our universe.

We refer to time as the fourth dimension, although we have very vague notions about what we actually mean by that, especially since Einstein demonstrated that time is relative. We can visualize four dimensions quite easily: think of a fish moving forwards, backwards, up, down, left and right – the fact that it is moving gives us an understanding of the fourth dimension.

All empirical science is confined to these four dimensions. But pure mathematics (and some modern theoretical physics) is not. Current number theory deals with up to 11 dimensions, and there are potentially an infinite number of dimensions, and an infinite number of the sizes of the infinite numbers of different dimensions. Like the poor dot stuck on the conceptual line which cannot even begin to understand the concepts of left and right, we find it extremely difficult to conceptualize what life in 11 or more dimensions must feel like, but mathematicians do it routinely.

At best, we can only make informed guesses about how other species view number and dimension in the universe. A humming bird is aware of three dimensions, one would imagine, but quite how it perceives time is another question. If we forget conjuring tricks like Hans the counting horse mentioned in the previous chapter, there are still many aspects of animal cognition which are beyond our understanding. What urgent message tells lemmings to leap, and how do they receive it, and how is the clock reset after they have all swum away from shore into oblivion? Why do whales swim into shallow bays to die, refusing frantic persuasions to head back out to sea? Does an ant know its birthday? Does an ant have *any* conception of time?

There have been many studies of the homing instinct in pigeons, because there seems to be some cognitive ability in them which humans do not share. A study conducted in Pisa, Italy, in 1993 subjected a group of pigeons to surgery to see what effects, if any, would be produced in their homing ability (see note 1). Each of the experimental birds had a part of its brain removed – the posterodorsolateral neostriatum and the overlying corticoid, to be precise – the underlying assumption being that this part of the brain in pigeons corresponds to the prefrontal cortex in humans. The experiment produced some peculiar results. Over a familiar route established in training flights, the operated-on birds were slower than a control group of non-operated-on birds from the same loft, but they still found their way home. However, when all the birds were taken to an unfamiliar site, the operated-on birds oriented in the original training flight direction, not the necessary new direction. They were still able to orientate themselves, demonstrating an internal compass or sensitivity to the Earth's magnetic fields which is, as yet, quite beyond human capability, but they were on auto-pilot in the wrong direction. A similar experiment conducted in 1990 had identified the hippocampus area of the pigeon's brain as also an essential part of the central neural structures involved in homing ability (see note 2). While there is some evidence that sense of smell contributes towards a pigeon's homing ability, there is also clearly some cognitive apparatus which pigeons have, but which humans either do not have, or have but do not fully understand as yet.

Bees and other insects also have very sophisticated orientation skills. Like homing pigeons, honey-bees seem to be able to 'read' the Earth's magnetic field. In an experiment conducted at the University of Sussex in 1994, bees were trained in the open air to collect sucrose from a small bottle-cap (see note 3). After the bees had undergone a day's training, the sucrose was periodically removed and a videotaped study recorded the bees' efforts to locate it. The bees consistently faced in one compass direction while they hovered and manoeuvred. Bees seem to have the ability to recognize complex geometrical patterns, and the consistency and accuracy of their perception seems to be based on awareness of the geometrical orientation of the pattern's features. Bees communicate detailed information about distant food sources to other bees in the hive by performing what look like ritualized dance movements; they are, in fact, physical repetitions and representations of the changes in orientation necessary to reach the food. It has been shown that bees can not only identify specific flowers, sometimes many hundreds of metres away from the hive, as good sources of nectar, but they can also indicate the time of day when that particular flower is likely to deliver the highest yield. An experiment conducted in New Haven, Connecticut, suggests that bees are aware of the sun's position even when they are flying by moonlight and the sun is below the horizon (see note 4). Although we cannot say that bees are using numbers as such, they appear to be capable of measuring and indicating times, positions, orientations, distances and quantities, which is more or less all we do with numbers for most of the time.

We humans perceive numbers at a very early stage in our cognitive development. One of the classic experiments in number recognition was first conducted many years ago by the eminent developmental psychologist Jean Piaget. Piaget observed that until a certain stage of cognitive development has been reached, children cannot conceptually grasp the phenomenon known as *conservation of number*. The child is shown two rows of coins, thus:

O O O O O
O O O O O

The child agrees that each row has the same number of coins. Then the second row is spread out, thus:

O O O O O
O O O O O

The child now believes that the second row has more coins. Even putting the coins back as they were originally, then repeating the transformation, does not necessarily convince the child that each row has the same number of coins. In other words, very young children perceive bigness before they perceive fiveness, and the first perception overpowers the second for a while until the new idea of conservation of number has become fully internalized.

Even so, number recognition of some sort happens at an early stage in our developing understanding of the world. An interesting investigation in Rome in 1985 showed that children from poor backgrounds tend to master number recognition before they have begun to master any kind of notation of number, and that all number representation tasks are easier than verbal representation tasks (see note 5). The significance of the poor backgrounds is that these are children who have been exposed to little formal education or richly cultured home environments, so we would expect to see in them a more natural or innate pattern of number recognition. A more recent experiment with adults at Winston-Salem State University in North Carolina sheds some light on where in the brain number recognition – or at least recognition of number symbols – takes place (see note 6). Twenty-four right-handed, blindfolded volunteers attempted to identify the digits 0 to 9, using active or passive touch on a vibrotactile display. The fact that for all subjects the active left hand produced the greatest number of correct identifications suggests that the right hemisphere of the brain was most influential in identifying the digits. This is significant, because the right hemisphere is not associated with language. If recognizing digits takes place mostly in the right hemisphere of the brain, perhaps recognizing the abstract notion of fiveness takes place there, too. The link with visual as opposed to verbal ability (the right half of the brain is associated with the visual, the creative, the spontaneous, while the left half of the brain is associated with the verbal, the analytical, the formal) may also explain why we can 'see' fiveness faster than we can 'see' two-hundred-and-thirty-fourness. Do those savants who can instantly visualize, recall and manipulate large numbers in their heads without pen or paper have something more active happening in their right hemispheres than the rest of us? An article in the *New Yorker* (see note 7) describes an autistic savant, Stephen Wiltshire, whose extraordinary talent seems almost entirely visual-spatial: this young prodigy had virtually no understanding of or interest in language as a growing child, yet by the age of ten he had produced a series of drawings of London buildings showing an astonishing capacity for remembering and reproducing extremely complex detail. The same article mentions the well-known prodigious calculating gift which the novelist Vladimir Nabokov had until the age of seven, when it suddenly disappeared after a high fever with delirium. Nobody knows how such a gift appears in some individuals, nor how it can disappear. The only thing we know for certain is that, as yet, we have only the sketchiest notions of how the human brain receives, understands and manipulates all operations dealing with numbers. The occasional glimpses we see of extraordinary intuition or astonishing ability in metal calculation suggest that the human brain has the capacity to deal with numbers in ways which would seem impossible to most of us at present.

There are some curious anomalies revealed by anthropological studies of how different peoples perceive and use numbers. The Wedda tribe of Sri Lanka, for example, can only count a quantity of objects by pairing them one by one with some other objects – a primitive tally system (see note 8). Australian aborigines have no system of numerals: they use parts of the hand to indicate periods of time, the only unit of measurement in which they appear to have any interest (see note 9). The Plateau Tonga people of southern Africa have a language which contains a full range of equivalents for ordinal positions (first, third, twentieth, etc.), but they have no words for cardinal numbers (see note 10).

At the other end of the spectrum, access to information about numbers is now more complex and sophisticated than ever before in history. It is a routine affair for modern school children to carry in their pockets electronic calculators, the capacities and capabilities of which would have astounded mathematicians of only 50 or so years ago. Leibnitz, Newton and even Einstein would have paid a king's ransom for the cheapest version of the modern calculator. The American communications company AT&T now offers an e-mail service called the Online Encyclopedia of Integer Sequences (see note 11), which provides by almost instantaneous e-mail response lists of numerical information which in previous generations would have taken a lifetime to work out.

All human measurement units are derived from some natural feature or other. The old units of length were based mostly on the human body. A digit was the width of a finger (about 2 cm/three-quarters of an inch); a palm was the width of a hand (about 10 cm/4 in); a hand, which was the length from the tip of the middle finger to the wrist (about 20 cm/8 in); a foot (about 30 cm/12 in); a cubit, which was the length from the tip of the middle finger to the elbow (about 45 cm/18 in); and the fathom, which was the length of rope a sailor could hold between his outstretched hands (about 2m/6 ft). Modern units of measurement are also based on natural phenomena, but of a much more esoteric nature. The metre (length) is equal to 1,650,763.73 wavelengths of the isotope krypton 86; the kilogram (mass) is measured against the mass of a platinum-iridium cylinder stored at Serres in France; and the second (time) is the duration of 9,192,631,770 periods of radiation corresponding to a specific transition of the cesium-133 atom (see note 12).

So far, we have only been discussing how different creatures, including humans, may perceive numbers and dimension. When we begin to examine the diversity and regularity of number sequences occurring in the natural world, a fascinating series of patterns begins to emerge. As the Pythagoreans asserted 2,500 years ago, nature appears to adore numbers.

We can start with rabbits, as Leonardo of Pisa, or Fibonacci, did in 1202. In his *Liber Abaci* (see page 25), Fibonacci wrote this problem:

A man puts a pair of rabbits in a certain place surrounded by a wall. How many pairs of rabbits can be produced from that pair in a year, if the nature of these rabbits is such that every month each pair bears a new pair which from the second month on becomes productive?

We assume that there is no sickness or mortality in this rabbit colony, and that there is an endless food supply (and that no rabbits tunnel out under the wall). Conveniently ignoring the moral problem of all the incestuous liaisons involved, we observe that Mummy Rabbit and Daddy Rabbit produce Baby Rabbit, and that Baby Rabbit and one or other parent produce Baby Rabbit Two; so we now have a full new breeding generation. However, next month Mummy Rabbit and Daddy Rabbit are still doing their thing as well, so the numbers increase fairly rapidly. As a mathematical sequence, the numbers begin thus:

1, 1, 2, 3, 5, 8, 13 ...

To obtain the next number in the series, we simply add together the last two numbers obtained so far. The series therefore continues:

21 (8 + 13), 34 (13 + 21), 55, 89, 144, 233, 377, 610 ... and so on.

This simple sequence – known commonly as the Fibonacci sequence ever since Eduard Lucas first used that term in 1877 – is highly significant in numerology. Whenever a numerological analysis generates a Fibonacci number, that result is particularly noteworthy. The sequence is also important in general mathematics: it is applied to the theory of computer databases, for example. There are two reasons for the significance. The first is that several of the numbers in the sequence are, in and of themselves, particularly interesting or potent numbers, associated with many complex numerological attributes – we shall examine these in detail in later chapters. The second, more general, significance, is that adjacent numbers in the Fibonacci sequence produce closer and closer approximations to a highly significant number known as the Golden Ratio, Golden Section, or Divine Proportion (which will be described in more detail shortly) and, furthermore, that there appears to be a correspondence between the ratios in the sequence

Figure 4 An apple sliced horizontally reveals five seed compartments

and the dimensional ratios of many living things, especially plants.

The mathematician and astronomer Kepler first observed the significance of the number 5, the fifth number in the Fibonacci series, in nature. He believed that almost all trees and bushes have flowers with five petals and fruit with five compartments. Slice any apple horizontally to see for yourself (see figure 4).

The sixth number in the Fibonacci sequence, which we can label F_6, is the number 8. If we divide 8 by 5, using decimal notation, we obtain the answer 1.6. Now, consider the next pair in the sequence, F_7, or 13 and F_6, or 8. If we divide 13 by 8, the result is 1.625. If we continue this process of dividing each consecutive Fibonacci number by its predecessor in the series, a pattern emerges:

F_2 divided by F_1 1 divided by 1 answer: 1
F_3 divided by F_2 2 divided by 1 answer: 2
F_4 divided by F_3 3 divided by 2 answer: 1.5
F_5 divided by F_4 5 divided by 3 answer: 1.666666666...
F_6 divided by F_5 8 divided by 5 answer: 1.6
F_7 divided by F_6 13 divided by 8 answer: 1.625
F_8 divided by F_7 21 divided by 13 answer: 1.615384615...
F_9 divided by F_8 34 divided by 21 answer: 1.619047619...
F_{10} divided by F_9 55 divided by 34 answer: 1.617647059...
F_{11} divided by F_{10} 89 divided by 55 answer: 1.618181818...

... and so on. Each division produces a number which comes closer and closer to the Divine Proportion. We could continue the calculations endlessly, because the Divine Proportion is an irrational number – as was explained in Chapter One, irrational numbers cannot be expressed as a fraction with an integer (whole number) divided by another integer, and when irrational numbers are written in decimal notation the number of decimal places is infinite. To 50 decimal places, the Divine Proportion or Golden Ratio is:

1.61803398874989484820458683436563811772030917980576...

This unwieldy number has been venerated (as a fraction, generally) by many different cultures and for many ages, because of its geometric properties and its apparent presence in growth patterns in nature. The Rhind papyrus (see page 13), refers to a 'sacred ratio' which was important to the Egyptians. In the Great Pyramid built at Gizeh around 2650 BC, the ratio of an altitude of a face to half the side of the base is almost exactly 1.618. The Greeks almost certainly used the same ratio in their architecture, although it does not appear in any document. In 1509, Fra Luca Pacioli published a text on this number, called *De Divina Proportione*, which was illustrated by his friend Leonardo da Vinci. Leonardo called the number *sectio aurea*, or the Golden Section. The number is too complicated to repeat, so it is known nowadays by the names Golden Ratio, etc., or by two Greek letters. Some mathematicians call it T (pronounced 'tau' or 'to') the Greek equivalent of our letter t, although in America the number is more commonly called φ (pronounced 'phi'), following the suggestion of Mark Barr, an American mathematician, who named it after Phidias, a classical Greek sculptor.

It is possible to represent fractional approximations to φ, as in figure 5. The ratio is represented more accurately, however, whenever we draw a pentangle or a pentagram. In figure 6, the ratio between segment AB and segment BC is exactly φ. Since this is a regular figure, the ratio is represented five times. (This is just one of the reasons why the pentangle is such a potent spiritual symbol.)

Within the five arms of the pentangle is a regular pentagon, and the Golden Ratio is present within this figure, too, although it is concealed. It appears (five times of course) when we draw any of the diagonals which connect the five vertices (points where the sides meet). At each point where diagonals intersect, two segments are created, and the ratio of the larger segment to the smaller segment is φ. The five intersections

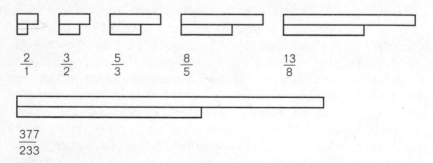

$$\frac{2}{1} \qquad \frac{3}{2} \qquad \frac{5}{3} \qquad \frac{8}{5} \qquad \frac{13}{8}$$

$$\frac{377}{233}$$

Figure 5 Fractional approximations to ø

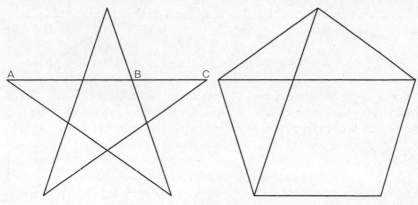

Figure 6 The pentangle   **Figure 7** Diagonals within a regular pentagon

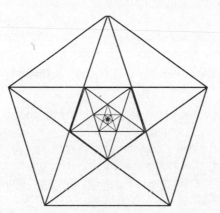

Figure 8 An infinity of Golden Ratios within nested pentagons

of diagonals create a new pentagon, and within *that* pentagon there are five more concealed diagonals, which in turn create a new pentagon, and within that pentagon there are five concealed diagonals, which create a new pentagon ... and so on to infinity – a strikingly beautiful geometrical property, and, numerologists would assert, a strikingly beautiful magical property (see figure 8).

A similar spiral down to infinitesimal smallness appears when we draw a rectangle with its length and width in the ratio of the Divine Proportion, square off one side and draw an arc across to connect the diagonals of the square, and then repeat the process in the remaining smaller rectangle, then repeat the process again – the process is infinite, and from it emerges the familiar spiral pattern shown in figure 9. The reason the spiral is familiar is because we observe it everywhere in nature: in the shell of a snail, in the shell of a nautilus under the sea, in the uncurling of a fern.

Wherever nature produces patterns which involve expansions or contractions by ratio, the ratio very often appears to be 1.618... . The

41

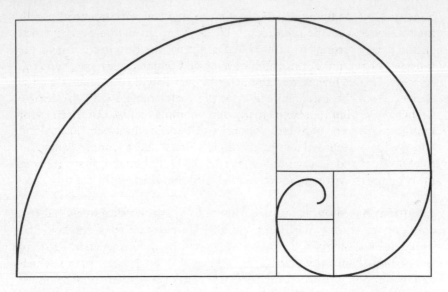

Figure 9 A spiral drawn from the Golden Ratio, or Divine Proportion

scales of a fir cone are set apart at increasing distances, and the ratio involved is φ. The parastichies (spiral rows) of a pineapple follow the same proportional ratio. The pattern is repeated in the florets of the sunflower. In many plants there are pairs of leaves around a central stem which tend to grow in a spiral, such that the angles between each successive pair of leaves are constant. The most common angles are 180°, 120°, 144°, 135°, 138° 27', 137° 8', 137° 27', 137° 31' .... This is a familiar pattern. If we express these angles as ratios of a complete circle, the following sequence emerges:

$$\frac{1}{1} \quad \frac{1}{3} \quad \frac{2}{5} \quad \frac{3}{8} \quad \frac{5}{13} \quad \frac{8}{21} \quad \frac{13}{34} \quad \frac{21}{55} \quad \frac{34}{89}$$ ... and so on (see note 11).

In other words, the leaf arrangements of many living plants also appear to be striving towards the Divine Proportion, the ratios consisting of alternate members of the Fibonacci series. As yet, botanists have no explanation for this mathematical consistency in plant growth; but for numerologists, this astonishing correspondence is not haphazard or meaningless. On the contrary: it represents convincing evidence that the whole created universe corresponds to number, and that through study of number may be obtained some glimpses of the eternal and divine purpose which animates all living things.

Nature deals in whole numbers, as well as in the irrational Divine Proportion. It is very common to find patterns in nature which are known by mathematicians as geometric tilings: these are patterns built on repeated shapes which interlock, like the hexagonal walls of the honeycomb (see figure 10). There is a simple and very practical reason for the success of the honeycomb hexagon: it can contain a great deal and it is very strong. In numerological terms, the number 6 represents (among other things) the union of male and female, marriage, bonding, stability. In the Jewish tradition, the Mogen David or Star of David is derived from the interconnection of the male triangle with the female triangle – the sign represents many other complex ideas, but marriage or bonding between man and woman, and bonding between humankind and God, are included among them. The first Zionist Congress adopted the Star of David as a symbol of Jewry in 1897, although it first appeared in rabbinical writings much earlier, in the thirteenth century (see note 13).

Patterns based on the numbers 2, 3 and 5, or their multiples, are very common in nature, partly for the obvious reason that a fundamental principle in biology is expansion or growth by division. Many growing things branch into two paths, or three paths. In flowers, plants which divide suddenly into many flower stalks are called umbel, those which branch off alternately on each side of a main stalk are called corymb, and those which produce paired branches either side of a continuining main stalk are called cyme (see figure 12). Even in simple

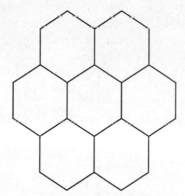
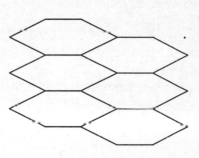

Figure 10 Geometrical tilings

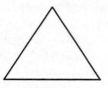
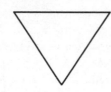

The male triangle   The female triangle   The Mogen David

Figure 11 The Mogen David

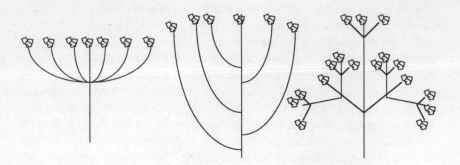

Figure 12 Umbel, corymb and cyme

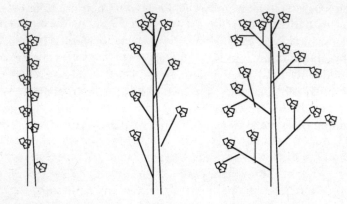

Figure 13 Spike, raceme and panicle

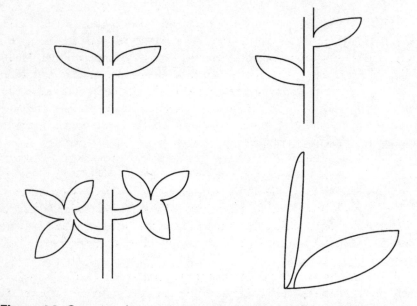

Figure 14 Opposite, alternate, compound and palmate leaf patterns

alternate branchings, there are different patterns, known as spike, raceme, and panicle (see figure 13).

Leaves themselves repeat the common 2, 3, 5 sequence. Although there are many different leaf shapes, and many different ways in which leaf and stalk are joined, the most common patterns are opposite and alternate (based on two), compound (usually based on three) and palmate (usually based on five), as illustrated in figure 14.

The numbers 3 and 5 (Fibonacci numbers F_4 and F_5) recur with great frequency in the family of flowers: three-petalled or three-sepalled flower groups include the Arrowhead family (Alismataceae); all the Spiderworts (Commelinaceae); the Iris family (Iridaceae) which actually have three sepals, three petals, three stamens and three styles over the sepals; orchids (Orchidaceae) which have three sepals and two lateral petals irregularly related to a larger third petal; the Birthwort family (Aristolochiaceae); and the Wood-sorrels (Oxalidaceae). The Lily family (Liliaceae), which includes lilies, trilliums, onions, tulips and hyacinths, presents a special case in that the flower plan may be either bell-like or triangular, in six or three. Typical lilies have six-parted flowers with six stamens and a long pistil ending in a three-lobed stigma.

Flower families with a pattern of five include: the Purslanes (Portulacaceae); Pinks (Caryophyllaceae) including the hothouse carnation; the Pitcher-Plant family (Sarraceniaceae); the Sundew family (Droseraceae); the Rose family (Rosaceae), a very large group which includes wild roses, strawberries, blackberries and apples; the Pea family (Leguminosae), another large group which includes peas, beans and clovers; the Flax family (Linaceae); Geraniums (Gerianiaceae); the Milkwort family (Polygalaceae); the Mallow family (Malvaceae), which includes the popular garden hollyhock; the St Johnswort family (Guttiferae); the Violet family (Violaceae), which includes the pansy; the Ginseng family (Araliaceae); Wintergreens (Pyrolaceae); the Heath family (Ericaceae), which includes rhododendrons, azaleas and blueberries; Primroses (Primulaceae); the Milkweed family (Asclepiadaceae); the Morning-Glory family (Convolvulaceae); Phloxes (Polemoniaceae); and the Tomato or Nightshade family (Solanaceae), a large group which includes tomatoes, potatoes and peppers.

Nature also seems fond of the Golden Ratio and of the number 5 under the ocean. Mention has already been made of the shell of the nautilus, the spiral of which is related to the Divine Proportion or ø. There are many varieties of starfishes and featherfishes with five arms. The Purple Sunstar (Solaster endeca) has eight arms, and the Common Sunstar (Solaster papposus) has twelve, but these are exceptions to the pattern.

There are many traditions of natural stones and metals having or relating to number characteristics. Certain crystals have definite and regular geometric shapes in which the underlying number relationship is immediately obvious: quartz, for example. Historically, numerology has 'borrowed' these tables of relationships from alchemy, which in turn relates different stones to different planets. I have compiled a table of correspondences (see table 1) from a variety of sources, but especially from the work of the late Scott Cunningham (see note 14). As will be explained in much more detail later, there are many different correspondences for numbers and planets, according to which numerological tradition we follow. The numbers given in table 1 are the numbers of the planetary magic squares, which will be discussed in detail in Chapter Four. The planetary/metal correspondences are very old, and common to almost all alchemical systems.

Table 1

Number	Planet	Metal	Stone
3	Saturn	lead	alum, black tourmaline, brown jasper, coal, hematite, jet, obsidian, onyx, salt, serpentine
4	Jupiter	tin	amethyst, lepidolite, lugilite
5	Mars	iron	asbestos, bloodstone, flint, garnet, lava, onyx, pipestone, red jasper, red tourmaline, rhodocrosite, rhodonite, ruby, sard, sardonyx, watermelon tourmaline
6	Sun	gold	amber, carnelian, diamond, orange calcite, pipestone, quartz crystal, sulphur, sunstone, tiger's-eye, topaz, zircon
7	Venus	copper	azurite, blue calcite, blue-green calcite, green jasper, green tourmaline, jade, kunzite, lapis lazuli, malachite, olivine, peridot, pink calcite, pink tourmaline, sodalite, turquoise
8	Mercury	quicksilver	agate, aventurine, mica, mottled jasper, pumice
9	Moon	silver	aquamarine, beryl, chalcedony, moonstone, mother-of-pearl, pearl, quartz crystal, sapphire, selenite
10*	Uranus	uranium	amber, coral, jet
11*	Neptune	caesium	amethyst, celestite, lepidolite, mother-of-pearl
13*	Pluto	plutonium	kunzite, spinel, tourmalated quartz

Traditional alchemy, which is many centuries old, knew nothing of the more recently discovered planets Uranus, Neptune and Pluto, but alchemy is a living tradition, and these additional correspondences are now widely accepted.

Nature is so teemingly diverse, it would be a simple matter to conjure up numerical correspondences across a very wide range of natural phenomena. What is more interesting is to note that there are certain numbers which nature appears to abhor, as she reportedly abhors a vacuum. No creature has 11 legs. There are countless examples of patterns of 6 in nature, and patterns of 8, but patterns of 7 and 9 are extremely rare, as are patterns of 13 or 17.

When we transfer our attention from the macrocosm to the microcosm, we begin to observe some very peculiar number properties in nature, many of which are still highly disputed by physicists. Quantum physics and quantum mechanics, which are now almost a century old, are predicated on a theoretical model of physical properties which are still barely understood.

Around the turn of the century, Max Planck began some experiments involving the radiation of light by hot, black objects. Until those experiments, theories of light were essentially Newtonian: they assumed that light was a wave form of energy, and all experiments seemed to confirm that model. Planck's observation was that light appeared to emanate not, after all, in waves, but in small bursts of energy, which he called 'quanta', the plural of 'quantum', the Latin for 'how much'. The Danish physicist Niels Bohr applied Planck's theory to the emerging theory of how atoms behaved. In 1913, Bohr asserted that energy is released from an atom in the form of a quantum of light (called a 'photon') when electrons leap from one orbit to another around the central nucleus of protons and neutrons. This 'leap' is very peculiar: according to Bohr, it is instantaneous, so that one instant the electron exists in one orbit, and the next it exists in another orbit, but in between it does not exist at all. Hence, this extraordinary transfer is called a 'quantum leap', although modern physicists prefer to use the term 'quantum jump' when discussing Bohr's theory.

From this notion of the quantum leap developed a very important modern mathematical idea: the so-called 'uncertainty principle', associated with Werner Heisenberg. Extremely simplified, Heisenberg's argument is that by the very act of observing particles, or quanta, we change the way they behave. By Planck's quantum hypothesis, we need at least one quantum of light in order to be able to observe the position of a particle, but the very presence of the quantum disturbs the particle and changes its velocity in a way that cannot be predicted. Heisenberg demonstrated that the uncertainty in the position of the particle times the uncertainty in its velocity times the mass of the particle can never be smaller than a certain quantity, which is now known as Planck's constant.

For centuries, empirical science has had as its underpinning the belief that the universe does adhere to predictable and reliable rules, even if we are not yet fully competent in observing and determining what those rules are precisely. The uncertainty principle, inevitably, introduces profound confusion. There are no longer any absolutes. The clockwork model is no longer appropriate. The universe is fuzzy. Einstein was so dismayed by this notion, that he repudiated the uncertainty principle: in a letter to Max Born in 1926, he remarked, 'At any rate, I am convinced that He [God] does not play dice.'

Even more recently, particles smaller than protons and neutrons have been discovered. They were named 'quarks' by the Caltech physicist Murray Gell-Mann, who was awarded the Nobel prize in 1969 for his work on them. Quarks are very mysterious beasts indeed. There are at least six types: up, down, strange, charmed, bottom and top. Each of the six types is further subdivided into three 'colours' – red, green and blue – although these objects are so small that they do not have real colour in the normal sense.

The mathematics involved in quantum physics is too complicated to describe here, but one number deserves brief mention: the imaginary number i, which will be discussed more fully later. The space-time continuum as we have known it until very recently is called Euclidean – it follows the familiar axioms of the geometry first set out by the ancient Greek mathematician Euclid. The modern physicist's conception of the universe, however, which assumes an expanding universe which originated in a big bang, and in which the principle of relativity is observed, breaks down if it is confined to Euclidean geometry: it just will not work. The modern mathematician has to use imaginary numbers, including i, and indeed numbers which are far more abstruse and complicated than i, and as soon as they are used, the distinction between time and space disappears very conveniently. This may sound like an ultra-sophisticated scientific trick, but it actually makes consistent sense within itself, and has led to many further exciting discoveries in the realms of modern mathematics and modern physics. At the smallest extreme of the universe, at the sub-atomic level, we observe electrons changing orbits instantaneously. At the largest extreme of the universe, we observe space-time as a curve. In both instances, we have to use imaginary numbers either for time or for space for space-time to make sense. These imaginary numbers have only very recently gained wide acceptance, so they of course do not appear in traditional numerology, but they will be taken into account in this book, particularly in Chapter Eight.

Planck's constant of uncertainty, chaos theory and other very modern mathematical conceptions actually bring us, paradoxically, full circle back to a very ancient idea: the notion of the infinite within the finite, familiar to Pythagoras and to Plato. One realm of modern mathematics which deals specifically with this question is known as the study of fractals. The beauty of fractals, about which whole books continue to be written, is that we see in their patterns some very striking symmetries and asymmetries which, for very good reasons, remind us of much that we see in nature.

The father of the modern study of fractals is Benoit Mandelbrot, a French mathematician who worked for IBM in New York. Mandelbrot's description was first published in an article in *Science* in 1967, although he did not introduce the term fractals until 1977. The article begins by asking us to consider a fairly straightforward geographical task: we are to measure accurately a given stretch of coastline. First, we fly over the coastline at 10,000 m (33,000 ft) and take photographs. Bays and headlands appear, but not in any great detail. Nevertheless, we are able to give at least an estimate of the given length of coastline. So we fly over the same stretch of coastline again, this time at 500 m (1,600 ft). Now the indentations are much clearer. This time, our measurement estimate is considerably longer, because we now take into account all those extra indentations and headlands which we failed to observe fully before. As it happens, this stretch of coastline is part of the very crinkly Norwegian coastline which gave Slartibartfast such delight (see note 15). So we give this stretch of coastline a really close examination, this time from only 5 m (16 ft). Now we have vast amounts of detail to work with. From 5 cm (2 in), we have even more. From the width of 5 atoms, even more. And so on, to infinity. This is very similar to the idea of the infinity of numbers between 2 and 3 discussed at the beginning of the chapter. The physicist would argue that there is a physical limit to the possible measurement, but mathematically there is no limit. The coastline cannot be accurately measured: we can only produce increasingly accurate approximations, and the limit of the tendency is infinite. In other words, this concrete and finite physical reality, a real piece of coastline, has no real limit but is infinitely long. This is a fairly startling idea.

The mathematical pattern behind the extreme irregularity of a real physical coastline is actually an extremely orderly and predictable pattern of scaling and transformation. We can represent the basic idea very simply. Take a line. Transform the line by an operation. For each new line generated, repeat the transformation, at the new scale. Repeat to infinity. These repeated steps are called iterations.

Machine-generated fractals are now commonplace. Many readers will be familiar with the screensavers which prevent burn-out on computer

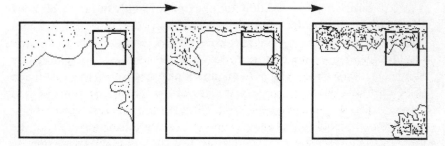

Figure 15 A coastline is finite, but it has an infinite length

screens, whose patterns are often generated by fractal algorithms. Software to generate fractals on home computers is already widely available (see note 16). The principle by which fractals are generated is very simple, although the mathematics become very complicated quite quickly.

The significance of fractals for the numerologist, apart from their intrinsic beauty, is the further confirmation they appear to give to the notion of a relationship between life and number: creation, extension, propagation and diversification in the natural living world seem driven by the same elemental patterns which are observed in numbers. Figure 16, for example, is a fairly convincing fern leaf, generated by a very simple four-step transformation sequence on a computer.

In 1845, a mathematician called P.F. Verhulst formulated a growth law for computations involving populations which increase towards a maximum limit. (A brief account of the formula is given in Appendix Nine.) Some very peculiar results emerge from the application of this formula, which is related to fractal geometry. When the rate of growth in the Verhulst formula is less than 2 (i.e., a 200 per cent growth rate), all is comparatively normal: the maximum population is reached, the numbers level off. If the population declines, numbers increase until the maximum is reached again, and the whole process repeats itself. However, when the rate goes slightly above 2, the obtained values begin to oscillate between two figures. (The rate 2.1 gives values of 0.82 and 1.13 alternately.) When the rate approaches 2.5, the values oscillate between four figures or points. When the rate equals 2.55, a new cycle begins, with oscillation between eight points. At 2.565, there are 16 points. When the rate reaches 2.57, something very strange happens. The points of oscillation have now doubled to infinity, and the whole dynamic pattern now becomes completely chaotic, with no observable pattern. However, even within this chaos there is a kind of order. The chaos divides itself into separate bands of chaotic behaviour. When the rate is around 3 there is only one chaotic band, but between 2.57 and 3 an infinitely large series of bands of chaos has been generated. At 2.679 there are two bands of chaos, at 2.593 four bands of chaos, then eight, then sixteen, and so on, to infinity.

These rather obscure and difficult observations only began to gain real significance when Mandelbrot began using very powerful modern computers to generate fractal patterns. The mathematical processes are too complicated to describe here, but they are very clearly explained by Keith Devlin (see note 17). What Mandelbrot discovered was that when the computers produced graphic images of the fractal equations he had programmed into them, in some of the images tiny islands, which at first he mistook as dots or smudges, began appearing in isolated areas of the image. On closer inspection, it became clear that these dots were minute replicas of the main image, somehow replicating themselves in separate

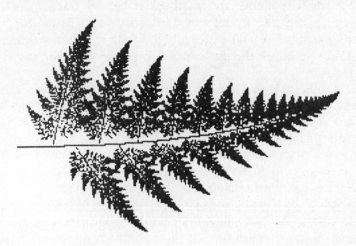

Figure 16 A fractal fern leaf

areas. Later still, it became apparent that the location of these apparently self-generating images was directly related to the gaps in the chaotic regions of the Verhulst process.

We do not yet fully understand the process of creation and regeneration in nature, nor do we yet fully understand the mathematics of fractal geometry, but the similarities between the processes we have observed in both are striking and beautiful. Numerologists believe that the more we discover about the natural dynamic processes occurring in the universe, the greater and clearer will be our observations of the eternal numerical patterns underpinning them.

Through countless ages, humans have attributed certain characteristics or qualities to certain numbers. In the next chapter, we look more closely at the attributes which different cultures, religions and mythologies have given to different numbers.

51

three

NUMBER ATTRIBUTES

0·1·2·3·4·5·6·7·8·9·0·1·2·3·4·5·6·7·8·9·0·1·2·3·4·5·6·7·8·9·0·1·2·3·4·5·6·7·8·9

For numerologists, the most widely accepted basis for an understanding of the significance of number attributes is the Hebrew or Jewish Kabbalah (also spelt Qabalah), which is so full of important information that it will be dealt with separately (see Chapter Five). Similarly, there are many important correspondences between numbers and letters in different alphabet traditions, particularly in the Greek, Coptic, Irish Ogham, Celtic, Runic and Latin alphabets, and these are so numerous that they, too, will have a chapter to themselves (Chapter Six). In the mean time, we can briefly examine how each of the numbers 0 to 9 has been symbolically interpreted in different cultures, and look at some other numbers of particular note.

0

Nought, or zero, also called null, was not known to the Greeks. As described in Chapter One, it originated in India, was taken up in 773 AD at the court of Caliph Al-Mansur in Baghdad, and only came into use in the West after 1202, when merchants got news of Fibonacci's new system of arithmetic in his *Liber Abaci*, and began to see the advantages of such a system. Accordingly, 0 has very little tradition of number mysticism. It begins to appear in alchemy from the fourteenth century onwards, and its emergence coincided with the introduction of the first Tarot cards, from which time it has always been associated with the card known as The Fool. The name null, used mostly in Germanic traditions, is derived from Latin *nulla figura*, which means 'not a real figure'. The Mayans – and perhaps before them the Olmec – appear to have independently achieved an understanding of 0. They represented the number pictorially with the sign of an empty oyster, called *xok*, which also means 'hollow' (see note 1).

1

The Pythagoreans gave 1 a name: they called it the *monad*. However, they thought of it not so much as a number in and of itself, but as the prime cause of all other numbers. Even as late as 1537, the German mathematician Kobel wrote: 'Wherefrom thou understandest that 1 is no number, but it is a generatrix, beginning and foundation for all other numbers' (see note 2). Even more recently, Euler noted that the simplest way to deal with 1 in relation to prime numbers (to be dealt with more fully in the next chapter) was to deny that 1 is a prime number at all.

However, despite its 'non-existence' as a true number, 1 was associated with many characteristics and symbolic interpretations by the Greeks and other cultures. Geometrically, 1 represents the point, a curious figure since it has no dimension of its own but, by its very existence, it defines a dimension. One represents the present, the here and now, and the same curiosity appears in time as in space: 'now' is constantly coming into existence, and immediately ceasing to exist as a new 'now' takes its place. Like the point which has no dimension, the 1 of time has no dimension of its own, yet it defines all eternity. This sounds very nebulous and metaphysical, but modern physics is very much preoccupied with the 1 of 'now-ness'. A research machine called the Large Hadron Collider is about to be built in a 27-km (17-mile) tunnel under the Franco-Swiss border near Geneva – at an estimated cost of £1.4 billion – to accelerate fragments of matter and smash them together at almost the speed of light in order to recreate the conditions that existed in the first million millionth of a second of the universe's existence (see note 3).

Greek culture was polytheistic, so 1 did not represent the unity of Godhead, as it has done subsequently for Christianity and Islam. 1 was associated with fire (the first element), with Cronos (Saturn in Rome) as the first god and originator of time, and both with the Moon and with the Sun. The other gods associated with 1 were Androgynos (because he/she contained both odd and even, male and female); Apollo, a precursor of the male-deity hegemony later typified by Zeus (Deus Pater or Jupiter in Rome); Atlas (the supporter of all things); Lethe (oblivion); and Vesta (the deification of the first element, fire).

The Hebrew notion of 1, as exemplified in the Kabbalah, will be discussed in Chapter Five, but from it is derived a vast philosophical tradition, first in Christianity, later in Islam, about the significance of the Oneness or Unity of God: 'There is no God but Allah', or 'The Lord thy God is one God'. In the radical Sufi tradition, there can be no separateness from God, and it is only when the seeker is completely annihilated and absorbed within the unity of the godhead that God can speak through His own mouth the expression of His existence and unity. There are countless Christian tracts, pamphlets and books, written over centuries, discussing the mystery of the Trinity, in which the three elements of Father, Son and Holy Ghost become the One, the Unity of God.

The fifteenth-century magician and mystic, Henricus Cornelius Agrippa von Nettesheim wrote of 1:

One therefore is referred to the High God, who seeing he is one, and innumerable, yet creates innumerable things of himself, and contains them within himself. There is therefore one God, one world of the one God, one Sun of the one world, also one phoenix in the world, one king amongst bees, one leader amongst flocks of cattle, one ruler amongst herds of beasts, and cranes follow one, and many other animals honour unity (see note 4).

The odd reference to the king of bees arises because classical and medieval writers thought the queen bee was a king bee. The reference to cranes is taken from a famous description by the classical Roman author, Pliny the Elder.

In a sense, 1 is so omnipresent, so all-consuming, that it is difficult even to discuss it. When the Greeks considered the behaviour of sets of objects, the smallest set they could think of was a set of two. How could you say that a set of one object even had a behaviour? That same indeterminacy appears in many subsequent cultures. One is the Ineffable, the Unutterable, the eternal source of the fountain, the beginning of the unfolding.

Eastern creation myths begin clearly with 1. The Chinese conceptualized a tiny egg, within which the entire universe was a chaotic mass. This is not so far removed from modern theory about the origins of the Big Bang. From within this dark and chaotic mass, Pangu, the first being, emerged. When Pangu broke open the universal egg, the lighter part (the *yang*, or masculine force) rose and became the heavens, while the heavier part (the *yin*, or female force) sank and became the Earth and its waters: 1 became 2 and creation had begun. The Japanese creation myth is very similar, except that from the world egg emerges first an unnamed god in the shape of a reed-shoot, followed by the two gods, Izanagi no Mikoto and Izanami no Mikoto.

The Egyptians, whose pantheon was vast, also had a nameless, formless god who preceded all the other gods; this god was called Neter, which simply means 'the god', and from Neter the two eldest gods, Shu and Tefnut, were parthenogenetically brought into creation, and from them Osiris and all the other gods were descended.

In Inca mythology, the god of 1, the primogenitor, is Lord Con Ticci Viracocha, who emerged from the void to create all matter, then later made his home in Lake Titicaca. This is the same Con Ticci or Kon Tiki commemorated in Thor Heyerdahl's famous boat.

The hermetic alchemists coined the name Azoth to signify the hidden essence of oneness which pervades the universe. The name is combinatory, derived from Latin, Greek and Hebrew letters. The sixteenth-century physician, magician and alchemist, Theophrastus Bombast von Hohenheim, known as Paracelsus, had the name engraved on the pommel of his sword. For alchemists, 1 was the number of the Philosopher's

Stone, the mysterious catalyst which turns base metal into gold. In the body, 1 represented the heart.

There is an unusual group of numbers known as the 'repunits' (short for 'repeated units'), which consists of all the numbers apart from 1 itself which only have 1 as digits: 11, 111, 1,111, 11,111, 111,111, etc. They have many curious features. Here is one example:

$$1^2 = 1$$
$$11^2 = 121$$
$$111^2 = 12,321$$
$$1,111^2 = 1,234,321$$
$$11,111^2 = 123,454,321 \text{ etc.}$$

In modern numerology, 1 is associated with certain personality traits and attributes. First, however, a brief explanatory note about number and 'character' is required.

Poor numerology books – and there are plenty of them about – tell the reader his or her number (birth number, lucky number, soul number, astral number, character number, etc.) and then launch into broad character descriptions: 'You are an aggressive go-getter who stands no nonsense; you are Mr Idea, but you should keep your plans to yourself because you work best alone', and so on. These are modelled on astrological descriptions by birth sign, and most of them are of very little use or validity, for two main reasons.

The first is that it is very rare for any one person to have just one number absolutely dominant throughout life. It is true that many people consider themselves to have lucky numbers, or one special number. A famous case is the Russian author Leo Tolstoy, who firmly believed 28 to be his special number. He was born on 28 August 1828, his son was born on 28 June and he left his home for the last time, before his death, on 28 October. For the composer Richard Wagner, 13 was especially significant. Wagner was born in 1813 (the digits of which add to 13), his name contains 13 letters, he wrote 13 great works and he died on 13 February. Nevertheless, serious modern numerologists believe that an individual's life is governed by a complex divine purpose in which many different numbers will play a significant part. The same number may recur with great frequency, or the individual may perceive enough of the underlying pattern to gain an attachment to a particular number and think of it as a special or lucky number; but in reality, serious numerologists believe, many numbers (often related numerically) work together in the underlying harmonies of life.

The second reason is that to say that one number alone determines a person's life is simplistic. It is neither possible nor reasonable to deduce an entire character and personality simply from one number or even from a group of numbers: 'You are a 7, so your character is this ....' Life is much more complicated than that. Serious numerology asserts that certain numbers are associated with certain attributes and – for a person in whose life a particular number is markedly dominant – some of the associated attributes may also appear; no more than that. These ideas will be clarified in the later chapters of the book which deal with practical numerology.

1 is, of course, associated with independence, single-mindedness, creativity, instigation, and so on. It is also associated with androgyny (it is the only number in the Pythagorean system which is both male and female) and with sexual hermaphroditism and neutrality. It is unusual for an individual to have 1 as a dominant life number. 1 is like the 'Go' in Monopoly: the player collects £200 for passing it, but its real purpose is to lead into the game proper. 11 is a prime number, the two digits of which yield 2 when added, and it quite often happens in numerological analysis that 1 yields 11 or 2. Like the Chinese primordial egg, 1 appears not to want to rest as 1: it wants to become 2 or another number. For that reason, 1 is also associated with material wealth, loneliness, seclusion, the contemplative or monastic life, isolation, and so on.

Esoterically, 1 is visualized as a great White Flame, as a stone from which living seed miraculously springs, as a pillar of fire, as a blazing crown, and as the burning bush which Moses beheld.

2

2 is the first number, according to some interpretations of the Pythagorean system, while others wait for 3. It is female. Some Greeks had reservations about its numberhood, thinking of it as a beginning and end with no middle. They were aware that in most cases multiplication does something greater than mere addition, so noting that $2 + 2 = 4$ and $2 \times 2 = 4$ – in fact that multiplying any number by 2 is the same as adding the number to itself – was something of a disappointment. However, the classification of 2 as female persisted. In the Pythagorean system, all even numbers are female, all odd numbers male.

The classical gods and goddesses associated with 2 are: Ceres (because there were two harvests in the classical world, the harvest of spring-sown wheat and the harvest of winter-sown wheat, or, in some cultures, the harvest of wheat and the harvest of barley); Cupid, the god of sexual love; Diana (as the Moon); Rhea (mother of Jupiter); but, above all, Aphrodite or Venus, the personification of all that is female.

A curious number pattern of 2, 6 and 12 is found in the story of Romulus and Remus, the mythological twin founders of Rome. Most people are familiar with the story of the twin babes, supposedly fathered by Mars, being left to drown in the River Tiber, but then being rescued and suckled by a mother wolf, until they survived and eventually founded the city. Because they were twins, they could not decide which of them was rightful King of Rome, so they prayed to the gods for an answer. Romulus and his followers stood on the Palatine hill, Remus and his followers on the Aventine hill. Six vultures descended to Remus, and he claimed the throne. Then 12 vultures descended to Romulus, which led him to assert that his claim was clearly twice as strong. After a bitter argument, Romulus killed Remus and became king. Numerologically, 6 represents stability, harmony, marriage and concord. The numerological interpretation of the Romulus and Remus legend, therefore, is that the discord of 2 is subsumed by the harmony of 6 to produce 12, the resolution of the discord.

2 is probably the most widely represented number in the natural world. Division into two parts, often opposites in character, is so commonplace as to be unremarkable. There are male and female, night and day, dark and light, high and low, young and old, strong and weak, and so on. Many plants and animals, including humans, are bilaterally symmetrical. There is a mathematical theory, called Goldbach's conjecture, which relates to the numerological theory of the pervading influence of 2. Goldbach conjectured (his conjecture has never yet been proven) that every number greater than 2 is the sum of two prime numbers. 2 is the only even prime number. (Prime numbers are discussed more fully in the next chapter.) In other words, in every positive number greater than 2 there is some element of 2 present.

The importance of 2 is recognized even in the structure of many languages, including all Indo-European languages, Arabic, Sanskrit and Hebrew, all of which have dual cases for nouns. Many languages have several synonyms for 2: in English, we have pair, brace, duo, twain, couplet, doublet, twin.

In many cultures, 2 signifies discord, disharmony or dissension. In English, there are many pejorative expressions based on 2: 'two-faced', 'double-dealing' and 'duplicitous' are examples. In other cultures, the duality does not have pejorative connotations. The Chinese *yin* and *yang* have already been mentioned. A more personified dualistic view of the universe is found in Zoroastrianism, which flourished in ancient Iran, in which all that is good and light is represented by the god Ahura Mazda and all that is evil and dark is represented by the god Ahriman. The Greek διαβολς (DIABOLOS) originally meant 'two-sayer' or 'slanderer' and it is the root of the Latin *diabolus* and English 'devil'.

In monotheistic religions, 2 implies the antithesis of the unique, eternal One. 2 is Lucifer, or the Anti-Christ. Because the nature of 2 as female (and its attribution to Venus) were known to medieval Christian exegetes, they called 2 the number of sex. They also noted in Genesis that the formula 'and it was good' is missing for the second day, because the creation of the second day was the creation of the waters, which was not completed until the third day. In the Christian view, 2 represents the female, and the female represents incompleteness.

57

Agrippa of Nettesheim makes the following observations about other Biblical aspects of 2:

Hence there were two tables of the Law in Sinai, two cherubins looking to the propitiatory in *Moses*, two olives dropping oil in *Zachariah*, two natures in Christ, divine and human; hence Moses saw two appearances of God, viz, his face and back parts, also two testaments, two commands of love, two first dignities, two first people, two kinds of spirits, good and bad, two intellectual creatures, and angel and soul, two great lights, two solsticia, two equinoctials, two poles, two elements producing a living soul, viz, Earth, and Water (see note 5).

The curious reference to God's 'back parts' is derived from Exodus 33:11 and 20–23:

And the Lord spake unto Moses face to face, as a man speaketh unto his friend .... And he said, 'Thou canst not see my face: for there shall no man see me, and live.' And the Lord said, 'Behold, there is a place by me, and thou shalt stand upon a rock: And it shall come to pass, while my glory passeth by, that I will put thee in a clift of the rock, and will cover thee with my hand while I pass by: And I will take away mine hand, and thou shalt see my back parts: but my face shall not be seen.'

As Agrippa's list suggests, medieval alchemists saw 2 represented in the intellectual sphere by the angel and the soul, in the celestial sphere by the Sun and the Moon, and in the elementary world by the elements of earth and water. The heart and the brain represent 1 and 2 in the physical body.

Modern numerological attributes of 2 are largely derived from these traditions. 2 is associated with archetypal female attributes: sensitivity, tact, emotional nature, timidity, tolerance, cooperativity, patience, diplomacy, receptivity, etc. Many of these attributes are denigratory to women, as are the attributes of duplicity, dissension, discord, and so on, which are also traditionally associated with 2. In almost every circumstance, these negative attributes can be traced back to some aspect of male chauvinistic or misogynistic thinking in the monotheistic religious traditions, particularly medieval Christianity. As modern paganism has evolved, and in particular as modern Wicca has emphasized the duality and equality of the God and of the Goddess, numerology has thrown off many of these traditional attitudes, and most modern numerologists interpret the characteristics and attributes of 2 more positively and less chauvinistically.

Esoterically, 2 is the descent of spirit into matter, the great feminine mystery of recreation, the waters under the firmament divided from the waters above the firmament, the silent and secret, the innermost, the sleeping princess, Snow White, Leah and Rachel, Martha and Mary, Mary Magdalene and the blessed Virgin Mary, the two columns of the Masonic Lodge, the Jachin and Boaz; where 1 is the head and the crown, 2 is the heart and the cross. 2 is also associated with tolerance, tact and stillness.

3

3 is the holiest of numbers in a very wide range of cultures. It is the first Pythagorean number, and it is male. It is the first odd number, after 1. Proclus, the chief representative of the Neoplatonists, noted in 475 AD that 3×3 is greater than $3 + 3$. Three dimensions encapsulate physical space. Numbers with three factors can be visualized as solids. 3 is mystically related to the circle, since a circle can be drawn through any three points which do not lie on a straight line.

The human mind seems to have an innate conception of 3 relating to completeness. 3 represents yesterday, today and tomorrow, or past, present and future. 3 represents positive, comparative and superlative. 3 represents beginning, middle and end. Mathematically, the pervasive influence of 3 is recognized in the observation of Carl Friedrich Gauss (1777–1855) that every integer (whole number) can be represented as the sum of at most three triangular numbers. Numbers can be thought of as having geometrical shapes (see figure 17). The sequence of triangular numbers begins 1, 3, 6, 10 .... The point made by Gauss, in a very elegant but complex proof, is that *every* whole number can be represented as the sum of three triangular numbers. The formula for determining figurate numbers, as these geometrical number sequences are known, is given in Appendix Ten.

The secret and holy symbol of Pythagoreanism, the *tetraktys*, venerated as an icon of the entire universe, is triangular in form (see figure 18). The top dot represents unity, position, eternity. The two dots below represent distance, separation, distinction, opposition, movement. The three dots represent all surfaces, maps, plans, arrangements, extensions in two-dimensions, and all geometric figures. The four dots represent three-dimensional space, the entirety of the universe. The mystic dimension of time is represented on each side of the pyramid by the combination of the four dots on the side with the one dot at the centre, the number 5 also representing colour, volume, everything susceptible to the five senses. The number of life, 6, is found in the hexagon of six dots formed by the central pair of dots on each side, and the number 7, the number of intelligence, health, light and inspiration, associated with the goddess Athene, is found by adding the central dot to this hexagon. The total of all the dots is 10, the number of perfection.

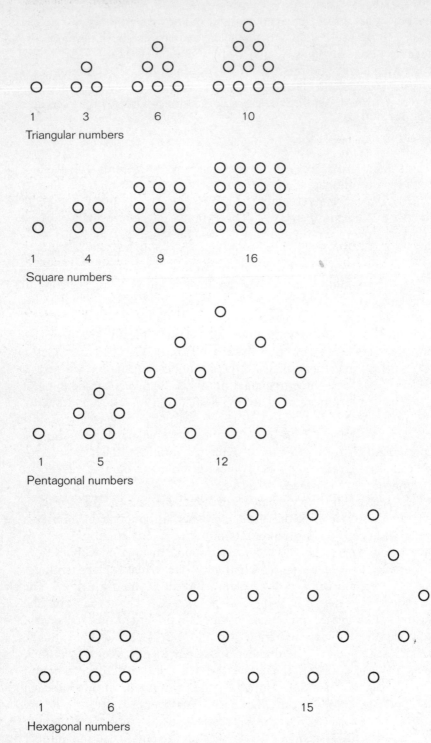

Figure 17 Triangular, square, pentagonal and hexagonal numbers

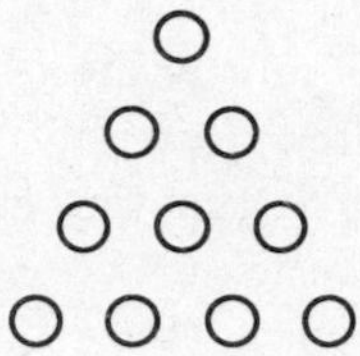

Figure 18 The tetraktys

The hegemony of 3 in Greek mythology is found in the number of deities and semi-deities who appear in threes: the Fates, the Furies and the Graces, for example. The first three immortal beings were Gaea (Mother Earth), Tartarus, ruler of the underworld, and Eros (Love). Gaea gave birth parthenogenetically to Uranus (Sky), Ourea (Mountains) and Pontus (Sea). The first children of Gaea and Uranus were the 300-handed Giants. Their next offspring were the three one-eyed Cyclopes.

Some of the classical gods associated with 3 are male, most notably Mars, Roman god of war, and Pluto, god of the underworld, but 3 is also the number of the Triple Goddess, whose names and aspects are many. In classical mythology she is Hecate or Helice; in Celtic mythology she is Cerridwen and Brigid and Rhiannon, or a score of other names. The goddess is triple because she appears in three aspects: first as the pure maiden; second as the mother who gives birth to all humankind; thirdly as the crone or wise woman who lays out the dead.

Yet the notion of divine trinity is much older than the Triple Goddess as she is known in Europe, much older even than the Greeks. The Babylonian creation myth begins with a trinity: Father Apsu rules the sweet waters, Mother Tiamat rules the salt waters, and their son Mummu is the mist that lies between them. In the epic of *Gilgamesh*, the earliest recorded work of literature, dating from the Sumeria of about 2700 BC, the hero is two-thirds god by his mother Ninsun and one-third man by his father Lugalbanda, King of Uruk. The Yoruba people of Nigeria have a creation myth which begins with Olorun the Father, Olokun the Mother and Obatala the Son. Clearly, this widespread mythographic pattern is derived from the archetypal image of regeneration: father and mother beget child, and there is a completeness.

Egypt had many gods and goddesses, but Isis, Osiris and their son Horus were the three principal deities; their Greek counterparts were Athena, Zeus and Apollo. The pattern is a little different in Hinduism, where Brahma the creator, Shiva the destroyer and Vishnu the sustainer do not have such clear sexual or regenerative roles: they are more abstract and complex figures, as are the Japanese trinity in Mahayana Buddhism of Amida, Sheishi and Kwannon. In Northern mythology, 3 represents the three worlds of Midgard (where Earth is), Asgard (where the gods are), and Nilfheim (the land of frozen fog). There are also three

61

Norns, or Fates, like the three Moiras of Greece, three female powers who spin and cut the thread of mortal life.

The Christian trinity is Pater, Filius and Spiritus Sanctus: God the Father, Son, and Holy Spirit. St Ignatius of Loyola is reputed to have wept with joy whenever he saw the number 3, because it was the number of the Holy Trinity. In practice, the Holy Spirit is too vague and intellectual a concept for some Christians, and adoration of the Virgin Mary, the Holy Mother, restores a pattern closer to the familial pattern found in many other world mythologies and religions. Biblical threes are legion: the darkness over Egypt lasted three days; Jonah spent three days in the belly of the whale; there are three Magi who bring three gifts to the infant Jesus, who is crucified but returns from death on the third day.

Hindu prayers end with *shantih shantih shantih* (peace), a three-fold invocation. The Grand Bard of Cornwall opens and closes the Cornish Gorsedh with a thrice-spoken question, *Eus kres?* (Is there peace?). As Aladdin learns from the Genie, wishes come in threes. Throughout the world's many cultures, 3 is a number of immense power and significance. As Agrippa of Nettesheim says: 'The number of three is an incompounded number, a holy number, a number of perfection, a most powerful number ... this number conduceth to the ceremonies of God' (see note 6).

In medieval alchemy, 3 represented the belly and genitals. The 1 of the head corresponds to the sphere of the intellect, the 2 of the heart to the celestial sphere, and the 3 of the belly and genitals to the elemental world.

In modern numerology, 3 is always auspicious and welcome. 3 is associated with fertility, creativity, generation and regeneration, completeness, fulfilment, youth and accomplishment. Multiples of 3 are very potent, particularly 9, which is 3×3; 33, or 3×11, which is the number of the *mahatma*, or great spiritual leader, in Hindu tradition (Christ lived to be 33); and 33,333, which is the number of deities in the *Mahabharata*, the Hindu epic. Multiples of 3 are easily found: add together the digits of the number, and if they are divisible by 3, then the whole number is divisible by 3. For example, 16,791 is divisible by 3 because $1 + 6 + 7 + 9 + 1 = 24$, which is divisible by 3 (and $2 + 4 = 6$, which is divisible by 3). The most potent multiples include all those which have three digits: for example, 102, 201, 300, 333. If a numerological analysis is directed at whether a certain activity or change is likely to be successful, a 3 or any combination of 3 in the answer is always propitious.

Esoterically, 3 represents perfection, harmony, family, equilibrium; the primary colours, blue, red and yellow; the fruit of the tree; resurrection from death; enlightenment. It is the paradigm of life itself: father, mother, child; seed, spirit, new growth; beginning, middle, end; the eternal cycle.

4

4 is the second number, according to Pythagoreans. It is female. It is the first composite number, the first number obtained by multiplication other than by 1. The Pythagoreans called 4 even-even, and both 4 and 8 were associated with harmony, truth, perfection and justice. There are four cardinal points of the compass, four elements: earth, air, fire and water, represented respectively by the cube, octahedron, tetrahedron and icosahedron (these three-dimensional figures are discussed more fully under 5). The Greeks associated 4 with solids: 1 for a point, 2 for a line, 3 for a surface, 4 for a three-dimensional solid.

The classical gods associated with 4 are Bacchus the god of wine, Zeus or Jupiter (because of the magic square of Jupiter, which will be described later), and Hermes or Mercury, the messenger of the gods. 4 is the alchemical number of the metal mercury.

In most cultures, 4 is associated with order: four directions, four winds, four phases of the Moon, four elements, four directions at a crossroads – all of these suggesting a complete and ordered sequence. It is very common in many religions for obeisance to be made in four directions, or for real or symbolic gates or watchtowers to be created in four directions. Crossroads are traditionally associated with supernatural occurrences. The Romans took from the earlier Etruscans the practice of laying out the foundations of a new city in a square, with four guarded gates, and the foundations were consecrated by priests as they were laid. In Malaysia, it is still common practice for small villages to be guarded by four shrines set at four sides of the village outskirts.

In the Bible, Ezekiel has a vision of four creatures close to God's throne: they are man, lion, bullock and eagle. 4 is also associated with the tetragrammaton, YHWH, the unutterable name of God, which will be discussed in more detail in later chapters. There are four archangels ruling over the corners of the world: Michael, Raphael, Gabriel and Uriel. They have four corresponding princes of Spirits, ruling over the four angels of the world – namely Oriens, Paymon, Egyn and Amaymon – and four corresponding demons or princes of Devils in the infernal world: namely Samael, Azazel, Azael and Mahazael.

As Anne-Marie Schimmel observes, the theme of four rivers is shared by more than one religion:

According to medieval Christian interpretation, the 4 rivers in paradise flow from Moses through the 4 great prophets of the Old Testament, and from Jesus through the 4 Gospels. The 4 rivers of paradise are also known in Hinduism; there, the heavenly cow is said to have produced 4 streams of milk from her 4 udders. The 4 rivers likewise form an important aspect of Islamic ideas concerning paradise, and for this reason, many gardens in Iran and Moghul India were divided by 4 canals into the so-called *charbagh* (4 gardens); this motif was often applied to mausoleums to suggest an earthly representation of paradisiacal bliss (see note 7).

The attributes associated with 4 in modern numerology are order, discipline, dependability, stability, practicality, homeliness and patriotism. In numerological analysis, 4 represents directness, the straight solution – like Nike, 4 says: 'Just do it.'

Esoterically, 4 is the real, the physical, the mundane, the material, the Lords of Destiny, the guardian angels and guardian beasts, a blue star, loving action or protection, charity, community service and dedication.

5

The Pythagoreans considered 5 the number of marriage, since it is the sum of female 2 and male 3. Pythagoras's right-triangle theorem is sometimes known as the Theorem of the Bride: the 3-4-5 triangle representing 3 for male, 4 for female and 5, the hypotenuse, for the child. Five was so important to the Pythagoreans that the five-pointed star, or pentagram, was a secret and sacred symbol of membership of the order. In later Celtic number mythology, the circle of five vowels represented the life cycle of the Goddess, each vowel relating to a particular tree. A, or Ailm (these letter names are Irish), stands for the silver fir, the tree of birth; O, or Onn, is gorse, the flower of spring; U, or Ura, is heather, the plant of high summer; E, or Eadha, is aspen, the tree of old age, since the undersides of its leaves are silver-white in the autumn winds; and I, or Idho, is yew, the tree of death.

Since humans have five digits per hand, 5 might seem a natural base for a counting system, but, in fact, only one language uses a counting system based exclusively on 5: Saraveka, a South American Arawakan language. In many Central American languages, the numbers 6 to 9 are expressed as 5 + 1, 5 + 2 and so on (see note 8).

There are five, and only five, Platonic solids (see figure 19). These are three-dimensional figures constructed from congruent regular polygons (congruent means equal in all dimensions). The most familiar is the cube, constructed from six squares. The other four are the regular tetrahedron, consisting of four equilateral triangles (equilateral means all sides of the same length); the octahedron (eight equilateral triangles); the dodecahedron (12 regular pentagons); and the icosahedron (20 equilateral triangles).

In classical cosmology, 5 is associated with Aphrodite or Venus, since Venus is fifth in a mystic sequence known as the Orphic ladder, and also because the planet Venus was earlier worshipped by the Babylonians as a representation of the goddess Ishtar, whose number was 5. However, 5 also represented Mars, because of the Martian magic square, which is 5 by 5. The Romans thought of the rainbow as consisting of five colours: white, red, green, blue and black.

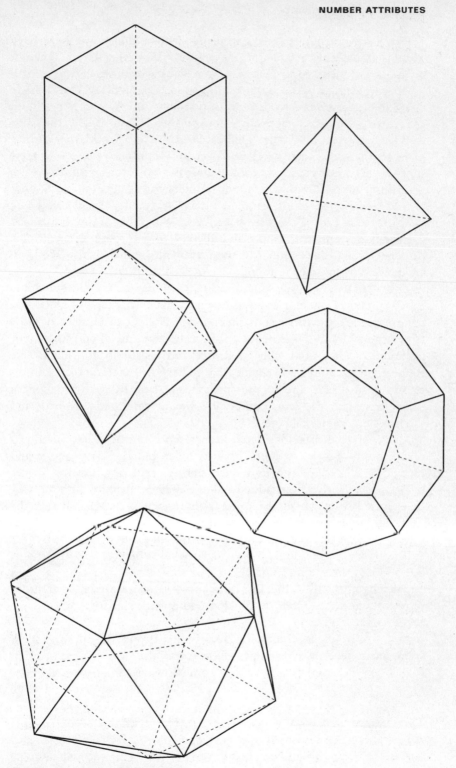

Figure 19 The five Platonic solids

The Navajo, a native American people who settled in northern New Mexico and north-eastern Arizona around 1000 AD, have a creation myth based on five worlds. The first was Black World, which was a small island surrounded by burning resin. The insects of Black World made wings for themselves and flew up to discover Blue World. When food grew short, the insects and birds flew on into Yellow World, the third world where men and other animals lived. Yellow World was harmonious and peaceful, and was ruled over by Mountain Lion. Food grew short again, however, so the First People moved into the fourth world, Black and White World, which they found already populated with other human beings: the Hopi, Zuni, Acoma, Comanche, Apache and Ute peoples. Here, Lazy Coyote provoked trouble and dissension. He caused a great flood, and the people and all the animals were forced to flee through a long, dark tunnel to the fifth world, which is this world in which we now live (see note 9).

There are five senses: seeing, hearing, smelling, tasting and touching. As was noted in Chapter Two, many plants have five petals or a five-fold pattern in their growth or construction. The ancient Chinese recognized five, rather than four, elements: earth, water, fire, metal and wood. 5 is traditionally associated with good luck and prosperity in China. The Sikh religion requires every male Sikh to have five sacred objects on his person at all times: the *kes* (uncut hair and beard); the *kach* (special undergarments); the *kara* (knife); the *kripan* (ceremonial sword); and the *kanjha* (ceremonial comb).

Medieval occultists considered human nature to be determined by a combination of four humours – black choler, blood, yellow choler and phlegm – related to the four elements of earth, air, fire and water respectively. To these was added a *quinta essentia*, meaning fifth humour or element, from which the word quintessence is derived. It was the secret and mysterious fifth essence which gave the spark of life to all the others – without it, man would remain made of clay.

In modern numerology, 5 is associated with heterosexual marriage, but also with hermaphroditism and homosexuality, since it is male and female together. It is the first number of innovation: in analysis, 5 represents new directions, rethinking, radicalism, curiosity, impulsivity, restlessness.

Esoterically, 5 is the spirit resurrected from the flesh; Christ ascending; a pink or crimson five-pointed star; the voice of God heard in the temple; Botticelli's Venus rising from the waves; the new Creation.

6

The Pythagoreans considered 6, like 5, as representative of marriage. It is female, but it is also the product of female 2 and male 3. It also represented equilibrium and good health, its icon being the male triangle (point uppermost) and female triangle (base uppermost) interlinked, which later was adopted in Jewish iconography as the Mogen David, or Star of David.

6 is the first perfect number. Perfect numbers are very unusual mathematically, and very significant numerologically. A perfect number, as originally defined by Euclid, is one in which the factors of the number (numbers which divide into it) add up to the number itself. The factors of 6 are 1, 2 and 3, and $1 + 2 + 3 = 6$. St Augustine wrote, 'Six is a number perfect in itself. God created all things in six days because this number is perfect.' Medieval Christian mystics made much of the fact that the six sides of a cube can be opened out to create the shape of the Cross. The Hebrew *b'reshit* ('in the beginning'), with which Genesis opens, was read by some as *bara shith*, meaning, 'He created Six' (in Hebrew, vowels are not indicated).

Zeus or Jupiter ruled 6 in the classical world, and the 6-by-6 magic square is dedicated to the Sun as the symbol of the god. The Chaldeans and Babylonians had long established 60 as an important number in measurement – it persists to this day in the way we measure time. A group of numbers, in which 6 is prominently included as a factor, are related to measurement, principally because for ages they have been practical, useful numbers for dividing quantities into smaller quantities. In numerical sequence, these numbers are: 2, 3, 5, 6, 7, 8, 10, 12, 20, 24, 28, 36, 48, 60, 72, 120 and 360. Sixty is still an important base for division: we use it in seconds, minutes and degrees. The classical zodiac consists of twelve houses, six above the Earth and six below it.

In Greece, 6 was strongly associated with Amphitrite, the sea-goddess daughter of Oceanus and wife of Poseidon, whose sacred dolphin brought her to him, and was later set among the stars as the constellation Delphinus. Classical sailors worshipped 6 as a lucky number against storms and shipwreck. This belief reappears in later Celtic mythology. In the sixth age of the world, the Children of Mil, or Milesians, are intent on invading Ireland, but the Druids of the Tuatha de Danaan, or People of Danaan, have raised a magical fog which prevents the ships from landing. The Milesians are forced to sail around Ireland three times, but eventually they are able to land safely because the number of their ships is 36, or 6×6.

The sixth hour, or *sexta hora* in Latin, was the hour in which Christ died on the Cross. In Christian Rome, and later throughout the world, it became the sexta or *siesta*, a time of quiet contemplation.

Cornelius Agrippa writes of 6:

It is also called the number of man, because the sixth day man was created; and it is also the number of our redemption, for the sixth day Christ suffered for our redemption; whence there is great affinity betwixt the number six and the cross, labour and servitude (see note 10).

In modern numerology, 6 represents marriage, harmony, perfection, devotion, tolerance, public service and orderliness.

Esoterically, 6 is beauty, bloodstone, violet, heliotrope (and all red flowers), the six jars of miraculous wine at the feast of Cana, intoxication, the wings of the Recording Angels, partnership, and emotional warmth. Through Amphitrite, it is also the number of seaworthiness and protection from harm by storm.

7

7 has long been considered a magically charged number. An ancient folk belief is that the seventh son of a seventh son will have special powers of clairvoyance and healing – this is derived from ancient Celtic mythology, in which 7 is the number of the archetypal male hero or god. Cu Chulainn, son of the god Lugh, has seven pupils in each eye, seven fingers on each hand and seven toes on each foot. Ferghus, the lover of Queen Medb, requires seven women to satisfy him, consumes seven pigs, seven deer, seven cows and seven vats of liquor at a sitting, and has the strength of 700 men (see note 11).

Although 7 is a male number, according to the Pythagorean classification, it is also associated with the female because it is a factor of 28, the number of the menstrual cycle. Robert Graves and others have argued that the ancient British calendar consisted of 13 months of 28 days, making 364, with the extra day commemorated in the stock phrase 'a year and a day' (see note 12).

The Greeks revered 7 because it came close to solving the exasperating problem of numbers which could not be expressed as integer fractions (i.e., irrational numbers). They observed that a square with sides of unit length 5 has a diagonal which is very close to 7: for that reason the Greeks called 7 the rational diagonal. Apollo and Athena are both associated with 7.

The cult of the sun-god Mithras was particularly strong among Roman legionaries, and so it took hold vigorously in Britain during the Roman occupation in the first four centuries AD. In Mithraism, which is Babylonian in origin, the soul is believed to ascend through seven planetary spheres before attaining heaven. This was ritually symbolized in Mithraic ceremony by the shedding of garments every seventh day, each garment being symbolically left at one of the gateways through which the supplicant passes before arriving, in naked glory, at the eighth gate, the gate of paradise. The famous erotic Dance of the Seven Veils is a corruption of this ancient ceremonial practice. The later Christian notion of seven levels of purgatory through which the soul must pass also ultimately derives from Mithraism. Mithras himself was a warrior/hero-type god which would make his association with 7 even more acceptable to the Romano-British Celts.

7 features in the famous children's riddle:

As I was going to St Ives,
I met a man with seven wives.
Every wife had seven sacks,
And every sack had seven cats,
Every cat had seven kittens.
Kittens, cats, sacks and wives,
How many were going to St Ives?

The answer, of course, is one – all the others were coming *from* St Ives. David Wells points out that this riddle is remarkably similar to one found in the Rhind papyrus, written by the scribe Ahmes or Amos 3,500 years ago (see note 13).

Medieval scholars saw in 7 the combination of the holy 3 with the mundane 4, and so 7 was seen as the number of all living sequences. Shakespeare writes of the seven ages of man, a notion first articulated much earlier. We still talk about the 'seven-year itch' in marriages, which is founded on the notion that 7 represents the end of a sequence, a time for change. The musical octave is built from seven notes – the eighth is really the first note of the next sequence, or octave.

The Bible abounds in events which occur in sequences of 7, particularly in the Book of Revelation, in which are mentioned: seven stars, seven churches of Asia, seven spirits before God's throne, seven horns, seven vials and seven plagues. The Apocalypse is revealed to St John in seven visions, and the end of the world will come when the seven angels open the seven seals which release retribution on the Earth, seven trumpets sound, and the scarlet woman rests upon seven hills. In Genesis, the seventh generation after Adam yielded Lamech, who lived 777 years and was to be avenged seventy-sevenfold, in the same way that Cain's murder was to be avenged seven times.

The first sura of the Qur'an has seven verses: three addressed to God and four to human aspirations. The Islamic declaration, 'There is no God but Allah, Muhammad is the messenger of Allah', consists of seven words: *la ilaha illa Allah Muhammad rasul Allah.*

The seven days of the week are named in English after a mixture of Roman and Teutonic gods: Sun for Sunday, Moon for Monday, Tiw for Tuesday, Odin or Woden for Wednesday, Thor for Thursday, Freya for Friday, and Saturn for Saturday. The pattern is probably established on the lunar cycle, in which the Moon achieves a recognizably distinct shape every seven days. In China, the periodicity of 7 is particularly associated with women: in the menstrual cycle, already mentioned; in the belief that girls become women (i.e., the menarche takes place) at 14, or 2×7, and the menopause begins at 49, or 7×7. The Chinese also associated 7 with spirituality.

Cornelius Agrippa gives a more detailed account of the presence of 7 in the human cycle:

Table 2

Seven angels which stand before God	Seven planets	Seven birds of the planets	Seven fish of the planets	Seven animals of the planets	Seven metals of the planets	Seven stones of the planets
Zaphkiel	Saturn	lapwing	cuttlefish	mole	lead	onyx
Zadkiel	Jupiter	eagle	dolphin	hart	tin	sapphire
Camael	Mars	vulture	pike	wolf	iron	diamond
Raphael	Sol (the Sun)	swan	seacalf (seal)	lion	gold	carbuncle
Haniel	Venus	dove	thymallus (grayling)	goat	copper	emerald
Michael	Mercury	stork	mullet	ape	quicksilver	achates
Gabriel	Luna (the Moon)	owl	seacat	cat	silver	crystal

For when the genital seed is received in the womb of the woman, if it remain there seven hours after the effusion of it, it is certain that it will abide there for good: then the first seven days it is coagulated, and is fit to receive the shape of a man: then it produceth mature infants .... After the birth, the seventh hour tries whether it will live or no: for that which shall bear the breath of the air after that hour is conceived will live. After seven days it casts off the relics of the navel. After twice seven days its sight begins to move after the light. In the third seventh, it turns its eyes, and whole face freely. After seven months it breeds teeth: after the second seventh month it sits without fear of falling: after the third seventh month it begins to speak: after the fourth seventh month it stands strongly, and walks: after the fifth seventh month it begins to refrain from sucking its nurse. After seven years its first teeth fall, and new are bred fitter for harder meat, and its speech is perfected: after the second seventh year boys wax ripe, and then is a beginning of generation: at the third seventh year they grow to be men in stature, and begin to be hairy, and become able, and strong for generation: at the fourth seventh year they barnish [grow stout], and cease to grow taller: in the fifth seventh year they attain to the perfection of their strength: the sixth seventh year they keep their strength: the seventh seventh year they attain to their utmost discretion, and wisdom, and the perfect age of men. But when they come to the tenth seventh year, where the number seven is taken for a complete number, then they come to the common term of life, the prophet saying, our age is seventy years' (see note 14).

Readers will perhaps be reminded of Jacques' speech in Shakespeare's *As You Like It* which describes the seven ages of man.

Agrippa gives a series of correspondences for 7, widely recognized in ancient mythology, medieval exegesis, and, indeed, in modern occultism. The correspondences can be seen in table 2.

In modern numerology, 7 is associated with spirituality, meditation, quietude, intuition, global perspective, transcendentalism and aloofness. Through Athena, and through the Celtic warrior-gods, it is paradoxically also associated with military prowess and physical strength, and with impressive physical attractiveness. The colour of 7 is a rich purple, as much blue as red; it is often associated with royalty.

8

8 is the number of paradise. The Greeks considered 8 the first cube or cubic number: $2 \times 2 \times 2 = 8$. They also noted the curious property that every odd number above 1, when squared, can be expressed as a multiple of 8, plus 1. For example, 7^2 is 49, which is $(6 \times 8) + 1$. The whole sequence begins:

$$3^2 = 9 - (1 \times 8) + 1$$
$$5^2 = 25 = (3 \times 8) + 1$$
$$7^2 = 49 = (6 \times 8) + 1$$
$$9^2 = 81 = (10 \times 8) + 1$$
$$11^2 = 121 = (15 \times 8) + 1$$
$$13^2 = 169 = (20 \times 8) + 1 \ldots \text{ and so on.}$$

It can be seen that the sequence of multipliers of 8 is the triangular sequence 1, 3, 6, 10, 15, 20 … etc. The Greeks also knew of another connection between sacred 3 and 8, in the sense that the three intersecting planes of the three dimensions create eight regions of space (see figure 20).

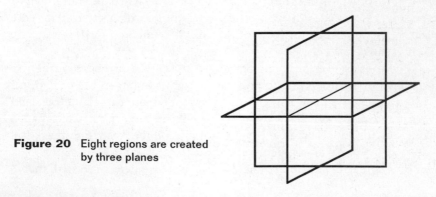

Figure 20 Eight regions are created by three planes

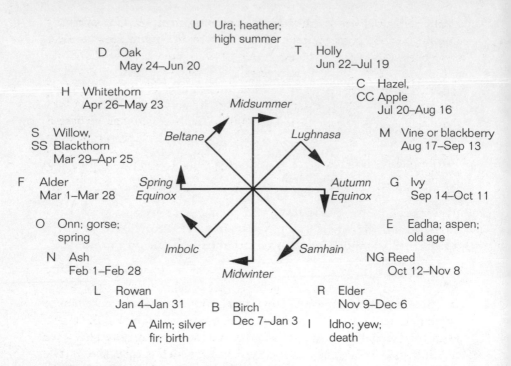

U   Ura; heather;
     high summer

D   Oak
     May 24–Jun 20

T   Holly
     Jun 22–Jul 19

H   Whitethorn
     Apr 26–May 23

Midsummer

C   Hazel,
CC Apple
     Jul 20–Aug 16

S   Willow,
SS Blackthorn
     Mar 29–Apr 25

Beltane

Lughnasa

M   Vine or blackberry
     Aug 17–Sep 13

F   Alder
     Mar 1–Mar 28

*Spring
Equinox*

*Autumn
Equinox*

G   Ivy
     Sep 14–Oct 11

O   Onn; gorse;
     spring

E   Eadha; aspen;
     old age

N   Ash
     Feb 1–Feb 28

Imbolc

Samhain

NG Reed
     Oct 12–Nov 8

Midwinter

L   Rowan
     Jan 4–Jan 31

B   Birch
     Dec 7–Jan 3

R   Elder
     Nov 9–Dec 6

A   Ailm; silver
     fir; birth

I   Idho; yew;
     death

Figure 21 The Celtic cycle of festivals

Another curious property of 8 known to the Greeks is that all squares of odd numbers above 1 differ by a multiple of 8. For example:

$$9^2 - 3^2 = 81 - 9 = 72 = 9 \times 8$$
$$13^2 - 5^2 = 169 - 25 = 144 = 18 \times 8 \dots \text{and so on.}$$

Euclid comments on this property.

8 was the holiest of female numbers to the Greeks, since it is the cube or third power of the first female number 2. It symbolized Gaea, or the Grand Matriarch, or Holy Mother. 8 was especially associated in classical Rome with the goddess Cybele, originally a Phrygian goddess, who was worshipped by the Romans under the name Magna Mater, or Great Mother. Partly through reverence for Cybele, the number 8 became associated with divine justice, a tradition which survived into the early medieval Tarot, where the card numbered VIII originally represented Justice.

The most universal mythological attributes of 8 are based either on the idea of eight compass points, or of eight stations in the calendrical cycle. In Norse mythology, Odin's horse Sleipnir has eight legs, and Odin's trial by fire lasts eight days. The ancient tribal Celts had a religious calendar based on eight stations of the year, a pattern still recognized in part in modern neopaganism (see figure 21).

Emmanuel Swedenborg, the Danish philosopher, suggested that 8 would be a far more useful base for counting than 10. Our everyday counting system is to the base of 10, or base-10. There are countless other possible bases. The binary system, base-2, which will be discussed in Chapter Eight, has the great advantage that its two terms, 0 and 1, can be related to positions or electrical states, like off and on. Its chief disadvantage, however, is that the numbers are very long and difficult to remember – 100 in base-10 is 1100100 in binary. The octal, or base-8 system proposed by Swedenborg is also very useful, and the numbers are easier to recognize and remember. The general public has ignored Swedenborg's proposal, but computers have been using octal and base-16 (hexadecimal) systems for decades. The first few numbers in the octal system are:

Decimal 1 2 3 4 5 6 7 8 9 10 11 12 13 14 15 16 17 18 19 20 ...
Octal 1 2 3 4 5 6 7 10 11 12 13 14 15 16 17 20 21 22 23 24 ...

To the untrained eye, the sequence looks as though it has some peculiar omissions, jumping straight from 7 to 10, but in octal notation that is perfectly correct, because we are counting in eights, not in tens.

Modern numerologists interpret 8 in a variety of ways. First and foremost, it is the number of the female or 2; then it is the number of the female and the mundane, or 2 and 4; and lastly, it is the number of the Magna Mater or Holy Mother, the three 2s which make 8 when multiplied. It also represents fecundity, fertility, prosperity, good fortune, law, divine and secular justice, proportion, foundation and regenerativity.

Esoterically, 8 is intuition, Moses the emancipator, the Magi who brought gifts to the Christ-child, the great trees (oak, beech, maple, sycamore, elm), blindfolded Justice holding her scales, clear crystal, the intellect soaring above the mundane.

9

9 is 3×3, therefore three times sacred. Numerically, 9 has some interesting properties. A well-known classroom trick is to have students write the digits 0 through 9 vertically, thus:

0
1
2
3
4
5
6
7
8
9

Then, starting at the bottom, the students write the same sequence upwards, generating the following:

09
18
27
36
45
54
63
72
81
90

This is the multiplication table for 9. Each pair of digits sums to 9.

The Arabs introduced to Europe a system of checking sums called 'casting out nines', although the method is probably Indian in origin. Replace each number in a sum by the sum of its digits (the original formula was to replace each number by the remainder on dividing by 9, which produces the same result). If the resulting sum is correct, then the original sum is correct.

There are many curious patterns associated with 9, which is one reason why it is so frequently associated with magic. Here are some of the better known curiosities:

$$(0 \times 9) + 1 = 1$$
$$(1 \times 9) + 2 = 11$$
$$(12 \times 9) + 3 = 111$$
$$(123 \times 9) + 4 = 1,111$$
$$(1,234 \times 9) + 5 = 11,111$$
$$(12,345 \times 9) + 6 = 111,111$$
$$(123,456 \times 9) + 7 = 1,111,111 \text{ etc.}$$

$$12,345,679 \times 9 = 111,111,111$$
$$12,345,679 \times 18 = 222,222,222$$
$$12,345,679 \times 27 = 333,333,333$$
$$12,345,679 \times 36 = 444,444,444 \text{ etc.}$$
$$\text{and} \ldots 12,345,679 \times 999,999,999 = 12,345,678,987,654,321$$

Magic squares will be discussed more fully later, but the magic square with the first nine digits, known to the ancient Chinese as the Lo Shu, is perhaps the best known. The Greeks called 9 the *ennead*, and revered particularly the nine-pointed star which is created by three intertwined equilateral triangles. There are nine Greek muses, of whom Terpsichore, muse of the sacred dance, is the ninth and most potent. In Norse mythology, Odin hangs in the world tree for nine days and nine nights, and in this period learns nine sacred songs. Nine is widely associated with charms, spells and invocations, because it is the number of change, motion, restlessness. The witches in *Macbeth* close their charm with:

Thrice to thine, and thrice to mine,
And thrice again, to make up nine.

Anne-Marie Schimmel points out that 9 is also traditionally associated with healing:

> In healing, a ritual act was often repeated 9 times; thus, a bewitched person had to count backward from 9 to 1, and 9 knots in a ribbon were thought to help in cases of a sprained foot or hand (this custom was known both in Scotland and in Germany). 9 kinds of ailments can be cured by a mixture of 9 special herbs, and in the area of Göttingen (Germany) one used to prepare, on Maundy Thursday, a soup called Negenstarke, 'ninefold strength,' which consisted of 9 different green vegetables' (see note 15).

To the Greeks, 9 was the number of imperfection and incompleteness, because it is one short of the perfection of 10, as exemplified and revered in the sacred icon of the *tetraktys*. In the Middle Ages, Cornelius Agrippa takes up this notion of imperfection by reference to the passage in Luke's gospel (17:12–19) in which Christ heals the ten lepers but only one, the Samaritan, returns to thank him, and the other nine, healed but unredeemed, fail to 'give glory to God.'

In modern numerology, also, 9 represents incompleteness, waiting, irresolution, change and transformation. It is a potent and sacred number, because it is 3×3. Its colour is sea-green (always changing, never resolving), and it is esoterically represented by the winged serpent or dragon – as will be explained later, the Hebrew letter Teth represents 9 and also means 'serpent', and it is associated with the miraculous brazen serpent which Moses created. 9 is traditionally associated with sexual energy, with healing, and with high magic and magicians, particularly Merlin. It is the number of Hecate, queen of witches, and it is the number of the Moon, queen of the heavens.

A mystery not yet completely resolved is the peculiar etymological relation between the word for 9 and the word for 'new' in many languages. It is certainly found in Sanskrit, Persian and Latin. French *nouveau* and *neuf* come from the same root (indeed *neuf* and *neuve* are used to mean 'new'), and German *neun* and *neu* come from the same root. The Spanish cognates are *nueve* and *nueve*, exactly the same word. Some writers have speculated that the historical basis was the prevalence of 8 as a counting base (so that 9 would be the first 'new' number), but the problem with that hypothesis is that, although 8 was used in some cultures – perhaps because there are only eight fingers if we discount the thumbs, or perhaps because people counted the spaces between the digits rather than the digits themselves – it was far less common than 10 as a counting base and does not seem to have been widespread enough to have caused such a marked linguistic effect. My personal view is that the connotation of 'newness' resonates with the very ancient numerological association of incompleteness, restlessness, imperfection and waiting to move on; but as yet there is no completely satisfactory answer to this interesting question.

10

10 is perfection. It is the target towards which the arrow of 1 was aimed. Like 1, it has initiatory and regenerative power. Its factors are 2 and 5, both of which are associated with spiritual essence.

In regular mathematics, 10 is so important that it is difficult to imagine the time before it was used as it is now. Our understanding of value by place – in which the addition of a zero to a digit means multiplication by 10 – is fundamental to our simplest arithmetical computation, yet, until the Arabs introduced it to the West, it was unknown to us. Most children understand the difference between 5, 50 and 500 quite easily and quickly, although it is a matter of opinion whether decimals are easier to teach than fractions; somehow it is easier to visualize a quarter of a pie or an eighth of a pizza than 0.25 of a pie or 0.125 of a pizza, although they mean the same thing.

In modern numerology, 10 is almost invariably reduced to 1, by the system of adding digits $(1 + 0 = 1)$. As will be explained in later chapters, I disagree with this system. I think 10 stands for 10, not for anything else. The numerological attributes of numbers above 9 will be discussed in greater detail later in the book.

Beyond 10

Some of the numbers beyond 10 deserve brief but special mention here.

12 would make a very useful and effective counting base. It is already firmly established in our daily lives because there are twelve months in a year and two times twelve hours in a day. There were twelve tribes of Israel in the Old Testament, and twelve Apostles in the New Testament. The ancient Hindus revered 12: it was common practice for a boy from a religious home to leave at the age of twelve and go to live for twelve years with a guru, or teacher.

13 is famous throughout the West as an unlucky number: the origin of the superstition is often given as the presence of thirteen at the Last Supper, the thirteenth being Judas Iscariot, Christ's betrayer. 13 is also associated with the principal god of the underworld, called Hades in Greek or Pluto in Roman mythology. A name has even been coined from Greek for the superstition: it is *triskaidekaphobia*, meaning 'fear of thirteen'. Ironically, 13 is an auspicious number in the Hebrew Kabbalah, which has many lists of 13, including the thirteen heavenly fountains, the thirteen gates of mercy, the thirteen rivers of balsam in paradise and the thirteen paths of love. In my view, 13 is a very powerful

and propitious number.

40 is an important Biblical number. The Flood lasted forty days, the Israelites spent forty years in the wilderness, and Christ spent forty days and forty nights in the wilderness. The number 40 seems always to imply a period of waiting, extension or trial.

Some curious squaring patterns begin with 34 and 67, as follows:

$34^2 = 1,156$
$334^2 = 111,556$
$3,334^2 = 11,115,556$
$33,334^2 = 1,111,155,556$ etc.

$67^2 = 4,489$
$667^2 = 444,889$
$6,667^2 = 44,448,889$
$66,667^2 = 4,444,488,889$ etc.

A famous puzzle number is 142,857, because each multiplication of it seems to produce the same digits rearranged:

$142,857 \times 1 = 142,857$
$142,857 \times 2 = 285,714$
$142,857 \times 3 = 428,571$
$142,857 \times 4 = 571,428$
$142,857 \times 5 = 714,285$
$142,857 \times 6 = 857,142$

Unfortunately, the pattern ends here, since 142,857 times 7 equals 999,999.

Many other numbers which are significant in numerology – for example the famous 666, or Number of the Beast – will be discussed in detail later, when we look more closely at the Kabbalah and Gematria. Appendix Four lists more attributes for other numbers higher than 10.

Now, however, we turn to prime numbers, imaginary numbers and other curious numbers and number patterns.

four

CURIOUS NUMBERS AND NUMBER PATTERNS

6986986986986986986986986986986986986986986986986986

Numbers are classified by type. The natural numbers are the ones we use for counting: 1, 2, 3, etc. They are classified as odd or even. The set of whole numbers is the set of the natural numbers and zero (0, 1, 2, 3 …). The set of integers is the set of whole numbers, their opposites (or negatives), and zero (… -3, -2, -1, 0, 1, 2, 3 …). Rational numbers are numbers which can be expressed as a fraction with both numerator (upper number) and denominator (lower number) being integers. When rational numbers are expressed in decimal notation, they either reach a definite end to the number of decimal places, or they end in a repeating decimal. For example, one-quarter is 0.25, one-third is $0.\overline{3}$. Irrational numbers are numbers which cannot be expressed as integer fractions. When irrational numbers are written in decimal form, the decimal figures never terminate or repeat, they just go on infinitely. The Pythagoreans hated them.

The classification of numbers, which can appear unnecessarily confusing at times, is summarized in figure 22.

A prime number is a number which can be divided only by 1 or by itself. Since time immemorial, the sequence of prime numbers has fascinated mystics and mathematicians. The Greek philosopher Eratosthenes devised a simple method for determining prime numbers, a method which is now commonly known as the Sieve of Eratosthenes. To find all the prime numbers between 1 and 100, first write out all the numbers:

1	2	3	4	5	6	7	8	9	10
11	12	13	14	15	16	17	18	19	20
21	22	23	24	25	26	27	28	29	30
31	32	33	34	35	36	37	38	39	40
41	42	43	44	45	46	47	48	49	50
51	52	53	54	55	56	57	58	59	60
61	62	63	64	65	66	67	68	69	70

71	72	73	74	75	76	77	78	79	80
81	82	83	84	85	86	87	88	89	90
91	92	93	94	95	96	97	98	99	100

We now 'sieve out' all the multiples of the first prime number, 2, by erasing every second number:

1	3	5	7	9
11	13	15	17	19
21	23	25	27	29
31	33	35	37	39
41	43	45	47	49
51	53	55	57	59
61	63	65	67	69
71	73	75	77	79
81	83	85	87	89
91	93	95	97	99

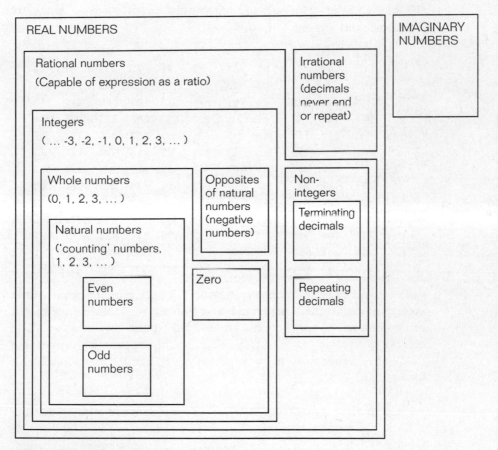

Figure 22 The classification of numbers

Now, beginning after 3, we erase every third number, or multiple of 3. The even multiples of 3, namely 6, 12, 18, etc., have already been erased, because they are also multiples of 2, so we erase 9, 15, etc.:

1			3	5	7
11	13			17	19
	23	25			29
31		35		37	
41	43			47	49
	53	55			59
61		65		67	
71	73			77	79
	83	85			89
91		95		97	

We repeat the sieving process for 5, 7, 11, and so on. Each multiple of a prime number cannot itself be prime, so as we eliminate the multiples. We are finally left with only the prime numbers themselves. These are the prime numbers below 1,000:

2	3	5	7	11	13	17	19	23	29	31	37
41	**43**	47	53	**59**	**61**	67	**71**	**73**	79	83	89
97	**101**	**103**	**107**	**109**	113	127	131	**137**	**139**	**149**	**151**
157	163	167	173	**179**	**181**	**191**	**193**	**197**	**199**	211	223
227	**229**	233	**239**	**241**	251	257	263	**269**	**271**	277	**281**
283	293	307	**311**	**313**	317	331	337	**347**	**349**	353	359
367	373	379	383	389	397	401	409	**419**	**421**	**431**	**433**
439	443	449	457	**461**	**463**	467	479	487	491	499	503
509	**521**	**523**	541	547	557	563	**569**	**571**	577	587	593
599	**601**	607	613	**617**	**619**	631	**641**	**643**	647	653	**659**
661	673	677	683	691	701	709	719	727	733	739	743
751	757	761	769	773	787	797	**809**	**811**	**821**	**823**	**827**
829	839	853	**857**	**859**	863	877	**881**	**883**	887	907	911
919	929	937	941	947	953	967	971	977	983	991	997

Two patterns are immediately striking. The first is that several primes seem to come in pairs, separated by a difference of two. These paired primes, known as twin primes, are in **bold** type in the list above. The second noticeable pattern is how frequently sequential primes are exactly ten higher than the previous prime: 181 and 191, 631 and 641, for example.

The twentieth-century mathematician Stanislaw Ulam has discovered some even more remarkable patterns in the sequence of primes (see note 1). The first pattern is observed in what is now known as Ulam's Little Doodle (see figure 23). Starting with 1, inscribe consecutive numbers in

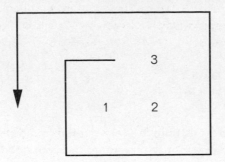

Figure 23 Beginning Ulam's Little Doodle

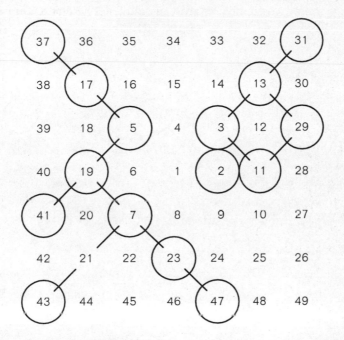

Figure 24 Ulam's Little Doodle

an anti-clockwise spiral. Very soon it becomes clear that, for some completely unknown reason, the prime numbers tend to fall on the diagonals of the figure created (see figure 24). When Ulam repeated the exercise, this time beginning with the prime number 41, he produced a pattern which is even more striking (see figure 25).

There are other distinct types of primes, apart from twin primes. Symmetric primes are primes which are the same distance from a given number on a number line. For example, 3 and 11, both primes, are equidistant from 7. There are no symmetric primes for 1, 2 and 3. The list of symmetric primes begins as follows:

4   3 and 5
5   3 and 7
6   5 and 7
7   3 and 11
8   5 and 11, 3 and 13
9   7 and 11, 5 and 13
10 7 and 13, 3 and 17

… and so on. It looks as though every natural number apart from 1, 2 and 3 has at least one pair of symmetric primes, but nobody has yet been able to prove it.

Emirps are primes which remain prime when their digits are reversed (emirp is 'prime' written backwards, of course). The first ten emirps are 11, 13, 17, 31, 37, 71, 73, 79, 97 and 101.

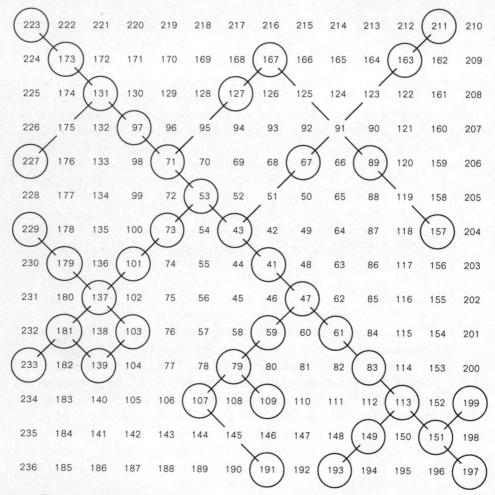

Figure 25 Ulam's Big Doodle

Primorials are not prime numbers: they are the products of a prime number and all the primes preceding it. Primorial 7, for example, is: $2 \times 3 \times 5 \times 7 = 210$.

The Mersenne primes are a subset of the Mersenne numbers. Father Marin Mersenne was a French Jesuit priest, a close friend of the philosopher Descartes and of the mathematicians Fermat and Pascal. Mersenne observed the sequence generated by raising 2 to different prime powers and then subtracting 1 from the result. In mathematical formula, that idea is expressed as $2^p - 1$. The number represented by p must be prime. When $p = 1$, we obtain $2^1 - 1$, $= 2 - 1 = 1$. When $p = 2$, the result is $2^2 - 1 = 4 - 1 = 3$. The list of Mersenne numbers begins as follows:

M_1	$2^1 - 1$	$= 1$
M_2	$2^2 - 1$	$= 3$
M_3	$2^3 - 1$	$= 7$
M_4	$2^5 - 1$	$= 31$
M_5	$2^7 - 1$	$= 127 \ldots$ and so on.

As the pattern begins, it looks as though every number produced by the Mersenne formula is itself going to be prime, as are 1, 3, 7, 31 and 127. However, this is not the case: for example, $2^{11} - 1 = 2,047$, which is not prime. The Mersenne primes are those Mersenne numbers which are prime. Mersenne himself actually made some errors and omissions in his original list, which is hardly surprising when one considers that some of these numbers are gigantic and all his calculations were done by mind and hand – there were no computers in 1644, when his *Cogitata Physico-Mathematica* was published.

There is a connection between Mersenne primes and the so-called perfect numbers. A perfect number is a number which is the sum of its divisors, including 1, but excluding itself. The first perfect number is 6, because the divisors of 6 (excluding 6 itself) are 1, 2 and 3, and $1 + 2 + 3 = 6$. The second perfect number is 28 ($1 + 2 + 4 + 7 + 14 = 28$), the third is 496 ($1 + 2 + 4 + 8 + 16 + 31 + 62 + 124 + 248$), and the fourth is 8,128 ($1 + 2 + 4 + 8 + 16 + 32 + 64 + 127 + 254 + 508 + 1,016 + 2,032 + 4,064$). It is obvious that it requires long and laborious calculation to discover these rare perfect numbers, yet all four of the numbers just described were known to the ancient Greeks. A peculiarity of perfect numbers is that they always end either in the digits ...28, or in the digit ...6 preceded by an odd number (apart from 6 itself). The four next perfect numbers after 8,128 are:

33,550,336
8,589,869,056
137,438,691,328
2,305,843,008,139,952,128

Even with supercomputers doing the number-crunching, only thirty perfect numbers have been discovered so far. The thirtieth perfect number has 130,099 digits. Needless to say, any numerological analysis which happened to produce a perfect number (apart from 6 and 28) would be extremely rare, extremely significant, and extremely auspicious.

The relationships between primes and other primes, and between primes and composite numbers, have fascinated mathematicians and numerologists in every age. The prime numbers are considered special, unusual and powerful. For instance, the Pythagoreans considered 17 a potent and evil prime number, because it lies between 16 and 18, the only two numbers which can simultaneously describe the perimeter and the area of a rectangle. Generally speaking in Pythagorean number mysticism, any number which is adjacent to a potent auspicious number is itself powerfully inauspicious. For example, 9 is the symbol of incompleteness because it falls one short of the divine 10. Similarly, 216 is a potent and auspicious number, as was mentioned in Chapter One, because it is the first cube which is the sum of three cubes, and, moreover, the cubes of the important right-triangle sequence 3, 4 and 5:

$$3^3 + 4^3 + 5^3 = 63$$
$$27 + 64 + 125 = 216$$

Since 216 is highly auspicious, 215 is highly *in*auspicious.

The Greeks classified any number whose factors (other than the number itself) are greater than the number as abundant, and a number which is greater than the sum of its factors (excluding itself) as deficient. There are many more deficient numbers than abundant numbers. For example, 8 is deficient, because $1 + 2 + 4 = 7$, and 8 is greater than 7; 12 is abundant, because $1 + 2 + 3 + 4 + 6 = 16$, and 16 is greater than 12.

Amicable numbers come in pairs, as the name suggests. They are numbers whose factors add up to the other number in the pair. For example, 220 and 284 are the first pair of amicable numbers. The factors of 220, excluding 220 itself, are 1, 2, 4, 5, 10, 11, 20, 22, 24, 55 and 110. Add these together, and the sum is 284. The factors of 284, apart from 284 itself, are 1, 2, 4, 71, and 142, which add up to 220. Amicable numbers are not as rare as perfect numbers – over a thousand pairs have been found – but they are still fairly rare. The first ten pairs of amicable numbers are:

220 and 284
1,184 and 1,210
2,620 and 2,924
5,020 and 5,564
6,232 and 6,368
10,744 and 10,856
12,285 and 14,595

17,296 and 18,416
63,020 and 76,084
66,928 and 66,992

Sociable numbers form wider relationships than amicable numbers, as their name suggests. They come in groups. The sum of the factors of the first number equals the second number. The sum of the factors of this number equals a third number. The process continues until the original number reappears, which determines the size of the group. Here is a group of five sociable numbers:

The sum of the factors of 12,496 = 14,288
The sum of the factors of 14,288 = 15,472
The sum of the factors of 15,472 = 14,536
The sum of the factors of 14,536 = 14,264
The sum of the factors of 14,264 = 12,496

Mathematicians also distinguish between algebraic numbers, meaning numbers which could appear as the solution of an algebraic equation, like 3 in the algebraic sum $2 + x = 5$, and transcendental numbers, which means any irrational numbers that are not algebraic numbers. The best known transcendental numbers are π and e, both of which we shall examine more closely later in this chapter. Irrational numbers which are algebraic are known as surds: examples are the irrationals $\sqrt{3}$ or $\sqrt{5}$.

A 'weird' number (serious mathematicians actually use this term) is an abundant number which cannot be written as the sum of any of its factors. The smallest weird number is 70 and it has 1, 2, 5, 7, 10, 14 and 35 as factors, which sum to 74, thus making 70 an abundant number, but no set of the factors sum to 70. Weird numbers are very rare. The first five weird numbers are 70, 836, 4,030, 5,830 and 7,192.

People are fascinated by very high numbers. The highest numbers used in modern mathematics actually have several special notations all of their own, but in ordinary decimal notation, the following are the most commonly used high numbers:

One million	$= 10^6$	$(= 1,000,000)$
One billion	$= 10^9$	$(= 1,000,000,000)$
One trillion	$= 10^{12}$	(etc.)
One quadrillion	$= 10^{15}$	
One quintillion	$= 10^{18}$	
One sextillion	$= 10^{21}$	
One septillion	$= 10^{24}$	
One octillion	$= 10^{27}$	
One nonillion	$= 10^{30}$	
One decillion	$= 10^{33}$	
One undecillion	$= 10^{36}$	
One duodecillion	$= 10^{39}$	

One tredecillion $= 10^{42}$
One quattuordecillion $= 10^{45}$
One quindecillion $= 10^{48}$
One sexdecillion $= 10^{51}$
One septendecillion $= 10^{54}$
One octodecillion $= 10^{57}$
One novemdecillion $= 10^{60}$
One vigintillion $= 10^{63}$
One googol $= 10^{100}$
One googolplex $= 10^{googol}$

There have been many attempts to ascertain why certain patterns emerge in the relationships between numbers. The twin primes, for example, start to thin out as we go higher and higher in the scale of natural numbers, until in very large numbers it becomes extremely rare to find twin primes at all; but why they should follow this pattern remains a mystery.

The Pythagorean Theorem, already mentioned, can be written formulaically as $a^2 + b^2 = c^2$, with a and b representing the sides of a right triangle adjacent to the right angle and c representing the hypotenuse. Pythagoras and his followers found many integer values which satisfy the equation, starting with the simplest, $3^2 + 4^2 = 5^2$. These groups of three numbers are known as Pythagorean triples, and if they occur naturally in sequence in any event or circumstance, that is numerologically very significant. Some Pythagorean triples are:

3–4–5
5–12–13
8–15–17
7–24–25
9–40–41
11–60–61
12–35–37
13–84–85
16–63–65
20–21–29
28–45–53
33–56–65
36–77–85
39–80–89
48–55–73
65–72–97

Multiples of these numbers obviously also form right triangles, as, for example, 6-8-10, which is twice 3-4-5.

There is a group of numbers which serious mathematicians refer to rather jovially as lucky numbers. We saw earlier how the Sieve of Eratosthenes is used to find prime numbers. A similar method is used to find the lucky numbers. We first eliminate every second number, so that only the odd numbers remain:

1 3 5 7 9 11 13 15 17 19 21 ....

After 1, the next number is 3, so now we erase every third number:

1 3 7 9 13 15 19 21 ....

After 3, the next number is 7, so now we erase every seventh number, starting with 19, and so on. The final sequence of lucky numbers begins:

1 3 7 9 13 15 21 25 31 33 37 43 49 51 ....

Whether these numbers are lucky in the conventional sense depends on whether you believe in lucky numbers or not. Many of them are prime – in fact, mathematicians are very interested in how the lucky numbers selection system and the Sieve of Eratosthenes both produce similar sequences – and almost all prime numbers are considered auspicious in numerology.

The Kaprekar numbers also produce an unusual sequence. A number is a Kaprekar number if it meets the following criteria: step one, square the number; step two, divide the resulting number into left-hand and right-hand digits, with the extra digit going on the right hand if the number of digits is odd; step three, add together the two numbers thus created. If the sum equals the original number, then it is a Kaprekar number. For example, $2,223^2$ is 4,941,729. Divide this number into left-hand and right-hand digits, to yield 494 and 1,729. Adding 494 and 1,729 gives us the original 2,223. The sequence of Kaprekar numbers begins 1, 9, 45, 55, 99, 297, 703, 999, 2,223, 2,728, 7,272, 7,777 .... Notice that the sequence 9, 99, 999, 9,999 ... lies within the Kaprekar sequence, and that adjacent pairs produce a sum pattern: $45 + 55 = 100$, $297 + 703 = 1,000$, $2,728 + 7,272 = 10,000$ .... If a Kaprekar number comes up in numerological analysis, it suggests a dead-end or closed loop, an unprofitable or redundant course. (Kaprekar numbers were discovered only in modern times, so they do not figure in traditional numerology.)

Perhaps the oldest of these interesting number patterns and sequences is the magic square. The 9-square, known to the ancient Chinese as the Lo Shu, was also revered by classical and medieval numerologists. In fact, there were seven magic squares, each dedicated to a planet or deity, and each associated with particular attributes (see note 2). These magic squares have been known for many centuries, and have played a central role in the development of numerology. The first is the Square of Saturn, which is the same as the Lo Shu (see figure 26). There are

4	9	2
3	5	7
8	1	6

Figure 26 The Square of Saturn

4	14	15	1
9	7	6	12
5	11	10	8
16	2	3	13

Figure 27 The Square of Jupiter

variations of this square, but they are all essentially the same square, with the variants being reflections or rotations of the original. The base number of the square is obviously 3, and it has 3^2 or 9 squares. The numbers in each line – horizontal, vertical and diagonal – sum to 15, and the sum of all numbers in the square is 45. 15 and 45 are both triangular numbers. 45 is also a Kaprekar number. Saturn, or Cronos, is the god of time, of first beginnings, of old age. Apart from zero (which the Greeks did not recognize), the Square of Saturn contains all the digits 1 to 9, from which all other numbers are made. Its proper colours are black for the squares, and white for the numbers.

The Square of Jupiter has 16 numbers (see figure 27). The sum of the numbers in each line is 34, which is the product of 2, the first female number, and 17, a male prime (considered unlucky by Pythagoreans). The sum of the square is 136, which is curiously related to 244: cube the digits of 136, and the sum is 244: $1^3 + 3^3 + 6^3 = 244$, then repeat for 244, and the original number returns: $2^3 + 4^3 + 4^3 = 136$. The powerful base number here is 4, which is the number of the real, the mundane, the practical, the actual as opposed to the idealized. In Albrecht Dürer's famous engraving *Melencolia* (1514), a variant of the magic square of Jupiter features prominently in the top-right corner of the engraving; the

11	24	7	20	3
4	12	25	8	16
17	5	13	21	9
10	18	1	14	22
23	6	19	2	15

Figure 28 The Square of Mars

6	32	3	34	35	1
7	11	27	28	8	30
19	14	16	15	23	24
18	20	22	21	17	13
25	29	10	9	26	12
36	5	33	4	2	31

Figure 29 The Square of the Sun

square signifies the oppressive influence of all things mundane. The proper colours of the Square of Jupiter are blue for the background and tawny-orange for the numbers.

The Square of Mars is 5 by 5 (see figure 28). The auspicious male prime 13 is at the centre of this magic square. Each line totals 65, which is the second number which can be expressed as the sum of two squares, since $8^2 + 1^2 = 65$ and $7^2 + 4^2 = 65$. 65 is also the product of 5 and 13, both of them highly potent numbers. The sum of the square is 325, which is the smallest number of the sum of two squares in three different ways, since $1^2 + 18^2 = 325$, $6^2 + 17^2 = 325$ and $10^2 + 15^2 = 325$. The proper colours of this square are red for the background and green for the numbers.

The 6 by 6 magic square is dedicated to Sol, or the Sun (see figure 29). The number of squares is 36, the sum of each line is 111, and the sum of the square is the infamous 666. 111 is the magic constant of the smallest magic square consisting of the first nine prime numbers, including 1 as a prime. It is also a repunit (see page 55). 666 is the Number of the Beast in the Book of Revelation – it will be discussed in detail in Chapter Six. The traditional colours for this magic square are yellow for the background and purple or magenta for the numbers.

The magic Square of Venus is next (see figure 30). There are 49 squares, the sum of each line is 175, and the sum of the square is 1,225. This square, in particular, is traditionally associated with healing. The 49 – holy 7 × holy 7 – is found within the sum of 175, since $175 = 1^1 + 7^2 + 5^3$; and 1,225 is 35^2. It is one of the rare numbers which is both square and triangular. The numbers are lemon yellow and the background squares are dark green.

The 8 by 8 square is dedicated to Mercury (see figure 31). It has 64 squares, with the sum of each line being 260 and the sum of all squares being 2,080. It is the least commonly used of all the magic squares. Its colours are pale blue for the numbers and tawny-orange for the squares.

22	47	16	41	10	35	4
5	23	48	17	42	11	29
30	6	24	49	18	36	12
13	31	7	25	43	19	37
38	14	32	1	26	4	20
21	39	8	33	2	27	45
46	15	40	9	34	3	28

Figure 30 The Square of Venus

8	58	59	5	4	62	63	1
49	15	14	52	53	11	10	56
41	23	22	44	45	19	18	48
32	34	35	29	28	38	39	25
40	26	27	37	36	30	31	33
17	47	46	20	21	43	42	24
9	55	54	12	13	51	50	16
64	2	3	61	60	6	7	57

Figure 31 The Square of Mercury

The last square is the magic square of Luna, or the Moon, which is 9 by 9 (see figure 32). Its colours are opposite to the colours of the Square of the Sun: lemon yellow numbers on a purple background. The sum of each line is 369, whose digits are holy 3 × 1, holy 3 × 2, and holy 3 × holy 3. The sum of the whole square is 3,321. The square is centered on 41, the prime number which Ulam discovered reveals the most striking diagonal pattern of primes (see Ulam's Big Doodle on page 82).

In medieval alchemy, each of the magic squares, and therefore each of the corresponding planets, was associated with a particular metal. The essential pursuit of alchemy was not merely the transformation of base metal into gold (although it is often portrayed as such), but rather the larger and more noble aim of transcending the mundane to achieve the spiritual. In each of these magic squares and its associated metal was seen a relationship between the soul or spirit and the body. Saturn's metal was lead, which represented the body concealing the light of the soul. We now know that lead does, indeed, provide a shield against many kinds of radiation, a fact which medieval alchemists appear to have known intuitively. Jupiter's metal was tin, which represented the soul emerging from the constraints of the body. Tin ore is dark and indistinct in rock, but, when heated, it flows silver-white. The metal corresponding to the Square of Mars is, naturally, iron. It was held to represent the

37	78	29	70	21	62	13	54	5
6	38	79	30	71	22	63	14	46
47	7	39	80	31	72	23	55	15
16	48	8	40	81	32	64	24	56
57	17	49	9	41	73	33	65	25
26	58	18	50	1	42	74	34	66
67	27	59	10	51	2	43	75	35
36	68	19	60	11	52	3	44	76
77	28	69	20	61	12	53	4	45

Figure 32 The Square of the Moon

dominance of the body over the spirit. The Sun's metal is gold, which represents the spiritual truth which lies at the heart of the universe. The metal of Venus is copper, the metal of mirrors, and it represents the very opposite of iron, namely the dominance of spirit over the body. Mercury's metal, quicksilver, was considered representative of the perfect balance of spirit and body, and the Moon's silver was the representation of the soul as the perfect reflector of the spirit.

Older even than the magic squares is the fascination with the irrational number π. The number was known to the Babylonians, Egyptians and Greeks (although not by that name). Ahmes or Amos, the scribe of the Rhind papyrus, states that the area of a circle is the same as the square of $\frac{8}{9}$ of its diameter, which would make π equal to $(\frac{16}{9})^2$, which is 3.16049..., a fair approximation. The First Book of Kings in the Old Testament includes the building of Solomon's palace, and chapter 7, verse 23 seems to imply that the builders used 3 as an approximation of π: 'And he made a molten sea, ten cubits from the one brim to the other: it was round all about, and his height was five cubits: and a line of thirty cubits did compass it round about.'

What, exactly, is π? The answer is, nobody knows exactly. The number

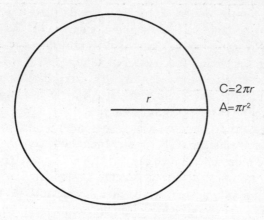

Figure 33 Circumference and area of a circle

has now been calculated to about 16 million decimal places, and there is no sign either of the number ever ending or of any repeating pattern emerging, although there are six consecutive 9s between decimal places 762 and 767. For a circle with radius r, the circumference (i.e., length all round) of the circle is $2 \times \pi \times r$, and the area of the circle is $\pi \times r^2$ (see figure 33). These relationships have fascinated mathematicians and philosophers for centuries. Pi has not played a very prominent role in numerology, although, as Euler demonstrated, it is related in an extraordinary way to the number e, which is the base of natural logarithms, and to the imaginary number i, both of which will be discussed shortly, and both of which ought to be included in a comprehensive, modern system of numerology.

There is a simple mnemonic for remembering the value of π to six decimal places. Learn the sentence: 'How I wish I could calculate pi ...'. Now substitute a number for the number of letters in each word, and put a decimal point after the first:

How I wish I could calculate pi ...
  3 . 1   4 1   5   9   2 ...

Unlike i, π is a real number, but it is transcendental, which means that it cannot be written as the solution of any equation which has integer coefficients, in other words, whole numbers. A common approximation for π is $\frac{22}{7}$, although $\frac{335}{113}$ is better, and $\frac{103,993}{331,102}$ is better still.

The Greeks – and many people after them – were obsessed with 'squaring the circle', meaning the accurate translation of the area of a given geometrical shape into a square. They began by squaring rectangles and triangles, which was fairly easy. Next they tackled regular and irregular polygons, and here, too, they achieved success. Hippocrates made the real breakthrough: he managed to square a lune (a crescent-shaped figure bounded by two circular arcs) which he had constructed. This generated tremendous excitement; if the lune could be squared, then squaring the circle could not be far away. Indeed, Simplicius, writing in the fifth century, reports that Alexander Aphrodisiensis (writing in the third century) had said that Hippocrates did manage the feat. However, 2,000 years later, we are certain that the circle never was squared, despite countless ingenious attempts.

The complex relationship between π, i and e is summarized in Euler's formula $e^{i\pi} = -1$, which is deceptively simple. First, however, we need to explain what i and e represent, and to say something about logarithms.

i is an imaginary number: it cannot actually exist. It represents that number which, multiplied by itself, would give the product -1, in other words $\sqrt{-1}$. The rule for multiplying negative numbers is very clear: negative times negative equals positive. The only way to obtain a negative product is if two different numbers – one negative and one positive – are multiplied together. So, there cannot actually be any number which, when multiplied by itself, equals negative 1. Nevertheless, the fact that i does not actually exist does not prevent us from using it in equations. Remember, it is just as difficult to prove the existence of, say, the number 5 – what constitutes fiveness is extremely difficult to define. We can add and multiply i, so $i + i = 2i$. We can factor i out of other numbers. So, for example, $\sqrt{-4}$ can be rewritten as $\sqrt{-1}$ times $\sqrt{4}$, which is i times 2, or $2i$. Numbers which combine a real number and some multiple of i are called complex numbers, and working with them can, indeed, become quite complex. A simple example would be $(2 + 3i) - (4 + 5i) = (2 - 4) + (3 - 5)i = -2 - 2i$. Multiplication and division are more complicated and involve what are known as conjugate complex numbers; that is, complex numbers in which the purely imaginary terms have opposite signs or are both zero. Although working with i can be tricky, it has become clear that this 'unreal' number has allowed mathematicians and physicists to describe much more fully the processes and phenomena at the extremes of the universe, in the tiniest particles of matter, the shortest periods of measurable time, and so on.

It was Leonhard Euler (1707–83) who named i, and he also named e. e has an actual value: to 30 decimal places it is 2.718281828459045235 360287471352.... The number is both irrational and transcendental. e is the base of natural logarithms, which themselves need some explanation.

Suppose we consider the numbers 100 and 1,000 as powers of 10 – they are 10^2 and 10^3 respectively. Now think about the number 500. It lies between 100 and 1,000, in other words between 10^2 and 10^3. The small number next to the 10 which indicates the power is called the exponent – the number 10 itself is the base. If we were to write 500 as a power of 10, it would be greater than 10^2, but less than 10^3. In other words, the exponent would have to be between 2 and 3. But we have two perfectly good systems for writing numbers which fall between whole numbers: we can either use fractions, or we can use decimals. In this case, we use decimals. The number 500 is actually 10 to the power of 2.698970004... which we could even write as $10^{2.698970004}$... The exponent created is a logarithm to the base 10. If you have a calculator with a logarithm key, try entering various numbers followed by log. You should observe that the logarithm of every number between 10 and 100 begins with a 1 followed by decimal places, every number between 100 and 1,000 with a 2 followed by decimal places, and so on. We shall look at logarithms and their uses in more detail in Chapter Eight.

Earlier, I described the kind of function where a variable is raised to a power. We can say, for example, that the function of x, or $f(x)$, is x^2. If x were 3, then $f(x)$ would be 3×3, or 9. If the roles are changed over, and instead of raising a variable to a constant power we raise a constant to a variable power, then a group of functions called exponential functions results. For example, we could write $f(x) = 2^x$. Now if $x = 3$, $f(x) = 2^3$, or 8. The only constant which cannot be used as the base of an exponential function is 1. The constant which is the base for exponential functions in calculus is e. The function $f(x) = e^x$ is the inverse of the natural logarithmic function. e plays an essential role in integral and differential calculus, and is the base of natural logarithms.

These terms are all very difficult to follow for the non-mathematician, and they are not easily explained in a short space. We can now, however, at least translate Euler's formula, even if we do not fully understand it. Euler says that $e^{\pi i} = -1$. The number 2.718281..., when raised to the power of π times $\sqrt{-1}$, equals -1.

We (general non-mathematicians) are as baffled by the meaning of imaginary and complex numbers as earlier observers were by the idea that numbers could be negative, but it is plain that without them much of our more recently acquired knowledge in theoretical physics and mathematics could not have been gained.

Lastly, a few individual numbers, apart from 666, have acquired a special history or significance in numerology, for a variety of reasons.

24 represents the number of hours in a day, but it is also 4!, a famous factorial. A factorial is a number times the number below it times the number below that, and so on all the way down to 1. 24 is factorial 4, since $4 \times 3 \times 2 \times 1 = 24$. Factorial 4 is written 4!, and is often read as 'four shriek' or 'four bang'. 10! is already a very big number (3,628,800) and 1,000,000!, recently calculated by Harry Nelson and David Slowinski, has 5,565,709 digits and its computer print out was 13 cm (5 in) thick (see note 3).

46 is famous because Psalm 46 in the Authorized Version of the Bible has 'shake' as its forty-sixth word, counting from the first word, and 'spear' as its forty-sixth word, counting backwards from the last word,

and the Authorized Version was completed in 1610, when Shakespeare was 46 years old.

153 is the number of fish in the net which Simon Peter drew from the sea of Tiberias in the New Testament. St Augustine considered the number special for that reason.

216, or Plato's number, already mentioned, is the smallest cube that is also the sum of three cubes, and it has been considered particularly significant since Plato says that it is the number of 'a human creature'. In Plato's *Republic* 729 appears when he says that a king lives 729 times more happily than a tyrant: 729 is 27^2, and it is also $364 + 365$, which suggests a calendrical connection. Plato gives 5,040 as the ideal number of inhabitants for a city, since it can be divided by any number from 1 to 10. 12,960,000 is another Platonic number, associated with 216, although its exact significance is unclear. It is 216 multiplied by 60,000, and it seems to be connected with a calendrical cycle which includes a Platonic or Great Year.

142,857 is well known because multiplication by any number from 1 to 6 produces the same digits in different orders:

$1 \times 142,857 = 142,857$
$2 \times 142,857 = 285,714$
$3 \times 142,857 = 428,571$
$4 \times 142,857 = 571,428$
$5 \times 142,857 = 714,285$
$6 \times 142,857 = 857,142$

1,234,567,891 is a prime number, as are 2,345,678,901,234,567,891 and 1,234,567,891,234,567,891,234,567,891. The highest prime number yet discovered – this time very much with the aid of computers – is $2^{756,839} - 1$, which has 227,809 digits.

18,446,744,073,709,551,615 is the solution to the ancient Indian legendary conundrum about how many grains of rice would be placed on the sixty-fourth and last square of a chess board if you began by placing one grain on the first square, two grains on the second, four grains on the third, and so on, doubling the number each time. The solution is $2^{64} - 1$ grains, enough rice, according to the legend, to cover the whole world to a depth of 2.5 cm (1 in).

2,235,197,406,895,366,368,301,560,000 to 1 against are the odds of four Bridge players each receiving a complete suit of cards in one deal. Although it is by no means obvious, this number is actually related to Euler's e.

The largest number, of course, is infinity, usually written ∞. But then, what do we mean if we write $\infty + 1$? Or how about $\infty + \infty$? Or how about ∞^∞? Number theorists have great fun messing around in the upper reaches of the multiples of infinity, where ordinary words and symbols break down and no longer seem capable of describing matters adequately. There have been some very clever (and abstruse) notations devised specifically to handle the infinite complex of infinities, in which the mathematical atmosphere thins out into the near-vacuum of pure philosophy.

Now that we have an outline of number history, and are more familiar with some number attributes and patterns, we can look in detail at the Hebrew Kabbalah, the rich and inspiring source of many of numerology's most important ideas.

five

THE KABBALAH AND BEYOND

A.E. Waite informs us that the word Kabbalah comes 'from a Hebrew root which signifies to receive ... Kabbalah equals reception' (see note1). Gershom Sholem prefers the translation 'tradition' (see note 2). Migene Gonzalez-Wippler also derives Kabbalah from the Hebrew root KBL (Kibel), meaning to receive, and gives us a simple introductory definition which clarifies why the Kabbalah is important to number magic:

> The Kabbalah is a philosophical and theosophical system that was originally designed to answer man's eternal questions on the nature of God and of the universe, and the ultimate destiny of mankind. As a practical system, it is based on the numerical correspondences between the various aspects of human life and the universal laws (see note 3).

The Kabbalah is not, in and of itself, a separate religion; it is, rather, an immensely complex Hebrew tradition which grew within, and alongside, the development of Judaism. A complete history of Judaism, even a very truncated one, is too detailed to be undertaken here, so many of the parallels and connections between the Kabbalah and the tenets of Judaism will not be fully described in this book. I recommend Rabbi Daniel J. Silver's *A History of Judaism* to any reader who wants to find out more about Judaism itself. The Kabbalah is a practical and an oral tradition, but it also has many texts – and commentaries on texts – and books about the texts and commentaries, and so on.

The history of the Jews begins with the Hebrew tribes who settled in the Fertile Crescent in the early part of the second millennium BC. They spoke West Semitic, a dialect closely related to Aramaic. They used donkeys for transport, herded sheep, traded in grain, wine and wool, and were semi-nomadic. They practised polygamy, with inheritance determined by complex legal procedure. Their society was patriarchal, with justice administered by the tribal chief and a council of male elders. Their Biblical archetype is Abraham.

From its very beginnings, that portion of the Old Testament which is the foundation of the Judaic sacred tradition has been subject to mistranslation and misinterpretation. Around 500 BC, original Hebrew died out and was replaced by Aramaic, the language eventually spoken by Jesus of Nazareth. The Jews spoke Aramaic during their 70 years' captivity in Babylon. When they returned to Palestine, the only men among them who understood Hebrew were Esdras and Daniel. The first five books of scripture, known as the Pentateuch, had to be accompanied by a series of books called the Targums ('interpretations'), in which portions of the Hebrew sacred texts were translated into Aramaic. Then Ptolemy II ordered that the Hebrew sacred texts be translated into Greek. This was done by the Essenes, a Hebrew sect of ascetics and mystics who lived near Alexandria between 200 BC and 200 AD. The Essenes were reluctant, however, to include all the esoteric lore of the original sacred texts in their translations, so they disguised some material and introduced some new material. The Old Testament stories of Adam and Eve and the serpent in the Garden of Eden, for example, were all Essene additions to the original Hebrew text. This Greek 'translation' was known as the Septuagint. Even where translation was accurate, and from the original, changes in language were influential. For example, the Greek word αναθεμα (ANATHEMA) originally meant 'offering' or 'dedication'. However, because it was associated with pagan votive offerings, it later came to signify ' all that which is unacceptable to God', exactly the opposite of its original meaning!

Following the inspiration of St Jerome, the Septuagint was translated into Latin, which version became known as the Vulgate. From 500 AD onwards, various versions of this Old Testament, added to the New Testament of the four evangelists, became the book we now refer to as the Bible, the most notable versions being John Wycliff's (d. 1384), William Tynsdale's (d. 1536), and the King James Authorized Version of 1610.

Judaism's principal religious texts are the Torah and the Talmud. Torah means literally 'doctrine' or 'teaching'. It refers to the five holy books of the Pentateuch specifically – namely Genesis, Exodus, Leviticus, Numbers and Deuteronomy, which are read aloud in synagogues – and also to the whole of Jewish law and religious studies. *Torah sheh-bik-sav* refers to written teachings and *Torah she-beal peh* refers to the oral tradition. The Jews have endured countless sacrifices and even martyrdom in order to preserve and transmit the Torah. The Talmud says, 'A single day devoted to the Torah outweighs a thousand sacrifices.'

The Talmud itself is a massive compendium of 63 books, representing a thousand years of commentary, interpretation and application of the Torah. Parts of the Talmud are in Aramaic. Included in this vast body of literature is a great deal of philosophy, astrology and numerology which also appears in the Kabbalah, although the texts of the Talmud are not actually Kabbalistic texts.

The first and most important text of the Kabbalah is the Sepher Yetzirah, which means the Book of Formation (Sepher, meaning 'book', is also sometimes written as Sefer). In legend, this short text is attributed to Abraham himself, although a more likely author is Rabbi Akiba, who lived about 130 AD in the reign of Emperor Hadrian. In 920 AD, Saadia Gaon translated the Sepher Yetzirah into Arabic, an important event for our purposes because, at that time, the Arabs ruled the mathematical world. In 1150 AD, a detailed commentary on the Sepher Yetzirah was written by Judah Halevi. The text, and some of Halevi's commentary, were translated into Latin by Postellus in 1552, but the first full English translation, *An Introduction to the Kabbalah* by W. Wynn Westcott, dates only from this century. The Sepher Yetzirah deals mostly with creation and the origins and nature of the universe and of humankind.

The second great written text of the Kabbalah is the Zohar, or Book of Splendour. The first written version of the Zohar is (arguably) that by Rabbi Simon ben Jochai, a disciple of Rabbi Akiba, who, persecuted by the Romans, fled to a life of secret exile in a cave in Israel, where he wrote the Zohar over a period of thirteen years, working entirely from memory, since he had no sacred texts with him. This explanation of the origin of the Zohar is given in the Zohar itself by Moses de Leon, an obscure Spanish rabbi who published his version of the work in the fourteenth century. Some scholars believe that Moses de Leon invented the story of Rabbi Simon, although it is accepted that the text of the Zohar includes material based on centuries of earlier oral tradition. The Zohar has had further centuries of commentary and analysis added to it, but its three most important elements are: the Siphra Dtzenioutha, or Book of Concealed Mystery; the Idra Rabba, or Great Assembly, which includes the description of the Adam Kadmon, or mystical Body of God; and the Idra Zutta, or Small Assembly, a philosophical meditation on death supposedly written by Rabbi Simon ben Jochai.

There are two other important Kabbalistic texts. These are the Sepher Sephiroth, literally Book of the Sapphires, which deals with the nature of God and includes the very important description of the Tree of Life, and the Aesch Metzareph, which is essentially an alchemical treatise.

The Kabbalah is more than just books, however; it is an unwritten system or school of philosophical thought, as well as a practical system of talismanic and ritual magic. Three particular aspects of the practical and magical Kabbalah concern us here: the Gematria, the Notarikon, and the Temura. All three will be explained in much more detail later, but, for the moment, these terms refer to the following: Gematria is the use of letters as numerals, and the vast interpretive system of numerology which results from it. Notarikon is the technique of creating new words or sentences from the first or last letters of a name or phrase, a magical technique which is highly developed in the Kabbalah. Temura is the practice of concealing sacred names or texts by coding or encryption, usually involving letter substitution.

We will look at the Gematria in more detail in the next chapter, but to understand the basis of the Kabbalah at all, it is necessary to be aware of the relationship between letters and numbers in the Hebrew alphabet. Like many other alphabets, Hebrew uses letters to signify numbers. The names of the letters are themselves words with meaning, so a system of correspondences is immediately established between numbers and the things which their names describe. For example, the Hebrew letter א or aleph, signifies the number 1, and the word itself means literally 'ox' or 'cow', but figuratively also means 'wealth'. There are 22 letters in all, each also serving as a number, plus five final versions of letters which have no separate meanings but do represent different numbers. The reader also needs to be aware of the significance of sound in both Judaism and in the Kabbalah: the universe was created by the articulation of sound – 'In the beginning was the Word ...'. Therefore, letters and words are more than just useful tools for communication; they are charged with the elemental magic (or divine intervention) which brought the whole of existence into being. The ancient Celts and the Pythagoreans also believed very strongly in the efficacy of the spoken word and in the power of correct utterance (and, therefore, in the extreme danger of false utterance).

Briefly tabulated, the Hebrew letter-number correspondences are shown in table 3 on page 103.

In this table, the literal meanings of each word are less important than their esoteric meanings. I have checked these against a variety of sources, but I am particularly indebted to Nigel Pennick's *Magical Alphabets* (see note 5).

Aleph (1), as we have already seen, means 'ox' literally, and 'wealth' figuratively. Esoterically, Aleph signifies independence, self-sufficiency, single-mindedness, creativity and innovation. In this respect, its attributes are very similar to those derived from the Pythagorean tradition. Gershom Scholem makes a very important point about the significance of Aleph; in reference to Rabbi Mendel's claim that Moses received the Commandments as a pure mystic utterance of God, he writes the following:

All that Israel heard was the *aleph* with which in the Hebrew text the first Commandment begins, the *aleph* of the word *anokhi*, 'I'. This strikes me as a highly remarkable statement, providing much food for thought. For in Hebrew the consonant *aleph* represents nothing more than the position taken by the larynx when a word begins with a vowel. Thus the *aleph* may be said to denote the source of all articulate sound, and indeed the Kabbalists always regarded it as the spiritual root of all other letters, encompassing in its essence the whole alphabet and hence all other elements of human discourse. To hear the *aleph* is to hear next to nothing; it is the preparation for all audible language, but in itself conveys no determinate, specific meaning. Thus, with his daring statement that the actual revelation to Israel consisted only of the *aleph*, Rabbi Mendel transformed the revelation on Mount Sinai into a mystical revelation, pregnant with infinite meaning, but without specific meaning. In order to become a foundation of religious authority, it had to be translated into human language, and that is what Moses did. In this light every statement on which authority is grounded would become a human interpretation, however valid and exalted, of something that transcends it (see note 4).

Beth (2) signifies not only 'house' as a building, but 'home' as a concept. It represents family, bloodline, inheritance. As in the Greek tradition, it signifies the archetypal female, the Great Mother. It is the first letter of the first word of Genesis.

Gimel (3) represents not just the camel, but all of nature. In the desert, camels were (and still are) possessions of great value, because they are so hardy in adverse conditions. The esoteric import of Gimel is harmony with nature, survival, the instinct to propagate and change.

The door of Daleth (4) represents access and denial, or authority. As Nigel Pennick points out (see note 5), the Irish Ogham and Norse Runic alphabets have identical meanings for their letter D also. In Celtic, D is Duir (Gaelic) or Derw (Brythonic), and means 'oak', the tree associated with the father-god who has many names, including Bran and the Dagda.

He (5), literally 'window', also means 'illumination' or 'insight' figuratively. Esoterically it represents intuition, inspiration, revelation, meditation and contemplation.

Vau (6) can mean 'door knob', as well as 'peg', 'nail' or 'hook'. Nigel Pennick gives its esoteric meaning as 'liberty' (the door knob opens the door), but the traditional attributes are more closely related to fertility. The corresponding sephira (this term will be explained shortly) is Binah, which represents female fertility, the Great Mother, the sea, and so on – it is not clear what the connection with the literal meaning is.

Zayin (7), sometimes written Zain, can mean 'sword', 'staff' or, more generally, 'weapon'. It therefore figuratively represents defence, and that which is defended, namely property. As with all wands and staves, it also signifies authority, including religious authority. We noted earlier that 7 is the number of the archetypal male hero or demigod in ancient Celtic mythology.

Cheth (8), sometimes written Heth, is the fence or barrier of discrimination. As in the Greek tradition, it is particularly associated with the

Table 3

Letter	English equivalent	Name	Meaning	Number value
א	A	Aleph	ox	1
ב	B	Beth	house	2
ג	G	Gimel	camel	3
ד	D	Daleth	door	4
ה	H	He	window	5
ו	V	Vau	peg, nail	6
ז	Z	Zayin	weapon	7
ח	CH	Cheth	enclosure	8
ט	T	Teth	snake	9
י	I	Yod	hand	10
כ	K	Caph	palm	20
ל	L	Lamed	ox-goad	30
מ	M	Mem	water	40
נ	N	Nun	fish	50
ס	S	Samekh	support	60
ע	O	Ayin	eye	70
פ	P	Pe	mouth	80
צ	TZ	Tzaddi	fishing hook	90
ק	Q	Qoph	back of head	100
ר	R	Resh	head	200
ש	SH	Shin	tooth	300
ת	TH	Tav	sign of cross	400
	Final Caph			500
	Final Mem			600
	Final Nun			700
	Final Pe			800
	Final Tzaddi			900

female. In the Kabbalah, it is also esoterically related to the powers of the intellect (the powers which are able to discern and discriminate) and to all high magic (which involves the placing and removing of barriers) and magical rituals.

Teth (9), meaning literally 'snake' or 'serpent', is strongly associated with the Moon and with sexual energy. The serpent is a very ancient symbol of power. It was used by Hippocrates to signify healing, and the sign of two winged serpents coiled about a staff, known also as the *caduceus* of Hermes or Mercury, survives to this day as a symbol for the practice of medicine. The ancient Celts portrayed curious serpents with rams' heads and horns. Dragons, which have forked tongues and lay eggs like snakes, are descended from the serpents of ancient mythologies.

Yod (10), sometimes written Jod, the hand, is the hand of God, or destiny.

Caph (20), also written Kaph, means 'the palm of the hand'. Nigel Pennick explains its esoteric meaning succinctly:

The palm is an important part of the body, for it is from there that radiates the bodily energy known variously as 'Pneuma', 'önd', 'Odyle' and 'Nwyvre'. It is best known from the oriental martial arts as 'Ki'. This is the subtle energy that is involved in healing from the 'laying on of the hands', and in the spectacular feats associated with the martial arts. In Christian symbolism, the palms of Jesus are pierced with the crucifying nails, destroying his ability to radiate beneficial healing energy' (see note 6).

Lamed (30) is a cattle-prod or ox-goad. It signifies progress and self-sacrifice.

Mem, which means 'water', represents the number 40, a number which appears very frequently in the Bible, in almost every case representing the completion of a significant period or transition. The Flood lasts 40 days, for example, the same period which Jesus spends in the wilderness. Mem has come to signify destiny as well as completion.

Nun (50) is esoterically related to Mem. Literally meaning 'fish', it represents escape from destiny, salvation, change of direction, new openings. The fish was a secret symbol of Jesus to early Christians.

Samekh (60) means 'prop' or 'support', both literally and figuratively, and is therefore associated with mutuality, communion, charitable acts and interdependence. Migene Gonzalez-Wippler relates it to the ovum and female fertility.

Ayin (70), sometimes written Ayn, means 'eye', and therefore represents vision, including clairvoyance and prediction. Nigel Pennick points out that Ayin parallels the Greek letter Omicron, which represents the Sun and light.

Pe (80) means 'mouth'. Its esoteric meaning is immortality, since it is connected to the idea of the Word which precedes all creation, and to the notion that a person's words may live after death.

Tzaddi (90), also written Tsade or Sadhe, means 'fish hook' literally, and its esoteric meaning is unclear. Nigel Pennick says that it represents one element being taken into another element, 'necessary opposites', while Migene Gonzalez-Wippler says it is 'a symbol of womanhood in a social sense.' Numerologically, 90 is a potent number: it is the product of complete 10, the number of perfection, and incomplete 9, the number of transformation and high magic.

Qoph, which represents 100, refers to the back of the head – it has no exact English translation. Esoterically, it means inspiration, inner illumination, intuition. To the Greeks, 100 was perfect 10 times perfect 10, and therefore a very blessed number.

Resh, representing 200, means 'head', and symbolizes outward appearance, the revealed persona, recognition, identity and individuality.

Shin, meaning 'tooth', and representing 300, has the esoteric meaning of transformation. Nigel Pennick calls it 'the divine fire that transforms one state into another.' Migene Gonzalez-Wippler calls it 'the spirit of God'.

The final letter, Tav (400), represents the phallus and the sign of the cross. It is related to the Egyptian *ankh*, or symbol of eternal life.

The finals of Caph, Mem, Nun, Pe and Tzaddi are special versions of the letters which appear only at the ends of words. They each have a numerical value – 500, 600, 700, 800 and 900 respectively – but they do not appear to have associations which are significantly different to those of the original letters.

When every letter also signifies a number, a word and an esoteric concept, the network of correspondences which can be established in even the simplest of utterances becomes extremely complex. Kabbalists have pursued these correspondences over many centuries and have built a vast compendium of commentary and interpretation.

Let us take a very simple example for the purposes of illustration, by looking at just one word: the first word in the Pentateuch, *Berashith*, 'In the beginning'. Berashith is written with six letters in Hebrew: Beth, Resh, Aleph, Shin, Yod and Teth. Numerically, it therefore represents $2 + 200 + 1 + 300 + 10 + 9$, and that sequence in itself is pregnant with meaning. 2 is the number of the archetypal female, the creatrix of all things, the symbol of all habitations and receptacles, the 'house', the bloodline, the Cosmic Mother, the beginning of all beginnings. 200 is all those attributes, or 2, raised by a factor of 100, the number of illumination, of the command, 'Let there be light!' 1, the number of Aleph, is the Cosmic Father, the unity of all creation. 300 is Shin, the divine fire of transformation, the 'spirit of God'. 10 is the hand of God. 9 is Teth, the flow of energy which winds, snake-like, through the universe. These number values, therefore, expand and illuminate the esoteric meaning of the word.

However, each letter is not only a number with esoteric correspondences: it is also a word. This sequence of literal meanings runs: house + head + ox + tooth + hand + serpent. The figurative equivalents of these words are: birthplace, origin, creation, bloodline + will, intention, conception + wealth, abundance, fertility, fecundity + transformation + completion, destiny, that which is ordained of God + unity, organic state, the flow of energy through the universe.

It is immediately apparent that the figurative and esoteric meanings of the sequence, both as numbers and as words, are peculiarly apposite and appropriate. The Kabbalah examines and relishes all such correspondences with enthusiasm for the minutest details of significance. The opening words, 'In the beginning God created the heaven and the earth …' are, in Hebrew, transliterated to Roman letters: *Berashith Bera Elohim Ath Ha Shamaim Va Ath Ha Aretz* …. Each and every word, and each of the millions of words which follow these, can be analysed and interpreted Kabbalistically.

The Sepher Yetzirah divides the Hebrew alphabet into three groups of letters: mothers, doubles and simples.

The three mother letters are Aleph, Mem and Shin (1, 40 and 300). They correspond to the three elements of air, water and fire. The heavens were created from fire, the earth from water, and air is the mediating element in between. In the seasons of the year, fire produces summer, water produces winter, and the mediating influence of air produces spring and autumn. In the creation of humankind, fire was used to form the head, water to create the belly, and air to form the chest between them. The three numbers sum to 341, which is a pseudoprime, a very rare kind of number, and the product of the primes 11 and 31. As David Wells notes, 'According to the latest physical theory of supersymmetry, space is most easily described as 11-dimensional' (see note 7).

The double letters are so called because each can be pronounced with a hard or soft sound. Each is associated with a pair of 'hard' and 'soft' attributes:

Beth (2) – wisdom and foolishness
Gimel (3) – patience and anger
Daleth (4) – fertility and isolation
Caph (20) – life and death
Pe (80) – power and servitude
Resh (200) – peace and war
Tau (400) – riches and poverty

These seven letters also correspond to the seven directions: above, below, centre, north, south, east and west; the seven days of the week; the seven planets; the seven orifices of perception: two eyes, two ears, two nostrils and the mouth. Their numbers are 2, 3, 4, 20, 80, 200 and 400, which sums to 709, which is prime.

Each of the remaining 12 simple letters is associated with a human attribute:

He (5, window) – sight
Vau (6, peg) – hearing
Zayin (7, weapon) – smell
Cheth (8, enclosure) – speech
Teth (9, snake) – taste
Yod (10, hand) – sexual appetite
Lamed (30, ox-goad) – work
Nun (50, fish) – movement
Samekh (60, support) – anger
Ayin (70, eye) – merriment
Tzaddi (90, fishing hook) – imagination
Qoph (100, back of head) – sleep

The sum of these simple letters is 445, which has as its factors the primes 5 and 89. The twelve letters also correspond to the twelve months of the year; the twelve signs of the zodiac; and the twelve organs: two hands, two feet, two kidneys, the spleen, the liver, the gall, the sexual organs, the stomach and the intestines.

At the heart of the Kabbalah is a profound philosophical idea which is common to all systems of magic, and to many religions: this is the notion that the sound of the spoken word has power. God (or the Goddess, or a divine spirit) created the universe by *speaking* it into existence. Many religions have special concerns or rules about the name or names of God, since being able to utter God's true name implies a divine power. In the Kabbalah, and thence in Judaism generally, God's true name is not uttered; it is represented by the holy tetragrammaton IHVH. This name is sometimes pronounced Yahweh, sometimes Jehovah, but neither pronunciation is the actual name of God, and no devout Jew would even attempt to pronounce the true name. Instead the epithet ADNI is used, pronounced Adonai, and usually translated as 'Lord'. Two other epithets are AHIH (meaning 'that which exists') and AGLA, which is formed by notarikon from the sentence, '*Atoh Gebore Leolahm Adonai*' ('Thou art mighty for ever, O Lord').

Against that background, we can understand more fully God's first recorded utterance, as written in Genesis: 'And God said, "Let there be light", and there was light.' The original Hebrew consists of six words (like *Berashith*, 'In the Beginning'), which is significant because 6 is the number of completion, of marriage, of harmony, of the created universe. The Hebrew sentence reads: *Viamr Alhim Ihi Aur Vihi Aur. Viamr*, meaning 'And said', is Vau, Yod, Aleph, Mem, Resh (6 + 10 + 1 + 40 + 200) and signifies the liberation (Vau) of the hand of God (Yod) in the unified creation (Aleph) of the archetypal creative principle (Mem) in the real universe (Resh). Alhim, meaning 'God', is Aleph, Lamed, He, Yod, Mem (1 + 30 + 5 + 10 + 40) and signifies the unified creation (Aleph) which is the directed energy or goad (Lamed) of illumination and life (He), revealed by the hand of God (Yod) in the act of creation (Mem). *Ihi*, which means 'Let there be', is Yod, He, Yod (10 + 5 + 10), signifying the hand of God (Yod) which illuminates and gives life (He) to itself (Yod). *Aur*, which means 'light', is Aleph, Vau, Resh (1 + 6 + 200), and signifies the unified creation (Aleph) in the liberation (Vau) of the real (Resh). *Vihi*, meaning 'And there was', is Vau, Yod, He, Yod (6 + 10 + 5 + 10), a repetition of the creation of unity in the liberation of the real. *Aur* is repeated. The sentence *Viamr Alhim Ihi Aur Vihi Aur* therefore literally means, 'And said God let there be light and there was light', but esoterically means: The hand of God moved freely in the creation of the universe, the creation of all that is real, and that flow of directed energy brought light with it, revealing God's own hand illuminated in the very act of creation, when all that is real was freed from non-existence.

We can now begin to approach the *sephiroth*, the spheres of influence in the four worlds of the Kabbalah, but first we need to understand the origins of the concept of the Adam Kadmon, or Body of God. In the Kabbalah, there are three infinities: the AIN or *Ain*, which means 'absence', the AIN SUP or *Ain Soph*, which is the mysterious vessel which contains the Ain (its literal meaning is 'not ending'), and, finally, the AIN SUP AUR, or *Ain Soph Aur*, which is the limitless point of light. All three are beyond human comprehension. However, the *Ain Soph Aur* is similar in many respects to the ancient Chinese concept of the cosmic egg, and, indeed, to our modern scientific conception of the entire universe contained within an infinitely small area in a time before time, the primordial point which produced the Big Bang which in turn created the universe.

According to the Kabbalah, the *Ain Soph Aur* first formed Adam Kadmon, which is the prototype of Adam, the 'red man', and of all humankind (see figure 34). The tetragrammaton, IHVH, is contained within the Adam Kadmon: Yod is the head, He is the arms, Vau is the trunk, and He is the legs. The head corresponds to Kether, the Crown, in the Tree of Life, which will be described shortly, and various attributes have been given to the other points of the body – beauty to the heart, justice to the left arm, foundation to the groin, and so on – although these attributions sometimes differ from text to text. They are derived from the sephiroth of the Tree of Life.

The idea of the containment of divine light is central to the concept of Adam Kadmon. Proverbs 25:2 expresses it: 'It is the glory of God to conceal a thing.' The light of Adam Kadmon is too bright for human-kind to behold: recall that God allowed Moses to see only his 'back parts' on Mount Sinai. The body of God, Adam Kadmon, therefore conceals or contains part of its light. In a succession of mystic conceal-ments, God's light is progressively veiled, with each separation creating a new world. These are the 'four worlds of the sephiroth'. The first descends directly from Adam Kadmon. It is called Atziluth, associated with the element of fire. The world of Atziluth is the world of pure spirit, of perfect archetypes – it is similar in some ways to the Platonic universe discussed earlier (see page 19). The second world is Briah, the world of creation, associated with water. Briah is peopled with archangels. The third world is Yetzirah, the world of formation, associated with air, and peopled with angelic forces. The fourth and final world is Assiah, the world of action, the element of which is earth. In Assiah live man and matter, time, and the 'shells' made of denser matter from the three timeless worlds of light. In Assiah also live the Qliphoth, or evil spirits. For many centuries, the four worlds had secret names, now revealed: Atziluth is Aub; Briah is Seg; Yetzirah is Mah; and Assiah is Ben.

One further concept, central to the Kabbalah, needs further explana-tion before we move on to the sephiroth and the Tree of Life; this is the

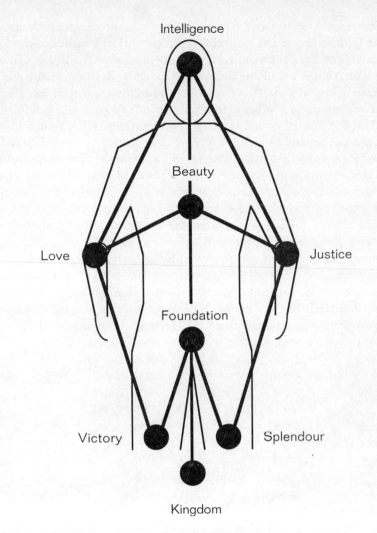

Figure 34 Adam Kadmon, the Body of God

Shekinah, also known as Matrona, the female aspect of God. Modern pagans, who conceive of the deity as male and female, god and goddess, have no difficulty understanding this concept; but the patriarchal religions, including Judaism, have wrestled with the concept to varying degree because it clashes with many of the misogynistic attitudes found in these religions. The Shekinah is believed by Kabbalists, and by some Jews, to hover over the marriage bed when a man and woman are engaged in sexual intercourse. In early Judaism and in the Kabbalah, sexual union is a mystery; the flesh becomes one flesh, a divine and sacred sacrament. The Shekinah is sometimes called the Divine Bride, the beloved of Jehovah. This explains why celibacy, which is highly

109

regarded in Christianity, is not similarly honoured by Jews – in the Hebrew tradition, marriage and sexual union are a required sacrament. According to the Kabbalah, when a child is conceived it is the man and the woman who provide the body, and God and His bride, the Shekinah, who provide the soul. These ideas are firmly ensconced in the Tree of Life, in which are placed the sephiroth, or spheres of influence. Malkuth, one of the divisions of the sephiroth, means the Kingdom, but also means the Bride.

The Tree of Life is called *Etz Hayim* in Hebrew. It is related to the Adam Kadmon, and looks quite similar, except that – and this is the element which most concerns us for the purposes of this book – each of its points and paths is associated with a specific number or number sequence and a great many interrelated numerological correspondences (see figure 35). Each sphere (the Hebrew singular is *sephira*, the plural *sephiroth* – the name actually means 'sapphire', and is a metaphor for the lucidity and brilliance of the divine spirit) has a name and a number. The sephiroth are connected by 22 paths, corresponding to the 22 letters of the Hebrew alphabet. The sephiroth have been likened to mirrors of different colours which each reflect God's radiance differently.

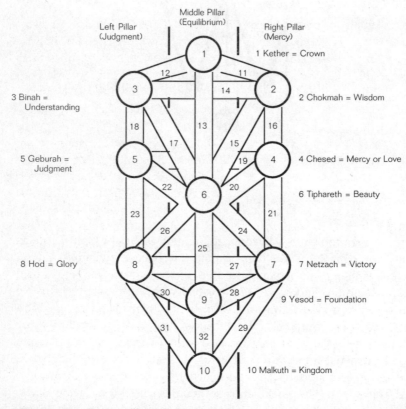

Figure 35 Etz Hayim, the Tree of Life

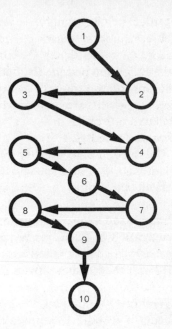

Figure 36 The Descent of Power, or
Flash of Lightning

All the sephiroth ultimately derive from the 1 of Kether, the Crown, also called the *ha-razon ad ein-soph* or 'infinite will'. Many Kabbalists conceptualize the pathways between the sephiroth as hollow tubes that glow incandescently as the light of God is diffused through them. The pathway of the counting sequence 1, 2, 3, etc. is known as the Descent of Power, or as the Flash of Lightning, on account of its shape (see figure 36).

Kether is the Crown, the head of the Middle Pillar of Mildness or Equilibrium. In the same way that the Greeks thought of 1 not as a true number, but as the divine source of all numbers, so Kether is often described as the source of all sephiroth. Kether is the mirror closest to the *Ain Soph Aur*, or Eternal Light, and therefore shines with the greatest brilliance. Each of the sephiroth contains and conceals the Light of God, because the human mind would be blinded by the full glory of the radiance of the Eternal Light even for an instant. (Paulus Ricius, a sixteenth-century German occultist, published in 1516 a commentary on the sephiroth called *Portae Lucis*, literally 'Gates of Light'.)

The light of the sephiroth flows in both directions, from God to the world and from the world to God. When the return flow is interrupted (by sin and ignorance), the interruption is called *shevirat ha-zinnorot*, which means literally 'breaking the channels'.

The Etz Hayim is divided into three columns or pillars. It is almost always represented as if viewed from the back, so the pillar on the right of the page (2 + 4 + 7, headed by Chokmah) is, indeed, the right-hand pillar. There are plenty of numerology books which print these columns the wrong way round.

The names of the sephiroth, which are in effect names of God, are cryptically encoded in Chapter 29 of the First Book of Chronicles, verse 11, in words which are later echoed in the prayer spoken by Jesus in the New Testament now known as the Lord's Prayer:

Thine, O Lord, is the greatness, and the power, and the glory, and the victory, and the majesty: for all that is in the heaven and in the earth is thine; thine is the kingdom, O Lord, and thou art exalted as head above all.

The kingdom at the end of the verse, for example, is number 10, called Malkuth, meaning 'kingdom'. It is also called many other names, and associated with many attributes. Here, then, are the ten sephiroth in full, with their names, attributes and associations.

1 Kether (The Crown)

Kether is also called Authiqa (the Ancient One); Authiqa Qadisha (the Most Holy Ancient One); Authiqa De-Authiqin (the Ancient of Ancients); Authiq Iomin (the Ancient of Days); and Risha Havura (the White Head). It has a divine (i.e., secret) name, which is Aheieh (Aleph, He, Yod, He = $1 + 5 + 10 + 5 = 21$), meaning 'I am'.

The number is associated with the archangel Metatron, and the Holy Beings or Chaioth Ha-Qadesh. The Kabbalah has demons as well as angels, and the archdemons of 1 are Satan and Moloch, who are accompanied by the Two Fighters, or Thamiel.

The sphere of the Crown is Rashith Ha-Gilgalim (the *Primum Mobile* or First Cause), and it corresponds to the head in the human body.

2 Chokmah (Wisdom)

Chokmah is also called Ab (the Father) or Abba (the Elevated, the Supernal). It has many divine names, including the now well-known Jah (Yod, He = $10 + 5 = 15$) and Jehovah (Yod, He, Vau, He = $10 + 5 + 6 + 5 = 26$), which were both closely guarded secrets at one time.

The archangel of 2 is Ratziel, who commands the Auphanim (the Wheels). Their demonic counterparts are the archdemon Beelzebub and the Ghogiel (the Hinderers).

The sphere of influence is the Mazloth, the Hebrew name for the zodiac, and the corresponding part of the body is the brain.

Chokmah is found on the right pillar of the Etz Hayim, and it is therefore associated with the active male principle – to the Greeks and the ancients, 2 was the first female number and represented the archetype of the female, Aphrodite or Venus, so this is an important anomaly between the two systems.

3 Binah (Understanding or Intelligence)

Binah was affectionately revered by early Kabbalists as Ama (the Mother) and as Aima (the Great Fertile Mother). Respect for intelligence and a deep love of learning have always been an important part of Jewish culture.

Despite the clearly feminine attribution to the Great Mother, the secret name of Binah was Alohim or Elohim (Aleph, Lamed, He, Yod, Mem = $1 + 30 + 5 + 10 + 40 = 86$), meaning 'Lord'. Michele Gonzalez-Wippler explains the gender discrepancy thus:

> The Hebrew word used to denote God in Genesis is Elohim. This word is a plural formed from the feminine singular of ALH (Eloh) by adding IM to it. Since IM is the termination of the masculine plural, added to a feminine noun it makes ELOHIM a female potency united to a male principle, and thus capable of having an offspring (see note 8).

The archangel of 3 is Tzaphkiel, of the angelic order of Aralim (the Thrones). The archdemon is Lucifuge, whose name is a later Latin interpolation for a now lost original, meaning 'he who flees from the light'. Appropriately, the demonic order is the Satariel (the Concealers).

Binah is attributed to Shabbathai (Saturn, the ancient god of wisdom), and corresponds to the heart. The planetary attribution to Saturn accords with Greek and classical tables. As with Chokmah, however, the gender is different – Binah is a feminine number, but to the Greeks, 3 was the first masculine number.

4 Chesed (Mercy or Love)

The number of Love is also called Gedulah (Greatness), and has the divine name El (Aleph, Lamed = $1 + 30 = 31$), meaning 'The Mighty One'.

Its archangel is Tzadkiel, of the Chasmalim (the Shining Beings), opposed by the archdemon Ashtaroth and the Agshekeloh (the Destroyers).

Chesed controls Tzadekh (Jupiter) and the right arm. The planetary attribution is classical. The 31 of the divine name is the fifth Mersenne number and the third Mersenne prime (see page 83). It is one of only two known numbers which can be written in two ways as the sum of successive powers ($1 + 5 + 5^2 = 31$ and $1 + 2 + 2^2 + 2^3 + 2^4 = 31$). (The other is 8,191.) It is interesting that 4 – the number of the world, the flesh and all things mundane in classical numerology – signifies 'love' in the Kabbalah. Chesed is sometimes translated as 'mercy' – like the *caritas* of St Paul, it means 'love' and 'loving-kindness', or 'the act of loving'; older versions of the Bible have St Paul praising 'faith, hope and charity', whereas more modern translations prefer the more accurate 'faith, hope and love'.

113

5 Geburah (Judgement or Strength)

Geburah is also known as Din (Judgment or Punishment) and Pachad (Fear). It contains the sense of a mighty, vengeful god, as evidenced by the secret names Eloh (Aleph, Lamed, He = $1 + 30 + 5 = 36$), meaning 'The Almighty' and Elohim Gibor (Aleph, Lamed, He, Yod, Mem, Gimel, Beth, Vau, Resh = $1 + 30 + 5 + 10 + 40 + 3 + 2 + 6 + 200 = 297$), meaning 'Lord of Battles'.

Its angelic order is the Seraphim (the Seraphs or Fiery Serpents), who are led by the archangel Khamael, in constant opposition to the archdemon Asmodeus and the Golohab (the Burning or Fiery Beings). Asmodeus is a favourite of diabolists and black magicians, because his fiery, blackened appearance is so terrifying.

The heavenly sphere of Geburah is Madim (Mars), which corresponds exactly with the classical image of Mars as the fiery god of war. The left arm is the bodily seat of Geburah.

The 297 of the divine name Elohim Gibor is the fifth Kaprekar number (see page 87), since $297^2 = 88,209$ and $88 + 209 = 297$. 5 is the number of Mars in classical numerology.

6 Tiphareth (Beauty)

Tiphareth is also called Rahamim (Compassion); Melekh (the King); and Zauir Anpin (the Smaller Countenance) – this last name is also given to the whole group of sephiroth from 4 to 9. The divine name is Eloah Va-Daath (Aleph, Lamed, Vau, He, Vau, Daleth, Aleph, Aleph, Tav = $1 + 30 + 6 + 5 + 6 + 4 + 1 + 1 + 400 = 454$), meaning 'God Manifest'.

The archangel of beauty is Raphael, served by the Malachim (the Kings). 6 is the number of beauty, order and harmony in almost all numerological traditions, and Raphael is far better known than his counterpart, the archdemon Belphegor, chief of the Tagiriron (the Arguers). 6 was the number of marriage to the Greeks, and, by extension, the number of all harmony between opposites.

The heavenly embodiment of beauty is Shemesh (the Sun), which corresponds to the chest in the human body. Tiphareth is drawn in the six-pointed Mogen David. The 454 of the divine name has two factors: 2 and 227, both prime.

7 Netzach (Victory)

The secret or divine name of victory is Jehovah Sabaoth (Yod, He, Vau, He, Tzaddi, Beth, Aleph, Vau, Tav = $10 + 5 + 6 + 5 + 90 + 2 + 1 + 6 + 400 = 525$), meaning 'God of Hosts'.

The archangel is Haniel, flanked by the Tarshishim (the Blazing Beings). Daniel sees one of the Tarshishim:

Then I lifted up mine eyes, and looked, and behold a certain man clothed in linen, whose loins were girded with fine gold of Uphaz:

his body also was like the beryl, and his face as the appearance of lightning, and his eyes as lamps of fire, and his arms and his feet like in colour of polished brass, and the voice of his words like the voice of a multitude (Daniel 10:5–6).

7 is the number of the warrior demigod in Celtic mythology. The description in Daniel is very reminiscent of the descriptions of Cu Chulainn, Ferghus, and others, with their blazing incandescence.

The archdemon is Baal. This name, written *ba'al* in ancient Canaanite, means nothing more sinister than 'master' – it is probably related to the name of the Celtic sun-god Bel or Belinus, also called Beli Mawr. Baal's demons are the Gharab Tzerek (the Raveners or Destroyers).

The heavenly sphere of Netzach is Nogah (Venus), and the corresponding part of the body is the right leg.

8 Hod (Glory or Splendour)

The number of Splendour is 8, and its divine name is Elohim Sabaoth (Aleph, Lamed, He, Yod, Mem, Tzaddi, Beth, Aleph, Vau, Tav = 1 + 30 + 5 + 10 + 40 + 90 + 2 + 1 + 6 + 400 = 585), meaning 'Lord of Hosts'.

The archangel is one of the most popular of all, Michael, and he leads the Beni Elohim (the Sons of the Lord) against the archdemon Adrammelech and the Samael (the False Accusers).

The heavenly sphere is Kokab (Mercury), and the corresponding part of the body is the left leg.

Hod is in the left pillar, the female side of the Etz Hayim, and this is in accord with the classical feminine attributes of 8.

9 Yesod (Foundation)

Yesod is also called Yesod Aalam (the Foundation of the World) and has the secret name Shaddai (Shin, Daleth, Yod = 300 + 4 + 10 = 314), meaning 'The Almighty'. The number 9 is traditionally associated with magical invocation and working, so the name Shaddai is considered particularly powerful.

The archangel of the Foundation is Gabriel, who will sound his horn at the ending of the world, and who is surrounded by the Cherubim (the Strong). Against Gabriel stands Lilith the Seducer, the only female archdemon (Lilith was created before Eve, a 'prototype' which went wrong). She is the leader of the Gamaliel (the Obscene Beings).

Yesod's sphere of influence is Levanah (the Moon), and it is not surprising that the corresponding body parts are the genitalia. 9 has strong sexual connotations in the Kabbalah, which are less apparent in classical numerology. In the 'good' sense, the foundation of the world is sexual union and procreation, but Yesod is also associated with several sexual negatives – in that sense, its attributes parallel those of classical 9, the imperfect number which falls just short of perfect 10.

10 Malkuth (Kingdom)

Malkuth, the number of perfection for the Hebrews as much as for the Greeks, is also called Atarah (the Diadem). Proverbs 12:4 tells us, 'A virtuous woman is a crown to her husband'; the original Hebrew is *atarah*. Ten is sometimes called the Shekinah (the Manifest Glory of God), a name rich with resonances, since the Shekinah is often envisaged as a real but invisible spiritual presence, not unlike the Holy Ghost in Christianity. This number is so important that it has many names. It is also called Kallah (the Bride) and Malkah (the Queen). Clearly feminine, its secret names nevertheless translate as masculine: Adonai (Aleph, Daleth, Nun, Yod = $1 + 4 + 50 + 10 = 65$), means 'Lord'; Adonai He-Aretz (Aleph, Daleth, Nun, Yod, He, Aleph, Resh, Tzaddi = $1 + 4 + 50 + 10 + 5 + 1 + 200 + 90 = 361$), means 'Lord of Earth'.

There is no ruling archangel of 10. The ruling angel is Sandalphon, an angel of the Earth, and the angelic order comprises the Ashim (the Souls of Flame). Psalm 104:4 describes the Lord 'who maketh his angels spirits, his ministers a flaming fire'. The corresponding archdemon is Nahema (the Strangler of Children), attended by the Nahemoth (the Wretched).

The heavenly sphere is the Aulam Yesodoth, which signifies all the material elements in the universe, all the matter that is, in other words, and the number therefore also represents the entire human body. This series of attributes is very much in accord with the classical Pythagorean notion of 10 as the number of perfection, the number of the completed universe.

There is some dispute about the demons and demonic orders of the Kabbalah, which does not really affect us very greatly here, but it ought to be mentioned for the sake of accuracy. The attributions given above are largely taken from Donald Tyson's excellent edition of *Cornelius Agrippa* (see note 9).

It is interesting to note that all commentaries agree that the emanations and correspondences within and between the sephiroth occur out of space and out of time – the transformations are instant from one state to another. This long-held conception, clearly described in the classic Kabbalistic commentaries, is highly reminiscent of Max Planck and the quantum leap and subsequent quantum theory of modern physics.

David Allen Hulse describes a sequence of correspondences between the paths of the Tree of Life and the minor and major arcana of the Tarot (see note 10). Table 4 of the major arcana is adapted from his description.

The pathways between the sephiroth generate a whole series of sequences. For example, Kether (1) of the middle pillar leads to Chokmah (2) via 11. Eleven is $10 + 1$, which is Yod plus Aleph, which spells Jah, a name of God. The combinatory sequences are countless,

Table 4

Path in the *Etz Hayim*	Connects numbers	Hebrew letter	Related Tarot card
11	1 and 2	Aleph (1)	0 The Fool
12	1 and 3	Beth (2)	I The Magician
13	1 and 6	Gimel (3)	II The High Priestess
14	2 and 3	Daleth (4)	III The Empress
15	2 and 6	He (5)	IV The Emperor
16	2 and 4	Vau (6)	V The Hierophant
17	3 and 6	Zayin (7)	VI The Lovers
18	3 and 5	Cheth (8)	VII The Chariot
19	4 and 5	Teth (9)	VIII Strength
20	4 and 6	Yod (10)	IX The Hermit
21	4 and 7	Caph (20)	X The Wheel of Fortune
22	5 and 6	Lamed (30)	XI Justice
23	5 and 8	Mem (40)	XII The Hanged Man
24	6 and 7	Nun (50)	XIII Death
25	6 and 9	Samekh (60)	XIV Temperance
26	6 and 8	Ayin (70)	XV The Devil
27	7 and 8	Pe (80)	XVI The Tower
28	7 and 9	Tzaddi (90)	XVII The Star
29	7 and 10	Qoph (100)	XVIII The Moon
30	8 and 9	Resh (200)	XIX The Sun
31	8 and 10	Shin (300)	XX Judgment
32	9 and 10	Tau (400)	XXI The World

and a whole lifetime could be devoted (many lifetimes already have been) to study of the Etz Hayim and sephiroth alone. Using some of the books on the Kabbalah mentioned in the bibliography as guides, the reader can pursue a more detailed study of this fascinating corner of numerology at will and at length, but here is just a brief example of sequence interpretation.

Binah (3), 'Understanding' or 'Intelligence', known as Ama, the Great Mother, leads through 17 to Tiphareth (6), which is Beauty. Seventeen can be Yod, Aleph and Vau (10 + 1 + 6), which has the esoteric meaning, 'The hand of God is the *primum mobile* of the unified creation'; or it can be Yod, Beth and He (10 + 2 + 5), which has the esoteric meaning, 'The hand of God is the progenitor of all illumination and insight'; or it can be Yod, Gimel and Daleth (10 + 3 + 4), which has the esoteric meaning, 'The hand of God is seen in all nature and is the authority of the universe'; or it can be Teth and Cheth (9 + 8), which has the esoteric meaning, 'Divine energy flows throughout the universe and is the source of the fertility of all created things'; and so on, and so on .... As this shows, even a three-number sequence can generate an incredibly complex sequence of interpretations. There is literally no end to this study: Kabbalists have been practising it avidly for many centuries, and will probably continue to do so for many more centuries. To end this chapter, here are some number sequences and 'translations' of my own. They are very personal to me, and are meant to be so. Each and every one of the interpretations could be replaced with a thousand equally valid alternatives, with an infinity of subtle nuances. Those of a nervous or sceptical disposition are welcome to skip ahead to Chapter Six. My own religious views include the conception of the supreme deity as female rather than male, so some of the words reflect that bias.

$$1 + 2 + 3 + 4 + 5 + 6 + 7 + 8 + 9 + 10 = 55$$

(Aleph, Beth, Gimel, Daleth, He, Vau, Zayin, Cheth, Teth, Yod, Nun, He)
'The one creator, beyond human understanding, is the source of all living things. She is a doorway to the eternal, and the opening and closing of the door are her authority. She is illumination, intuition and understanding, and knowledge of her love comes as blindingly as unimaginably great light. She is my support and my strength. She is the fertility of the Earth and of all living things, and her boundless energy flows throughout the universe. She lifts her hand and bestows understanding.'

$$2 + 4 + 8 + 16 + 32 \ldots$$

(Beth, Daleth, Cheth, Yod, Vau, Lamed, Beth ...)
'Here is my inheritance, my bloodline. By the authority of the Goddess, and through the fertility which is her gift to all living things, given by her hand, she sustains and encourages generation after generation through eternity ...'

$$3 + 9 + 27 + 81 + 243 = 363$$

(Gimel, Teth, Caph, Zayin, Pe, Aleph, Resh, Mem, Gimel, Shin, Samekh, Gimel)
'Goddess of Life, whose energy flows through the universe, whose palms radiate light and strength, whose mouth spoke the Word that began all things, whose mind conceived the waters of the creation, let your divine fire blaze within me and through me to all generations.'

six

GEMATRIA AND BEYOND

αβγδεϛζηθικλμνξοπϙϱστυφξψΔΛΞΠΣΥΦΨ

The reader will have gained some understanding of gematria from the previous chapter. The essential element is that letters represent numbers and numbers represent letters. Sentences can generate sums, which, in turn, can generate new sentences. Number sequences can be expanded and extrapolated by hermeneutics to create immensely detailed and complex statements. Of particular interest to Kabbalists are those correspondences where the same number total is generated by different words or phrases. For example, the phrase 'until Shiloh come' in Genesis (49:10) is interpreted as a prophecy of the coming of the Messiah, as evidenced by the following correspondence in Hebrew: 'until Shiloh come' is *Iba Shilh* (Yod, Beth, Aleph, Shin, Yod, Lamed, He) which corresponds to 10 + 2 + 1 + 300 + 10 + 30 + 5, which totals 358. The Hebrew for 'Messiah' is *Mshich* (Mem, Shin, Yod, Cheth), which is 40 + 300 + 10 + 8, again giving a total of 358. In Numbers (21:9), we are told how Moses fashioned a serpent of brass which had the magical power of curing anyone suffering from the bite of a real snake. The Hebrew name for the brazen serpent is *Nachash*: Nun plus Cheth plus Shin (50 + 8 + 300), which again totals 358.

In a moment we shall examine how this general idea of gematria has been adapted and adopted for use with other alphabets, and, in particular, how gematria works in English (not perfectly, by any means, but certainly well enough for many practical numerological purposes). First, however, we need to complete the explanation of notarikon and temurah, promised in the last chapter.

Notarikon is actually a Greek word, since the practice of it was common with the Greek alphabet long before the Kabbalah even existed. What made notarikon especially suited to the Kabbalah was the fact that ancient Hebrew omitted vowels, which allowed far greater freedom in interpreting short letter combinations. Imagine that a word could be written 'tn' in English: we could interpret it as 'tan', 'ten', 'tin', 'ton', or 'tune'. This advantage will become clearer in a moment. There are actually two kinds of notarikon. In the first one, the first, or last, or first and last letters of a word or sequence of words generate in turn a new word or words. An example is probably easier to understand than the explanation. Consider, for example, the following nonsense sentence: 'Bedside tiger unbelievable two mice.' The first and last letter of each word, by notarikon, spell out: 'Be true to me.' This is the harder version. Using just first letters, or just last letters, is much easier. For example, 'Take heart; every fool runs up into the inner sanctuary, rushes into peril expeditiously' conceals 'The fruit is ripe' in the sequence of first letters. The second kind of notarikon performs the same operation in reverse; a word or phrase is expanded by using its letters as the first (sometimes last) letters of a new phrase. For example, 'Arise!' becomes 'Awake, revolutionaries – inspiration strikes everywhere!'

Temurah is simply encryption or code-making. The most common in the Kabbalah is the split-alphabet code. The first 11 letters are written in their normal order (right to left), then the remaining 11 letters are written beneath them in reverse order (left to right), thus:

Vau	He	Daleth	Gimel	Beth	Aleph
Pe	Tzaddi	Qoph	Resh	Shin	Tav

Caph	Yod	Teth	Cheth	Zayin
Lamed	Mem	Nun	Samekh	Ayin

To encode or decode, each letter is paired with its partner. For example, the temurah name for Babel (Beth, Beth, Lamed) is Sheshak (Shin, Shin, Caph). Metzepetz (Mem, Tzaddi, Pe, Tzaddi) is the temurah version of the tetragrammaton, IHVH, the unutterable name of God.

Notarikon and temurah are really of only incidental interest to us here. Gematria, which is our main concern, occurs in any alphabet where letters also signify numbers. The Western magical tradition of gematria, on which much of the foundation of modern numerology is based, is found in all the following alphabets: Hebrew; Greek (pagan and Christian); Coptic (an alphabet descended from Egyptian hieroglyphics); Phoenician (also known as Punic); Irish and British Ogham; the Norse and Anglo-Saxon runic alphabets; Gothic; and Westphalian (Old High German).

In addition to these 'natural' systems of gematria, several others have been devised. The Romans used letters for numerals, but not in a way which could be used for gematria. However, from earliest times, various systems of gematria based on Roman letters have been devised and used. There are several systems in English, none of which is perfect, but all of which have their various merits. Finally, there is a complete esoteric system, known as Enochian, devised by modern numerologists working within the extensive tradition of the Golden Dawn, a modern magical system.

The oldest of all these alphabets is Phoenician. Phoenician is actually related to Hebrew. It is descended from ancient Canaanite. (In the Old

Table 5

Greek letter	Letter name	Hebrew parallel	English parallels	Number value
Α α	Alpha	Aleph	A	1
Β β	Beta	Beth	B	2
Γ γ	Gamma	Gimel	C/G	3
Δ δ	Delta	Daleth	D	4
Ε ε	Epsilon	He	E/H	5
ς	Stau	Vau	St/V	6
Ζ ζ	Zeta	Zayin	Z	7
Η η	Eta	Cheth	long E/Ch	8
θ Θ	Theta	Teth	Th/T	9
Ι ι	Iota	Yod	I	10
Κ κ	Kappa	Caph	K	20
Λ λ	Lambda	Lamed	L	30
Μ μ	Mu	Mem	M	40
Ν ν	Nu	Nun	N	50
Ξ ξ	Xi	Samekh	hard Ch/S	60
Ο ο	Omicron	Ayin	O	70
Π π	Pi	Pe	P	80
ϙ	Koppa	Tzaddi	Q/Tz	90
Ρ ρ	Rho	Qoph	R, Rh/Q	100
Σ σs	Sigma	Resh	S/R	200
Τ τ	Tau	Shin	T/Sh	300
Υ υ	Upsilon	Tau	Y, U/Th	400
Φ φ	Phi	Caph final	Ph	500
Χ χ	Chi	Mem final	Ch	600
Ψ ψ	Psi	Nun final	Ps	700
Ω ω	Omega	Pe final	long O	800
ϡ	Sampi	Tzaddi final	S	900

Testament, the Phoenicians are called Canaanites and Sidonians.) The Phoenician alphabet has had a very profound influence on all Western culture; it was the foundation for the Greek alphabet, and, subsequently, all Western writing.

Many of the early Greek characters are identical to the original Phoenician. (By 'early', I mean approximately 1700 BC.) Around 800 BC, the 16-character Greek alphabet developed into a 24-character series, and suddenly it was written from left to right instead of from right to left – there has been no satisfactory historical explanation for this change. The Homeric serial order (still used by some numerologists)

121

dates from about 775 BC, but it was superseded by the Herodianic correspondences in about 600 BC – like the later Roman code, this was not suitable for gematria. The Greek alphabet code which we shall deal with here is the Pythagorean code, introduced about 450 BC, but which remained a closely guarded secret for centuries. We are already familiar with the Hebrew correspondences, and the Pythagorean sequence is very similar, so both are given in table 5.

Stau, Koppa and Sampi were not used in later classical Greek. The correspondences between most of the Greek and Hebrew letters are very obvious. However, some of the pairs do not appear to correspond at all, and one part of the sequence – from Koppa to Tau – seems misaligned by one place: we would expect Rho and Resh to be paired, Sigma and Shin, and Tau and Tau, but they are not.

To anticipate a later argument, it is fairly obvious that certain English letters should be assigned particular number values for good historical reasons: there is not much argument that L should represent 30 (as do the related letters Lambda and Lamed). Nevertheless, there are many popular numerology books which promulgate the idea that each English letter is the equivalent of its ordinal position in the English alphabet: A = 1, B = 2, ... Y = 25, Z = 26. This is a simple mistake, which we shall discuss in more detail towards the end of this chapter.

As in Hebrew, certain letters (and their corresponding numbers) were ascribed to different parts of the body, but the Greeks also conceptualized the Soma Sophia ('Body of Wisdom'), in which letters (numbers) were also ascribed to the twelve signs of the zodiac. In the following summary of the Soma Sophia, the first letter (number) is on the right side of the body, the second on the left:

Alpha (1) – Omega (800) – Aries – the head
Beta (2) – Psi (700) – Taurus – the throat
Gamma (3) – Chi (600) – Gemini – the shoulders, arms, hands
Delta (4) – Phi (500) – Cancer – the chest
Epsilon (5) – Upsilon (400) – Leo – the heart
Zeta (7) – Tau (300) – Virgo – the stomach
Eta (8) – Sigma (200) – Libra – the intestines
Theta (9) – Rho (100) – Scorpio – the genitalia
Iota (10) – Pi (80) – Sagittarius – the thighs
Kappa (20) – Omicron (70) – Capricorn – the knees
Lambda (30) – Xi (60) – Aquarius – the ankles
Mu (40) – Nu (50) – Pisces – the feet

The number of the whole person, and of the whole zodiac, is therefore: 801 + 702 + 603 + 504 + 405 + 307 + 208 + 109 + 90 + 90 + 90 + 90 = 3,999.

Christian number mysticism was also based on Greek. The most famous example of Christian hermeneutics is the interpretation of the text of Revelation 13:18: 'Here is wisdom. Let him that hath understanding count the number of the beast: for it is the number of a man; and his number is six hundred threescore and six.' By adding the number values of each letter, Aleister Crowley came up with the ingenious but not very convincing Το Μεγα θεριον (TO MEGA THERION), which means 'The Great Wild Beast', as the source of the number. A much earlier interpretation was that of the second-century Bishop Ienaeus, who suggested Λατεινος LATEINOS ('The Latin One', signifying Romans in general); while for centuries the most popular interpretation has been Νερον Κεσαρ NERON KESAR (the Emperor Nero). Robert Graves points out the errors in this long-held interpretation:

The solution is based on the Hebrew. *Nun* = 50; *Resh* = 200; *Vav* = 6; *Nun* = 50 = *Neron*. *Koph* = 100; *Samech* = 60; *Resh* = 200 = *Kesar*. But Nero in Latin remains Nero when written in Hebrew, and Kaisar (which meant 'a head of hair' in Latin and 'a crown' in Hebrew – perhaps both words were borrowed from a common Aegean original) should be spelt with a *Kaph* (= 20), not a *Koph*, which makes the sum add up to only 626 (see note 1).

Graves himself favours TRIJON (which means 'little beast'). In Hebrew letters, that would be Tau = 400; Resh = 200; Yod = 10; Vau = 6; and Nun = 50: yielding 666.

David Allen Hulse points out the curious fact that the value of the Greek letters for NERON KESAR is 1,332, which is exactly twice 666 (see note 2). Hulse also lists many of the Greek words or phrases used by early Christian mystics to show associations with the key magical numbers 111, 222, 333, and so on. One example of each will suffice here:

111	Κλαξ	(KLAX) – key, home, bloodline
222	Ναζαρενε	(NAZARENE) – Jesus of Nazareth, the Nazarene
333	Καισαρα	(KAISARA) – Caesar
444	Σαρξ Και Αιμα	(SARX KAI AIMA) – flesh and blood, the material
555	Δρακουτι	(DRAKONTI) – the dragon, Satan
666	Λογος Αγαπες	(LOGOS AGAPES) – the word of love
777	Σταυρος	(STAVROS) – the Cross of the crucifixion
888	Ιεσους	(IESOUS) – Jesus
999	Θεος Αυεκλαλτος	(THEOS ANEKLALTOS) – the ineffable God

Many other numbers are attributed to Christ by Greek gematria. Among them are 808 (Ιεσου Ραββι IESOU RABBI, 'Rabbi Jesus'); 1,480 (Ξριστος XRISTOS, 'Christ'); and 2,368 (Ιεσους Ξριστος IESOUS XRISTOS, 'Jesus Christ'). The Greek for 'fish' is (Ιχθευς ICHTHEUS), which expands by notarikon to (Ιεσους Ξριστος θεου Ηυ'ιος Σωτερ IESOUS CHRISTOS THEOU EUHIOS SOTER), meaning 'Jesus Christ, Son of God and Saviour'.

The Greeks loved geometry (which literally means 'Earth measuring'), the Greek word for which was Γεομετρια (GEOMETRIA), which has the variant form Γαμετρια (GAMETRIA), which is also a Greek variant of 'gematria'.

Each Greek letter not only has its own number value, it also acquires a second number value through the process of gematria itself. For example, is α ALPHA (Alpha, Lambda, Phi, Alpha = 1 + 30 + 500 + 1 = 532). The letters, like the Hebrew letters, also have literal, figurative and esoteric meanings. These correspondences are summarized briefly below.

α is Alpha, number value 1, value by gematria 532, literal meaning 'cattle', figurative meaning 'wealth', which corresponds exactly with the Hebrew equivalent Aleph.

ß is Beta, number value 2, value by gematria 308 (Beta, Epsilon, Tau, Alpha) or 311 (Beta, Eta, Tau, Alpha). In Latin, the word beta has the humdrum meaning of 'beet' or 'beetroot'. In modern Greek, the letter is pronounced like [v] in English vase. Modern Greeks have to write μπ (Mu, Pi) to approximate a full [b] sound. Christian gematria has obscured whatever original pagan attributes this number may have had for the later Greeks – it is universally regarded as evil in Christian hermeneutics, the number of the Devil. This interpretation was heavily reinforced by Mithraism, in which the demon of evil, Angra Mainyu, is known as 'the second'. Modern numerology tends to prefer the early Greek and subsequent Hebrew attributes related to the eternal feminine principle, the Great Mother, and so on.

γ is Gamma, number value 3, value by gematria 85, figurative meaning 'the complete', which corresponds in meaning fairly well with the Hebrew equivalent Gimel, widely associated with prosperity. When the letter is doubled in Greek, the first Gamma is nasalized, producing a sound like the [ng] in a German's pronunciation of the word finger. In early Greek, two Gammas written on one staff (rather like an English capital F) were called the Digamma ('Two Gammas'), and pronounced like English [w], but the Digamma disappeared early from the Greek alphabet.

∂ is Delta, number value 4, value by gematria 340. The hard [d] sound of classical Greek has been voiced to a hard [th] sound (as in fa*th*er) in modern Greek, which has to use ντ (Nu, Tau) to reproduce the original [d] sound. The literal meaning is 'delta', which originally indicated any object shaped like a triangle and eventually came to mean (in English) a pattern of triangular alluvial deposits at the mouth of a river. In Hebrew, Daleth means 'door' because originally it meant 'tent-flap', the triangular piece of cloth which closed the tent entrance. In modern algebra, ∂ usually signifies a finite increment in a variable. The Greeks called a constellation Deltoton ('The Triangle'), which is also used later by the Roman author Cicero. The esoteric meaning is very similar to those in all other traditions: 4 is the number of the real, the material, the mundane, the four elements, and so on. Christian exegesis also makes much of the four great archangels, and the Four Horsemen of the Apocalypse.

ε is Epsilon, number value 5, value by gematria 865. The element *psilon* means literally 'simple', so the name means 'simple e'. The medieval concept of the *quinta essentia*, or fifth essence, heavily influenced interpretations of Epsilon. Apart from the attributes mentioned in Chapter Three, it is also associated with the spiritual within the material, the psyche, or the soul.

ς is Stau, number value 6, but this letter disappeared early from the Greek alphabet and does not appear in Greek gematria.

ζ is Zeta, number value 7, value by gematria 316, literal meaning 'offering', figurative meaning any kind of gift or sacrifice, and strongly associated with the archangel Michael in Christian Greek gematria. It so happens that this letter and the next three in sequence form a word in Greek, (ZETHI), which is an imperative, meaning 'Live!'

η Eta, number value 8, value by gematria 309, which is the number of the god Ares (later Mars). 8 is also considered a solar number. Nevertheless, the Pythagorean and subsequent medieval attributes of 8 as the number of Cybele, the Magna Mater, survive most strongly in modern numerology. Mention was made in Chapter Three of the Celtic eightfold division of the calendar, and the eight regions of space created by three intersecting planes.

θ is Theta, number value 9, value by gematria 18. Nigel Pennick gives 318 as the gematria value, which seems to be an error. He also lists positive attributes for it, which must be a mistake. Theta is the first letter of θανατος (THANATOS), the Greek for 'death', and the letter had ominous associations even in classical Greece; at a trial, a juror scratched

125

the letter into a potsherd to indicate his vote for the death-penalty. It was an inauspicious number for Pythagoreans, since it fell one short of perfect 10, but it also had the good fortune to be holy 3 times holy 3. In almost all numerological systems, 9 signifies incompleteness. It is particularly associated with patience and devotion (the thrice holy waiting and waiting and waiting for the coming of perfection).

ι is Iota, number value 10, value by gematria 1,111. The fact that it is the smallest of the Greek letters led to the coining of the English word 'jot', meaning 'the merest amount'. Two very strong influences have heavily impressed themselves on modern numerological interpretations of 10: the Pythagorean reverence for the number, idolized in the secret and sacred tetraktys (see page 59); and the universal hegemony of 10 as the base for practical counting systems.

κ is Kappa, number value 20, value by gematria 182. It is associated with Kronos, the god of time, and therefore with fate, death, the inexorable. It is interesting that many languages have counting systems which are based on 20, or the score – the origin seems likely to be nothing more complicated than the usual human complement of ten fingers and ten toes.

λ is Lambda, number value 30, value by gematria 78. It is a highly auspicious number in the Greek tradition, being holy 3 times perfect 10. It is associated with fertility. It is sometimes used to represent numerology itself.

μ is Mu, number value 40 (another very sacred number, commonly found in both the Old and the New Testaments), value by gematria 440 (sacred 40 times prime 11, plus many other interesting interpretive factorizations). The original capital form of this letter, which looks much like the English capital M, is found also in Phoenician and Etruscan, as well as Cretan and the earliest Greek. By gematria, 440 is equivalent to a Greek phrase meaning 'the house', which, like the Hebrew Beth, can also mean 'family' or 'bloodline'.

ν is Nu, number value 50, value by gematria 450. It corresponds almost exactly with the Hebrew Nun, except that in the Greek tradition it appears to have picked up some negative attributes from association with Nut, an Egyptian goddess of the underworld, later echoed in the Norse goddess Nott, a goddess of darkness, and the runic letter Nyd (we shall discuss runes shortly).

ξ is Xi, number value 60, value by gematria 70. (Pennick inexplicably gives the gematria value as 615.) 60 is an immensely practical and useful number. The Chaldeans, Babylonians and Egyptians discovered very early on that dividing a whole into 60 parts made recombination and distribution very flexible; all the following fractions are possible: $\frac{1}{2}, \frac{1}{3}, \frac{1}{4}, \frac{1}{5}, \frac{1}{6}, \frac{1}{10}, \frac{1}{12}, \frac{1}{15}, \frac{1}{20}, \frac{1}{30}$ and $\frac{1}{60}$. As a result, 60 has survived to this day in the seconds of a minute, the minutes of an hour and the degrees of a circle. Factorized as 3 and 20, the attributes might be unclear, but as 2 and 30, 60 is clearly an auspicious and blessed number.

o is Omicron, number value 70, value by gematria 360 (Pennick gives 1,090). The literal meaning is 'little o' (micron means 'little'). It corresponds to the Hebrew Ayin, which means 'eye' – very apt for a little o. It is associated with the Moon (the little o in the sky). Pennick relates Omicron to Christ, but I think he may have confused Omicron with Omega in this instance.

π is Pi, number value 80, value by gematria 90. The letter has represented the number 3.141592... for so long, and with such significance, that it is hard to untangle its original attributes. The Hebrew parallel is Pe, which had two forms, hard and soft, associated respectively with power and servitude. Remember, too, that the literal meaning of Pe is 'mouth', from which comes the figurative meaning of 'immortality', since that which is spoken (LOGOS in Greek) has power and lives for ever. Pythagoras must have had good reason for choosing π to represent the mysterious number with which he and his disciples wrestled – the suggestion is that the earliest Greek tradition also associated π with power.

ϙ is Koppa, number value 90. The name of this letter appears in later Latin texts, even spelled with a 'k', when the sound was otherwise universally represented by q. This letter disappeared from the Greek alphabet very early and does not figure in Greek gematria.

ρ is Rho, number value 100. Pennick gives the gematria value as 170, the same as the prayer ('Amen'), meaning 'Let it be so.' Presumably he reads Rho as Rho plus Omicron (100 + 70 = 170). I prefer Rho plus Omega, the long o, which gives a gematria value of 900 (100 + 800 = 900). We would expect Rho to pair up with Hebrew Resh, but it does not; its Hebrew parallel is Qoph, which describes the back of the head. The numerological attributes of this whole sequence of letters (Rho to Tau) are very uncertain, partly because there is this lack of correspondence.

σ is Sigma, number value 200, value by gematria 254. Sigma notation is used in modern mathematics to indicate the sum of a series, called arithmetic (emphasis on the third syllable), in which a constant difference produces each new term, such as 2 + 4 + 6 + 8 + 10 + 12 + ... If the sequence depends on multiplication by a constant ratio, rather than addition of a constant difference, then the sequence is called geometric, such as 2 + 4 + 8 + 16 + 32 + 64 + ... We would expect Sigma to partner Hebrew Shin, but, instead, it pairs with Resh, meaning 'head'. The cyrillic alphabet, used in Russian, and related to the early Greek alphabet, uses a capital C where English would use S – the C was a common alternative to Sigma in early Greek, but now survives only in cyrillic.

τ is Tau, number value 300, value by gematria 701. There are many numerological connections here. Tau is physically shaped like the crosses used for crucifixion, and possibly for The Crucifixion. A cross of that shape was certainly used for the crucifixion of St Anthony, so it is now often called a 'St Anthony cross', in the same way that the diagonal cross is a 'St Andrew cross'. Kabbalistic tradition has it that this was also the shape of the staff upon which Moses raised the magic brazen serpent which could heal snake bites. The gematria value of 701 is the same as that of the *Chrismon*, the monogram of Christ, which consists of the first two letters of his name in Greek (Chi, Rho, 600 + 100 = 700; by a tradition called *colel*, numbers one unit apart correspond). The Greek tradition, especially as influenced by Christian Greek hermeneutics, strongly overshadows the Hebrew tradition here. However, Shin (which is Tau's equivalent) is a mother letter, corresponding to the element of fire, signifying creation. Either way, the number 300 is numerologically extremely potent. The difficulty lies in deciding whether it would better be represented by S or by T in English, a problem to which we shall return shortly.

υ is Upsilon, number value 400, value by gematria 1,260. The *psilon* (as in Epsilon) means 'simple', so this is 'simple u'. It is the last of the 'misaligned' sequence of letters, in that its Hebrew correspondent is Tau. Pythagoras used capital Upsilon in his teachings of moral philosophy to indicate the divergent paths of knowledge and ignorance, or good and evil.

φ is Phi, number value 500, value by gematria 510. These last four letters – Phi, Chi, Psi and Omega – correspond to the Hebrew finals Caph, Mem, Nun and Pe, which have no independent word values or associations. Phi is well known in America because one of the largest college student fraternities is ΦΒΚ (Phi Beta Kappa), which derives its name from the Greek phrase Φιλοσοφια Βιου Κυβερνετες (PHILO-SOPHIA BIOU KUBERNETES), meaning, 'Philosophy (is) the Governor of Life.' As we saw earlier, φ is also used in mathematics to represent 1.61803..., the Golden Ratio or Divine Proportion (see pages 38 to 42).

χ is Chi, number value 600, value by gematria 610. As Nigel Pennick points out (see note 3), the same gematria value of 610 is also found in Κοσμος (KOSMOS), 'the Cosmos', and in Ηο Θηεοτες (HO THEOTES), 'the Godhead'. It is easy to confuse Chi with the English X, but they are quite different. The letter is pronounced with a back-of-the-throat [ch] sound, like Scottish lo*ch* or German a*ch*. There is a literary or poetic device called *chiasmus*, in which opposing ideas are expressed in a parallelism to make a figurate crossed shape like Chi. Examples are, 'Do not live to eat, but eat to live', or Alexander Pope's famous quatrain:

A little learning is a dangerous thing;
Drink deep, or taste not the Pierian spring:
There shallow draughts intoxicate the brain,
And drinking largely sobers us again.

The ideas cross over each other, so to speak: 'shallow draughts' crosses to 'sobers', 'intoxicate' crosses to 'drinking largely', hence the idea of chiasmus. 600 is an especially auspicious numerological number, for a number of interwoven reasons. It is the 6 of marriage and contentment and harmony, multiplied by perfect 10 multiplied by perfect 10. However, in Hebrew 600 is represented not by a Chi sound, but by final Mem, the final humming with which the universe is filled, the last remnant of the initial Word of the spoken creation (LOGOS in Greek), the first and last sound from God's lips (and incidentally the first sound of the word for 'mother' in almost every language in the world).

ψ is Psi, number value 700, value by gematria 710, the same as Πνευμα Αγιον (PNEUMA AGION), 'Holy Spirit'. It is familiar in English words like psalm and psychology. The original Greek word psyche has no exact equivalent in English – its nearest cognates are 'breath', 'life' and 'soul', but the full meaning is a mixture of all three.

ω is Omega, number value 800, value by gematria 849, the same as Κυριος (KYRIOS), 'Lord' and Σχηεμα (SCHEMA) 'plan' or 'design'. The mega element means 'large', so Omicron is 'little o' and Omega is 'large o'. Omega is the twenty-fourth and last letter of the classical Greek alphabet, from which is derived the significance of the description of Christ as the Alpha and Omega of creation, the First and Last of all things.

In early Greek, the last letter was ϡ or Sampi, number value 900, which, like Stau and Koppa, has no gematria value and no correspondent attributes.

It can be seen that many aspects of Hebrew gematria and Greek gematria are very similar, despite obvious misalignments and anomalies.

If there were enough space, we could repeat the exercise for other alphabets, and we would observe many similar correspondences. However, we will concentrate briefly on two other alphabets with very different letter orders – Nordic runes and Celtic Ogham – before we move on to the much trickier question of gematria in English. We need to examine these two in particular because English is the offspring of many parents – the southern, or Romance, elements are represented in all those English words which are derived from Latin, Greek, French, Spanish, Portuguese, Italian, and so on; but English is largely derived from the northern, or Teutonic, branch of Indo-European, which includes Old Norse, Swedish, Norwegian, German, Friesian and Dutch. As if this inheritance were not rich enough already, there is also a very ancient magical alphabet tradition which flourished among the Celts and their priests, the Druids, and which in turn may have connections and relations with Hebrew, Greek and Roman gematria, the origins of which are too complex to describe in detail here.

There are many different rune systems, and many good books written about them (as well as books about Ogham – see note 4). The most widely accepted Nordic rune alphabet is called the *futhark* (also *futhorc*), since its first letters are F, U, Th, A, R and K or hard C. The standardized alphabet of 24 characters is called the Elder Futhark (it probably dates from as early as 400 AD) to distinguish it from variants, and, in particular, from the 16-letter runic alphabet which developed in Scandinavia along slightly different lines from the earlier Anglo-Frisian futhark, and which is commonly known as the Younger Futhark.

What is immediately obvious is that the order of the Futhark is quite different to that of the Hebrew and Greek alphabets, in which there was a fair degree of correspondence. The runic order is by no means haphazard. The 24 letters are divided into three groups, each group being known as an *aett*. Here, very briefly listed, are the runes of the Elder Futhark, with some of their attributes.

ᚠ is Feoh or Fehu (Fe in the Younger Futhark), first letter of the first aett, phonetically F, meaning 'cattle' literally, and 'wealth' or 'power' figuratively, and so corresponding exactly with Hebrew Aleph and Greek Alpha. The English word 'fee' is etymologically related to Feoh.

ᚢ is Ur, phonetically U. It originally represented the wild ox or aurochs, now extinct. It represents a more abstract and magical (and therefore more potent) power than Feoh. It is considered a highly auspicious rune. (Vowels in all alphabetical-magical systems are especially sacred.) Two other literal meanings of Ur are 'drizzle' and 'slag'. It is always interpreted esoterically as representing vital, regenerative energy.

ᚦ is Thorn or Thurisaz (Thurs in the Younger Futhark). Its sound is always the [th] of thorn, never of *th*is. It literally signifies the thorn, and is also associated with the hammer wielded by Thor, the Nordic counterpart to Herakles, Mars, and others, and many similar warrior-gods in Celtic mythology. Handwritten thus þ in Old English, it was later confused with a capital Y: this explains the origin of the Ye in Ye Olde Booke Shoppe – the Y was actually a Thorn, representing 'The', but it was commonly misread. Thorn is masculine in character, and signifies wilful energy. Thursday takes its name from Thor and his futhark letter, Thurs – the word Thurs literally means 'giant'.

ᚠ is As, also known as Asc, Ash, Asa or Ansuz. The Old English word *aesc* meant 'ash', the tree, and also 'spear', since spears were made from that springy and resilient timber. The most sacred tree in Norse mythology is the world tree Yggdrasil, which is an ash tree. The letter is dedicated to Woden (Odin, Odhinn), the sovereign ancestral magician-god, who gives his name to Wednesday, or Woden's Day.

ᚱ is Raidho, Rad, Raed or Rit, related to English 'ride' and 'road', German 'rad' ('wheel') and the name Ritter ('rider'). It is often interpreted to signify movement, transformation and self-control, and, because 'ride' has obvious sexual connotations, with sexual energy. It is conceptualized as a chariot on a path of power, sometimes also as a clap of thunder.

ᚲ is Ken, Cen or Kennaz (Kaun in the Younger Futhark). English is confused about which letter it should use to represent this sound – we put dogs in kennels not cennels, but we drive cars, not kars. The Goidelic (northern Celtic) word *cenn* means 'head' (its Brythonic, or southern Celtic, cognate is *pen* or *penn*, as in Pennsans or Penzance, which means 'Holy Head'). In all cases, the meaning is figurative as well as literal. The rune Ken signifies action, and is often paired for contrast with the eleventh rune, Is, which signifies stasis or deadlock. Kaun literally means 'sore' (the noun), and the letter is often ritually conceptualized as a blazing torch.

ᚷ is Gyfu or Gebo, the parallel to Hebrew Gimel and Greek Gamma, phonetically a hard [g] as in gift, which is, in fact, one of its literal meanings. Esoterically, it often signifies the gift or gifts of the gods, divine patrimony, that which is fated or given. Nigel Pennick suggests that the cross we use in modern writing convention to indicate a kiss is not derived from X, but comes from Gyfu (see note 5).

ᚹ is Wyn, Wunjo or Wunnaz, phonetically W. The Romans represented this sound with V. The Greeks did not use the sound at all. A further complication is that Middle High German confused the [w] and [v] sounds, which is why the letter w is pronounced [v] by modern Germans and Austrians. There was a similar confusion between [v] and [w] in eighteenth- and nineteenth-century English – a Dickensian character might be *w*ery happy to be in*w*ited to dinner. Wunjo means joy, harmony and fellowship.

ᚺ is Hagalaz, Hagal or Haegl, the first letter of the second aett, phonetically H. It literally means 'hail', the cold, granular stuff that falls out of the sky. Metaphorically, it represents disruption, strife, and destruction.

ᚾ is Nauthiz, Nyd or Not, phonetically N. It means 'need'. It is said to represent pictorially the firebow used to ignite the needfire, the fire necessary to survival.

ᛁ is Is or Isa, phonetically I, meaning 'ice'. As mentioned earlier, it signifies stasis, contraction, deadlock, even death itself.

ᛃ is Jera, Jer, Gara or Yer. Its sound is [j] or soft [g]. It means 'year', but also signifies the harvest literally and providence, the cycle of fortune, and so on, figuratively.

ᛇ is Eihwaz, Ihwaz or Eoh. Its sound is that of the letter y in *y*acht. It represents the yew tree, which in all European traditions is associated with death. However, the rune itself is considered auspicious. Yew timber was used for hunting bows, but was also used, along with hazel and willow, for ritual wands and staves.

ᛈ is Perth, also called Peorth, Peord and Perthro, phonetically P. Edred Thorsson says that it means 'lotbox' (see note 6), which refers to a choosing or voting game. Perth is sometimes called the 'dice cup' or 'shaker'. Freya Aswynn says that it signifies the womb, the manifestation of that which was formerly concealed. In the Northern tradition, a person's fate is determined by Wyrd, which is a combination of the given and inevitably determined (the rules of the game) and what the person makes by free will of the allotted gifts (the player's skill within the game).

ᛉ is Elhaz or Algiz, corresponding to English Z, and literally meaning 'elk', the great deer of the North. It is the most powerful rune of protection, and is found throughout northern Europe, even in cultures where runes are not widely used, as a talisman to ward off evil influences.

ᛋ is Sowelu, Sowilo, Sigel or Sig, phonetically S, the rune of the Sun. The English word sigil, which means 'magical sign', is derived from Latin *sigillum*, a diminutive of *signum*, meaning 'sign'. The same word also refers to a seal or signet.

ᛏ is Tyr or Tywaz, the first letter of the third aett, phonetically T. Tyr is the northern sky-god, also known as Ziu or Tiw, after whom Tuesday is named. In Nordic legend, Tyr sacrificed his right hand to bind the Fenris-Wolf, a supernatural beast, so the rune signifies steadfastness, responsibility and sacrifice, the attributes of the noble warrior. The shape of the letter imitates a spear, and it points figuratively towards the pole star, the direction of Asgard, where the gods dwell.

ᛒ is Beorc, Birkana or Bar, phonetically B, signifying the birch tree. Birch is the tree of regeneration, new beginnings. Birch besoms, or brooms, have been used for centuries in Europe. The Roman Senate was swept with birch brooms before each new session. Witches fly on broomsticks made of birch.

ᛖ is Ehwaz or Eh, phonetically E, literally 'horse'. It is an auspicious rune, associated with fraternity and sorority, human intercourse and association in general, trust and cooperation.

ᛗ is Mannaz or Man, phonetically M, and signifies humankind.

ᛚ is Laguz or Lagu, phonetically L, and represents all water, but especially the sea. Figuratively and esoterically, this rune symbolizes organic growth and fecundity.

ᛜ is Ing or Ingaz, phonetically Ng. Ing is a god's name: he is the god of the hearth and inglenook, the male consort of the goddess of fertility, Nerthus. Ing therefore represents human fertility and regeneration.

ᛞ is Dagaz or Dag, phonetically D, literally 'day' or 'daylight', which is a sometimes precious commodity in the North.

ᛟ is Odal, Othil or Othila, phonetically long O, and signifying the home, ancestral land and possessions. The order of Dagaz and Othila is widely disputed, with many writers putting Othila before Dagaz. The ancient tradition of Omega (long O) as the last letter of the classical Greek alphabet may have influenced views on where Othila belongs.

The number correspondences of the runes are by no means clear. The most common systems of interpretation simply set out the 24 letters of the Elder Futhark in its three aetts and ascribe the counting numbers to them in sequence, so that Feoh is 1, and Othila is 24. David Allen Hulse applies an adapted Pythagorean system (after 9 come 10, 20, 30, etc.), but his classification inexplicably misses out the number 6 (see note 7). We shall return to this question after we have considered Ogham and the alphabet mysteries of the British Druids.

In the Druidic alphabet, each letter signifies a tree or shrub, and each tree or shrub is associated with an array of mythological attributions. Moreover, the letters in their sequence represent or symbolize portions of time ('months') in the calendar.

The original Beth-Luis-Nion, named after its first three letters, just as we call our modern alphabet the ABC, has thirteen consonants and five vowels, as follows:

B L N F S H D T C M G P R   A O U E I

B is the letter Beth (all these letter names are Goidelic, or Irish Gaelic words), which means 'birch'. It is identified as the tree of inception, exactly the same as Beorc in the runic alphabet.

L is the letter Luis, meaning 'rowan', also known as quickbeam, quicken and mountain ash. In Ireland, Druids lit fires of rowan wood to summon the spirits of the dead to assist warriors in battle.

N is the letter Nion, meaning 'ash'. In British folklore, the ash is a tree of rebirth and regeneration.

F is Fearn, meaning 'alder', the sacred tree of the British god Bendigeidfran, or Blessed Bran. The tree was held in high regard by the Celts for the charcoal it produced. It was also used for conduits and pipes to channel water, being especially resistant to decay. The tree stains reddish when cut, reminiscent of the shedding of blood. It also yields three important dye colours: red from the bark, green from the flowers and brown from the twigs.

S is for Saille, meaning 'willow', or osier. The willow is traditionally associated with witchcraft – so strongly in fact, that the words 'wicker' (meaning willow reed or osier), 'wicked' and 'witch' are all etymologically related. Its leaves and bark yield salicylic acid, a principal constituent of aspirin, and were infused since earliest times to relieve cramps, especially menstrual cramps, and other pain.

H is for (H)uath, meaning 'the hawthorn', also called whitethorn and may. It is an unlucky tree.

D is Duir, meaning 'oak'. The word is very similar in Goidelic and Brythonic, and the word Druid is almost certainly derived from it. It is the totem tree of the son-god, the maker of thunder, in all his manifestations – Zeus (and Herakles) in Greece, Jupiter (and Hercules) in Rome, Thor in Scandinavia, Bel (and a legion of heroes, including Finn, Ferghus and Cu Chulainn) in Britain and Gaul. It is common knowledge that the oak was specially venerated by the early Celts. Duir corresponds to runic Dagaz.

T stands for Tinne, meaning 'holly', the totem tree of the oak-god's twin (or father), the holly-god or Green Knight, represented by Bran in the British tradition and by Kronos in Greece and Saturn in Rome.

C is for Coll, meaning 'hazel'. In Celtic mythology it is always associated with wisdom. Then as now, hazel was the favoured wood for making divining rods. White hazel wands were carried by Druids as symbols of their authority.

M is the letter called Muin, meaning 'vine'. The vine is not native to Britain, but it was important in Mediterranean mythology, principally because it is the source of wine. The vine does figure in British art from the Bronze Age onward, which suggests that its mythology was understood and to some extent subsumed in Druidic culture.

G is for Gort, meaning 'ivy'. The vine and the ivy share the characteristic of growing spirally. Both are associated with resurrection. Ivy leaves, which are toxic, may have been chewed for their hallucinatory effects.

P is for Peith, meaning 'water-elder', also called whitten or guelder-rose. Peith is not the original letter. It was substituted for Ng, or Ngetal, which means 'reed'. In Egyptian and Mediterranean mythology, the reed symbolized royalty. A reed was pushed into Jesus's hand when he was mockingly robed in scarlet.

R is for Ruis, which means 'elder'. Although the flowers and bark of the elder yield therapeutic substances, and elder flowers and elder berries make good wine, the tree has a reputation for evil. It is associated with witchcraft and death, along with the yew, cypress and nightshade.

The five vowels form an esoteric sequence in their own right.

A in the Druidic alphabet stands for Ailm, which means 'silver fir'. Throughout northern Europe, it is associated with childbirth.

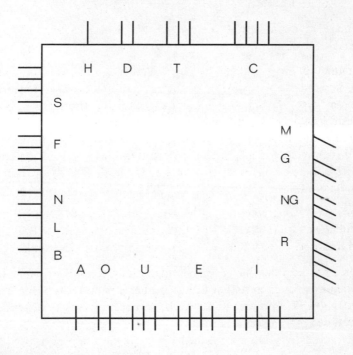

Figure 37 The Ogham alphabet

135

O stands for Onn, which means 'furze' or gorse. Known in Brythonic as 'eythin', this prickly bush with its bright golden flowers typifies the Sun at the vernal equinox. Gorse was highly regarded by the early Celts for its practical value in controlling livestock.

Heather is the plant of the third vowel, **U** or Ura. It also is associated with bees, and with midsummer. It was sacred to the Roman goddess Venus Erycina, the second part of her name being derived from the Greek name for heather, *ereice*.

E is Eadha, meaning 'aspen', also known as white poplar. It is the tree of old age. Its leaves are distinctively lighter on the underside than above – thus in a breeze, it 'turns white'.

I is for Idho, meaning 'yew'. In all European cultures, the yew is the tree of death.

The sequence of vowels therefore represents the cycle of life from birth to death.

The Druidic alphabet is the counterpart of Ogham, a graphic alphabet in which letters are represented by straight or diagonal notches cut on the corner angles of timber or stone (see figure 37). The Ogham or Druidic alphabet has much clearer numerical correspondences than the runes, although they are incomplete. They run as follows:

1	Ailm	silver fir	A
2	Eadha	aspen	E
3	Idho	yew	I
4	Onn	gorse	O
5	Beth	birch	B
6	Muin	vine	M
7	Peith	water-elder	P
8	Fearn	alder	F
9	Coll	hazel	C, K
10	Gort	ivy	G
11	Tinne	holly	T
12	Duir	oak	D
13	Nion	ash	N
14	Luis	rowan	L
15	Ruis	elder	R

It is interesting to note that these number attributions, which are well attested in the Celtic vernacular texts, seem completely independent of the fixed calendar/alphabet order.

Now, finally, we can approach the difficult question of how to devise an accurate system of gematria for the English language. The 1 to 24 identification with the runes seems more or less haphazard, and not very reliable. The Celtic number attributions are very clear, if deficient. The Hebrew and Greek letter correspondences are very close, although there is an obvious misalignment around the English corresponding letters P to V. Putting all these considerations together, we can observe the following possibilities for a gematria of the English alphabet:

	A	B	C	D	E	F	G	H	I	J	K	L	M
Hebrew	1	2		4			3	5	10		20	30	40
Greek	1	2		4	5		3		10		20	30	40
Runic	4	18		23	19	1	7	9	11	12	6	21	20
Druidic	1	5	9	12	2	8	10		3			14	6

	N	O	P	Q	R	S	T	U	V	W	X	Y	Z
Hebrew	50	70	80	100	200	60	9		6				7
Greek	50	70/800	80	100	200	300	400				60		7
Runic	10	24	14		5	16	17	2		8		12	15
Druidic	13	4	7		15	16	11						

The immediate and obvious difficulty is that there are several gaps, and not much clear agreement even when there are correspondences.

The English language, powerful, beautiful and fascinating as it is, is ill-suited to magic, and particularly to gematria, principally because its sounds and its orthography are so disparate. Some languages (Spanish, Welsh and modern Cornish are good examples) are almost purely phonemic: every letter almost always represents the same sound. The notorious spelling confusions in English, like all those acceptable pronunciations of the letter sequence *ough* which so baffle foreign students of the language, persist in the language for historical reasons. But magical systems are concerned with sound rather than with spelling – the Word which became all creation, the Logos, is a *spoken* word.

So how can these problems of orthography and phonology be reconciled? The answer is that there is no perfect answer. Most modern numerologists follow the easy road, A =1, B = 2, C = 3, etc. Using such a system, they would analyse the name Barry Knight as follows:

B A R R Y K N I G H T
$$2 + 1 + 18 + 18 + 25 + 11 + 14 + 9 + 7 + 8 + 20 = 133 = 1 + 3 + 3 = 7$$

They then inform us that Barry Knight is 'a 7', and tell us all about his strengths, weaknesses, preferences in underwear, and so on.

A second school of modern numerology reduces each number to the sum of its digits as soon as they go above 9: 10 becomes 1 (1 + 0), 11 becomes 2 (1 + 1), and so on.

B A R R Y K N I G H T
$$2 + 1 + 9 + 9 + 7 + 2 + 5 + 9 + 7 + 8 + 2 = 61 = 6 + 1 = 7$$

This does not make good sense. The essential numerological relationship in gematria is this: sounds are sacred. The true name of the supreme deity is unutterable. The universe and all of time was created by the Word, when the supreme deity spoke. Letters are representations of particular sounds, and are therefore sacred. Numbers correspond to letters, and therefore to sacred sounds.

It seems cruel to reduce Barry from a knight to a nit, but that, in essence, would make better numerological sense in some ways. If we imagined his name as a Hebrew phrase, we would have no difficulty writing it as Beth, Aleph, Resh, Yod, Nun, Yod, Teth $(2 + 1 + 200 + 10 + 50 + 10 + 9 = 282)$. We could do it in Greek, too: Beta, Alpha, Rho, Iota, Nu, Iota, Tau $(2 + 1 + 100 + 10 + 50 + 10 + 300 = 473)$. The ideal English system would allow us to make consistent transliterations and conversions from letter to number.

Having a clear understanding of the basis from which we should build does not make the task any easier, however. There have been many attempts, most notably those of the British occultist Aleister Crowley. He experimented with Enochian (the mystic language of the Golden Dawn); with a phonetic Hebrew transliteration; with a code based on the trigrams of the ancient Chinese oracular text, the *I Ching*; with a system called the English Qabalah of Liber Trigrammaton, in which the graphic shape of each number determines its letter equivalent ($H = 4$, because it can be contained within a square, $X = 5$ because it has four points and a centre, and so on); and in his *Book of the Law*, with a system of symbolic interpretation based on Sanskrit (the system was prophetically predicted, rather than analytically described). Apart from Crowley's, other systems include Graeco-English, in which the 26 English letters are ascribed to 26 of the 27 Greek letters (Sampi is not used), and the Fadic system, in which the 26 English letters are paired with only eight of the Hebrew letters, according to how closely they approximate them phonetically.

Each of these systems has some merit, but none of them is entirely satisfactory. Here are some examples of the attempts at an English system of gematria already described.

Serial English:
$A = 1, B = 2, C = 3, D = 4, E = 5, F = 6, G = 7, H = 8, I = 9, J = 10, K = 11, L = 12, M = 13, N = 14, O = 15, P = 16, Q = 17, R = 18, S = 19, T = 20, U = 21, V = 22, W = 23, X = 24, Y = 25, Z = 26.$

Crowley's English Qabalah of Liber Trigrammaton
(reconstructed by David Allen Hulse – see note 8):
$A = 9, B = 15, C = 3, D = 25, E = 20, F = 16, G = 13, H = 4, I = 1, J = 10, K = 24, L = 2, M = 18, N = 19, O = 12, P = 8, Q = 22, R = 21, S = 17, T = 6, U = 26, V = 23, W = 11, X = 5, Y = 7, Z = 14.$

Crowley's Sanskrit-English Qabalah
(reconstructed by David Allen Hulse):

A = no value, B = 3, C = 6, D = 8, E = no value, F = 2, G = 3, H = 8, I = no value, J = 9, K = 1, L = 3, M = 5, N = 0 (place value), O = no value, P = 1, Q = 2, R = 2, S = 7, T = 1, U = no value, V = 4, W = 4, X = 0 (place value), Y = 1, Z = 6.

Graeco-English:
A (Alpha) = 1, B (Beta) = 2, C (Gamma) = 3, D (Delta) = 4, E (Epsilon) = 5, F (Stau) = 6, G (Zeta) = 7, H (Eta) = 8, I (Theta) = 9, J (Iota) = 10, K (Kappa) = 20, L (Lambda) = 30, M (Mu) = 40, N (Nu) = 50, O (Xi) = 60, P (Omicron) = 70, Q (Pi) = 80, R (Koppa) = 90, S (Rho) = 100, T (Sigma) = 200, U (Tau) = 300, V (Upsilon) = 400, W (Phi) = 500, X (Chi) = 600, Y (Psi) = 700, Z (Omega) = 800.

Hebrew/Fadic:
A = 1, B = 2, C = 3, D = 4, E = 5, F = 80 (reduced Fadic value 8), G = 3, H = 5, I = 10 (Fadic 1), J = 10 (1), K = 20 (2), L = 30 (3), M = 40 (4), N = 50 (5), O = 70 (7), P = 80 (8), Q = 100 (1), R = 200 (2), S = 300 (3), T = 400 (4), U = 6, V = 6, W = 6, X = 500 (5), Y = 10 (1), Z = 7.

Modern Numerological:
A = 1, B = 2, C = 3, D = 4, E = 5, F = 6, G = 7, H = 8, I = 9, J = 10 = 1 + 0 = 1, K = 11 = 1 + 1 = 2, L = 12 = 1 + 2 = 3, M = 13 = 1 + 3 = 4, N = 14 = 1 + 4 = 5, O = 15 = 1 + 5 = 6, P = 16 = 1 + 6 = 7, Q = 17 = 1 + 7 = 8, R = 18 = 1 + 8 = 9, S = 19 = 1 + 9 = 10 = 1 + 0 = 1, T = 20 = 2 + 0 = 2, U = 21 = 2 + 1 = 3, V = 22 = 2 + 2 = 4, W = 23 = 2 + 3 = 5, X = 24 = 2 + 4 = 6, Y = 25 = 2 + 5 = 7, Z = 26 = 2 + 6 = 8.

I myself use a system which is based largely on the Greek and Hebrew models, but with some modifications; it has served me well for many years. In all the examples of gematria which follow in the remaining chapters, it is my own system which I shall be using, without further explanation. However, it is important to point out that I make no claims for the superiority of this system over any other. For me, Hendricks and Hendrix are the same name numerologically, and my system takes that into account, but other numerologists may consider the different spellings significant. The reader is welcome to investigate all systems of gematria further and to reach whatever conclusions seem apt; and, further, to review all the interpretations and analyses given later in this book using other systems, to see what correspondences or discrepancies are generated.

My system 'straightens out' the misalignment between the Greek and Hebrew correspondences, and includes some possibly obscure cross-references from other languages (for example, I give W the same value as Greek Omega because in Welsh the letter w represents the long o sound, similar to English cool). The languages with which I am familiar, in approximate order of fluency, are English, Cornish, French, Latin,

German, Greek, Russian and Welsh, so there is a fairly eclectic set of reasoning behind these choices. There is not space to explain fully how I arrived at this final system – it took many years of trial and error. In the following list, I have included very brief explanatory references, where it was simple to do so, in order to give some indication of my reasoning, plus some perfunctory headings for figurative and esoteric correspondences, but, in the end, all these selections and interpretations remain a matter of personal preference. Appendix One gives the correspondences in their simplest form for quick reference.

The author's system:

A = 1	Aleph in Hebrew, meaning 'ox' and 'wealth', Alpha in Greek, with the same meanings. The Celtic parallel is Ailm, 'silver fir'. The Futhark is As, or Asc, meaning 'ash' and 'spear', but with number value 4. A represents the first principle, the ineffable, the origin of all things.
B = 2	Beth in Hebrew, meaning 'house', 'family' and 'bloodline', number value 2. Beta in Greek, number value 2. Beth in Celtic, meaning 'birch', and signifying birth and inception in the Druidic alphabet, but with the number value of 5. Beorc in the Futhark has the same meanings. 2 represents the sacred female, the Magna Mater or Great Mother, in the Pythagorean system.
C, CH = 20	The hard [K] sound in castle or character. See K for parallels.
C = 60	The soft [S] sound in cement or police. See S for parallels.
CH = 8	If soft, as in church, parallels Hebrew Cheth = 8, enclosure or barrier, representing the eight regions of three-dimensional space and the perfection of womanhood, the perfect cube of 2.
CH = 600	The guttural [CH] of Scottish loch, or German Bach, not usually found in everyday English, parallels Greek Chi = 600, esoterically representing crossroads, astrological cusp or momentous change.
D = 4	Daleth in Hebrew, number value 4, meaning 'tent-flap', 'door', and esoterically representing religious authority. Delta is the Greek parallel, with the same number value and meanings. D is Duir in Irish, Derw or Derow ['oak'] in Welsh and Cornish, sacred to the father-god Bran and to Druids. The Futhark letter is Dagaz, number value 23, meaning 'day' or 'daylight'.
E = 5	Epsilon in Greek. Eadha, meaning 'aspen', in Celtic. Ehwaz, meaning 'horse' in the Futhark. 5 esoterically represents the quintessence, spirit within flesh.
F = 500	Phi in Greek, associated by the Pythagoreans with the phallus and regeneration. The Celtic parallel is Fearn, meaning 'alder', number value 8. The Futhark is Feoh, meaning 'cattle' and 'wealth', number value 1.
G = 3	Gimel in Hebrew, literally 'camel' but representing all living things, all of nature, number value 3. Gamma in Greek, also with the value 3. The Celtic parallel is Gort, meaning 'ivy'. The Futhark is Gyfu, 'gift' or 'fate'.

G, GE = 12   Soft G or GE, as in *G*iovanni or *G*eorge – see the parallels for J.

GH = 8   Silent GH, as in ni*gh*t, is equal to silent H – see H.

H = 5   If initial or aspirated, as in *h*at, parallels Hebrew He = 5, the window, illumination, inspiration. The Celtic parallel is Huath, 'hawthorn'. Futhark Hagalaz, number value 9, means 'hail' or 'destruction'.

H = 8   Silent H, as in o*h*m or raja*h*. Found occasionally in English, the number value parallels Greek Eta.

I = 10   Yod in Hebrew, meaning 'hand' or 'hand of God', number value 10. Iota in Greek, also 10. The same sound is found commonly in English as a final Y – see Y. The Celtic parallel is Idho, meaning 'yew'. The Futhark is Is, 'ice' or 'stasis'. Esoterically, 10 represents the hand of God or the Goddess, the completed and perfected universe, the tetraktys, the end of all things, summation.

-ING = 22   This is Northern, not classical. It is the Futhark letter Ing, value 22, which esoterically represents the gods and goddesses of the home and hearth.

J = 12   Also Northern. It is taken from Jera or Yer in the Futhark, which represents the year, harvest, cyclic patterns. This is also the value of consonantal Y – see Y.

K = 20   Caph in Hebrew, meaning 'palm of the hand', number value 20. Kappa in Greek, signifying fate, that which is ordained. The Celtic parallel is Coll, 'hazel', number value 9. The Futhark parallel is Ken, meaning 'torch' or 'action'. Esoterically, 20 represents the perfection (10) of the divine purpose (2).

L = 30   Lamed in Hebrew, meaning 'ox-goad' literally and 'energy' or 'initiative' figuratively, number value 30. Lambda in Greek, also 30, signifying fertility. The Celtic parallel is Luis, 'rowan', number value 14. Laguz in the Futhark means 'water'. Esoterically, 30 represents the perfection (10) of divine action or loving-kindness (3).

M = 40   Mem in Hebrew, meaning 'water', number value 40. Mu in Greek, signifying the family, number value also 40. The Celtic parallel is Muin, 'vine'. The Futhark is Mannaz, 'humankind'. Esoterically, 40 represents the number of aeons, long time passing, as in forty days and nights in the wilderness, the perfection (10) of the physical world (4).

N = 50   Nun in Hebrew, meaning 'support', number value 50. Nu in Greek, also 50. Nion in Celtic, meaning 'ash'. Nyd or Nauthiz in the Futhark, meaning 'necessity'. Esoterically signifies the perfection (10) of the living spirit (5).

O = 70   Omicron is Greek for short o, as in h*o*t, which corresponds with Hebrew Ayin, 'eye', number value 70. The Celtic parallel is Onn, 'gorse'. 70 signifies the perfection (10) of understanding (7). The 'eye' is the eye of witness, spiritual illumination and inspiration.

O, OO = 800   Omega in Greek for long O, as in r*o*se, = 800. The Futhark parallel is Odal, meaning 'home', 'land', 'possessions'.

141

Esoterically, long O signifies the end of all creation, the purpose of life, the divine plan, the perfect completion (100) of the universe (8). The letter W has the same value – see W.

P = 80 — Pe in Hebrew, meaning 'mouth', 'word' (and therefore figuratively 'immortality'), number value 80. Pi in Greek, signifying 'power', also 80. The Celtic parallel is Peith, 'water-elder'. Perth in the Futhark means 'lotbox' or 'womb'. Esoterically, 80 is the mouth, the Word which began creation, all prayer and sacred invocations, the perfection (10) of the universe (8).

PH = 500 — See F.

Q, QU = 100 — Qoph in Hebrew, meaning 'the back of the head', number value 100. Esoterically, the brain, the unique individual living behind the eyes, perfection (10) times perfection (10).

R = 200 — Resh in Hebrew, meaning literally 'head', and figuratively representing the whole head, the outward persona, that which is manifest, number value 200. The Greek parallel is Rho. The Celtic is Ruis, 'elder'. The Futhark is Raidho, literally 'wheel' or 'riding', but figuratively 'sex'. Esoterically, 200 is the complete perfection (100) of the female (2), the paradigm of beauty, and therefore a number sacred to the Goddess.

S, soft C = 60 — S as in snake is the parallel of Samekh in Hebrew, value 60, meaning 'support, sustenance', the number of courage. The Greek is Sigma. The Celtic parallel is Saille, meaning 'willow'. The Futhark is Sowelu, 'sun'. Esoterically, 60 is the perfection (10) of harmony (6).

S, Z = 7 — Vocalized S, as in rose, is the equivalent of Z – see Z.

SH = 300 — Shin in Hebrew, number value 300, literally 'tooth', signifying consumption, transformation, all patterns of change and regeneration, the complete perfection (100) of nature (3).

S, ZH = 15 — Vocalized SH or ZH, for example the sound in pleasure. A sound not found in Hebrew, nor in Greek. It is found in Russian, represented by the letter Ж. The Futhark number value equivalent is Elhaz, meaning 'elk' literally and 'protection' figuratively and esoterically.

T = 9 — Teth in Hebrew, 'serpent', number value 9, signifying the energy which courses throughout the universe, sexual energy, the divine will. The Greek parallel is Tau, meaning 'cross'. The Celtic parallel is Tinne, meaning 'holly', and associated with the transformation of the son-god Bel into the father-god Bran, hence with Jesus, since this transformation takes place on Midsummer's Day, the day of St John, who prefigures the advent of Jesus. The Futhark parallel, Tyr, is the name of a sky-god. Esoterically 9 represents magical transformations of all kinds – it is the number of Myrddyn or Merlin. In Pythagoreanism, 9 represents incompleteness.

TH = 9 — If unvoiced, as in thin, corresponds to Greek Theta, number value 9, associated with submission to the divine will, devotion, waiting for perfection, and death.

TH = 400 — If voiced, as in this, corresponds to Hebrew Tav, number value 400, signifying the sign of the cross, and therefore, in the Christian tradition, with sacrifice.

-TION = 350	This ending, common in English words, has the numerical value of SH plus N.
U = V = 6	Vau in Hebrew, meaning 'peg, nail', esoterically the opening of the door, liberty, freedom of spirit, creativity. The Celtic parallel is Ura, signifying the heather of high summer. In Latin, V is represented by U. In Pythagoreanism, 6 is the number of harmony, the perfect coupling of female 2 and male 3, and therefore of marriage.
W = 800	(Because W is the same as long O or Omega, cf. Welsh c*w*m)
X = 80 or 600	In most cases the value will be 20 + 60 (K + S); for example, Hendrix and Hendricks have the same number value. In very rare borrowings from some other languages, X has a [CH] sound or derivation, so then equals the guttural CH, as in Scottish lo*ch*, value 600.
Y = 10	As a final or intermediary vowel, e.g. happy or dysentery, parallels Greek Iota, number value 10, and Hebrew Yod, also 10, meaning 'hand of God'. Esoterically, the number of perfection.
Y = 12	The consonant, as in *y*ellow, is Jera or Yer from the Futhark, value 12.
Z = 7	Zeta in Greek, number value 7, meaning 'offering'. Zayin in Hebrew, number value also 7, meaning 'sword', and figuratively all weapons, military strength and authority. Esoterically, 7 represents the warrior or hero, religious authority, spirituality and royalty.

Workable though this system has proven itself to be, it is by no means perfect. It is essentially Pythagorean, but it also approximates the Hebrew and Greek systems, although there are no letter equivalents for the numbers 500, 600, 700 and 900. U and V share the number value 6, which a Roman would understand perfectly, but which is anomalous in English; sometimes I interpret a u or an ou in a word as the equivalent of Omega or long O, which itself is equivalent to W – in my system, the word 'would' and 'wood' only differ by the value of the letter l: 'would' = W + long O + L (even though it is silent, it has good historical and grammatical reasons for being present) + D = 800 + 800 + 30 + 4 = 1,634; 'wood' = 800 + 800 + 4 = 1,604. The value of 12 for J and Y is quite outside the pattern of the rest of the system, but that is because I consider J and consonantal Y separate Northern consonants – the value of 12 is taken from the Futhark. Whenever Y functions simply as a vowel, it is the equivalent of Iota or Yod, value 10. In my system, Barry and Barr*i* (or Tony and Ton*i*) are interchangeable, both ending in the Iota equivalent, value 10, but yesterday begins with consonantal Y, value 12. There would be a letter equivalent for the number 90 if the sound represented by the letter combination TS or TZ appeared in English – the Hebrew parallel is Tzaddi – but the sound only occurs incidentally, as in si*ts* – it is not a true single consonant which could be used initially.

143

I suppose it would not be unreasonable to read sits as $S + I + TZ = 60 + 10 + 90 = 160$, but I prefer $S + I + T + S = 60 + 10 + 9 + 60 = 139$.

It is important to remind the reader that this system is only one of many possible systems. Barry Knight, who troubled us earlier, is going to continue to trouble us (apologies to any real Barry Knight who happens to be reading this). However, that question can be carried forward to the next chapter; we now have enough background material under our belts to start tackling some practical numerology.

seven

PRACTICAL NUMEROLOGY

1234567890123456789012345678901234567890123456789012345678901234567890

The only essentials for practical numerology are pen or pencil, paper and an open mind. Other useful tools include: a good calculator (a graphing calculator if you want to get really sophisticated); two ordinary cubic playing dice; a dodecahedral die (see the figure on page 157); two packs of playing cards; a dartboard and darts; a binary conversion table (see Appendix Eleven); an abacus; graph paper; a ruler; a folder or ring-file.

We shall look at how these tools may be used shortly, but first we have to consider what practical numerology is used for. The five most common purposes of numerology are: interpretation; diagnosis; analysis; prediction or prognostication; invocation, charms and spells. Of these, only the first is included in most popular numerology texts.

Interpretation in numerology is essentially based on classical gematria – names are converted to numbers, or numbers are converted to letter sequences, and interpretations are made. As was explained before, almost all modern numerologists use a serial A = 1, B = 2, C = 3, etc. correspondence paradigm, which, in my view, makes most, if not all of the interpretation invalid. Interpretation in modern numerology is most often seen in the form of conversion of names or letters to numerical sequences, although classical gematria works in both directions.

Diagnosis differs from interpretation in that it usually works from numbers to letters, or directly on patterns in number sequences, and has a specific purpose in mind; for example, why does this number or number sequence keep appearing or recurring? Is a particular number exerting a special influence here?

Analysis is about recurring patterns and correspondences. Analysis can be applied to groups as well as to individuals. Where diagnosis concentrates on individual numbers, analysis looks at whole sequences.

The meaning of prediction is fairly obvious. Sceptics claim that prediction and prognostication are impossible, but common sense tells us that certain events are quite predictable – the sun will probably rise tomorrow, I am likely to have a cup of tea today, and the Pope probably won't be getting married this week. Numerology simply looks at recurring patterns and suggests how they might continue to develop.

Invocation, the working of magical prayers, charms and spells using the power of numbers, is probably the least understood and least used aspect of numerology, which is a pity, since it is potentially the most important. The reader will have observed, I hope, from the preceding chapters that numbers have had sacred significance in most ages and in most cultures. In every religion of the world, major and minor, certain numbers have held special meaning. For the true numerologist, numbers are holy. They express unassailable truths about the cosmos. They are metaphysical and metatemporal. They are God's thoughts, the living spirit of the Goddess. They have immense magical power.

We shall be looking in detail at these different types of numerology in this and subsequent chapters. Let us begin, however, by picking up the threads from the end of the last chapter, and continue the investigation of the practical applications of gematria. Here is an extract from a typical numerology guide:

> If you are a number eight, you should never rely on luck, for you must work hard to earn what you get. Justice should be your keynote. As a number eight, you may seem to be restricted. This need not be true if you have learned to discipline yourself. You can have outstanding success by moving cautiously and conservatively, relying on your own judgment, for as a number eight you are mental and should be well-balanced. If you live by the golden rule you can earn a place of authority.

This, and the 200 pages of similar stuff accompanying it, is so much hooey, in my view. I have deliberately not given the name of the author and publisher, but there are dozens of almost identical books selling the same kind of material. What the authors of these books have done is to take vague astrological descriptions and plagiarized and adapted them to numerology, with very little apparent understanding of the long traditions of numerology in Greece, in the Hebrew Kabbalah, in the medieval hermeneutic occult philosophers, and in the few serious numerologists of more modern times (see note 1). As has been already mentioned, virtually every contemporary numerological text uses the English alphabet serial gematria (A = 1 ... Z = 26), and the digit-addition simplification system (e.g., $369 = 3 + 6 + 9 = 18 = 1 + 8 = 9$). In my opinion, both these procedures are simplistic and inadequate –wrong, in other words.

Let us bring Barry Knight back on stage and subject him to the typical modern numerological analysis of his name:

B A R R Y K N I G H T
$2 + 1 + 18 + 18 + 25 + 11 + 14 + 9 + 7 + 8 + 20$
$=133 = 1 + 3 + 3 = 7$

'Barry, you are a seven. You dislike manual labour. You are not as domestic as a number six, or as practical as a number four. You believe that seeking knowledge is second only to acquiring understanding and wisdom. As a number seven, you should rely on your own intuition and follow your hunches ....'

And so on. Now let us see if we can do a better job (not easy – I deliberately chose Barry Knight because it is a very difficult name for a numerologist). We need to have the alphabet correspondences handy. If you intend using my system (thank you), I suggest you copy Appendices One and Two and keep them at the front of your ring-file or numerology workbook, where you can glance at them easily. You will find that you learn the correspondences very quickly and your tables will no longer be necessary, but it is useful when you start out. If you are using one of the other systems described in the last chapter, or a system of your own devising, the same practical method applies.

Even with a more accurate system, interpreting Barry Knight presents problems. Here is my suggested solution, followed by some explanatory notes:

B A R R Y K N I GH T
2 + 1 + 200 + 200 + 10 + 20 + 50 + 10 + 8 + 9 = 510

B, A and R are straightforward. The Y is a final vowel, not a consonant, so it is a 10 rather than a 12. The K is highly problematical. It is silent, so the question arises as to whether it should be represented by a number or not – if sound is the only factor (it is certainly the most important factor), then Barry can just as easily be a Night as a Knight. However, the silent K has a historical background. In the German Knecht, from which the name is derived, the K is pronounced. There is good evidence that the K was pronounced in early and medieval English, too. Chaucer's *Knyghtes Tale* is probably about a Knight with a sounded K. So, I include a number for K in the sequence. GH, which crops up very frequently in English, is the same sound as weak or silent H, and in my system (one of the reasons I chose it), G + H is 3 + 5, which equals 8, which is the number of the weak or silent H anyway.

So we now have a very different total for Barry Knight. He is not 'a seven': he is a 'five hundred and ten'. But, as is obvious from my comments in the paragraphs above, I do not believe in the simplistic idea that anyone can be classified in terms of a single number. Most contemporary numerologists would add the digits of 510 to make Barry 'a six'. So, if I do not believe that Barry Knight is 'an eight' or 'a six', what do I believe about the relationship between his name and his number? Is it all meaningless coincidence?

I believe not, but I want to repeat my caveat given in the Foreword: I am not trying to persuade anyone to share my beliefs; I am merely trying to describe them. I think that there is a correspondence between Barry

Knight the person (the many thousands of people with that name) and the letters of the name and the numbers that the letters represent. What follows, therefore, is an exposition of how I interpret those correspondences.

The first and most important element is the recognition that the single-digit addition method gets us nowhere. Adding the 5 to the 1 and the 0 has no meaning, and, furthermore, there is no evidence that that method was ever used in classical Greek, Kabbalistic, medieval or any other traditional systems. In all traditional systems the factors are the key to interpretation, yet this vital point seems to have been lost in the degradation of much modern numerology. A possible reason is that factorizing is much harder work than just adding digits.

The prime factors of 510 are 2, 3, 5 and 17. Each factor appears only once in the multiplication ($2 \times 3 \times 5 \times 17 = 510$). If a factor appears more than once, then its significance is greater. For example, if our total were 10,200, the prime factors would still be 2, 3, 5 and 17, but some of them would be raised to a higher power than others ($2^3 \times 3 \times 5^2 \times 17 = 10,200$). In this case, we would place greater emphasis on the interpretation of the 5, and yet more emphasis on the interpretation of the 2, since both these numbers are raised to a higher exponent than the other factors.

How do we obtain the prime factors of a number? We need two tools: first, a list of prime factors (see Appendix Five), and second, a good head for figures or a calculator. We begin by dividing the number by the first prime, 2 (we ignore 1, of course). We continue dividing by 2 as long as we can. When the dividend is no longer even, we try dividing by the next prime, 3, then by 5, then by 7, then by 11, and so on, until we have nothing left but the prime factors. For example, what are the prime factors of 107,640? Begin by dividing by 2:

$$107,640 = 2 \times 53,820 = 2 \times 2 \times 26,910 = 2 \times 2 \times 2 \times 13,455.$$

13,455 is an odd number, so we have reached the end of the sequence in which we can take out 2 as a factor. We can tidy up the $2 \times 2 \times 2$ sequence by writing it as 2^3. Now we try dividing by 3. A simple trick helps us – if the digits of any number add up to 3 or a multiple of 3, then the number itself is divisible by 3. $1 + 3 + 4 + 5 + 5 = 18$, which is a multiple of 3, so 13,455 is divisible by 3:

$$107,640 = 2^3 \times 3 \times 4,485 = 2^3 \times 3 \times 3 \times 1,495.$$

The digits of 1,495 add up to 19, so we have come to the end of the sequence of 3 as a factor. We tidy up the 3×3 into 3^2. We can tell by the last digit that 1,495 is divisible by 5:

$$107,640 = 2^3 \times 3^2 \times 5 \times 299.$$

The 299 is clearly not divisible by 5. It may be prime. We check in the list (Appendix Five), and see that it is not there, so we have to keep trying. We try 7 next:

299 divided by 7 gives 42.71428571..., an irrational number and not an integer, so 7 is not a factor.

The next prime number above 7 is 11, so we try 11:

299 divided by 11 gives 27.18181818.... That doesn't work either.

When we try the next prime, 13, it does work:

$$107,640 = 2^3 \times 3^2 \times 5 \times 13 \times 23.$$

Finally, we check the remaining 23 – the prime numbers table confirms that it is prime.

So, the prime factors of 107,640 are 2, 3, 5, 13 and 23. The 2 is cubed, the 3 is squared, which increases their influence. Try this exercise on any large number particular to you – your telephone number, perhaps – and note the factors. Now try it again on a group of numbers which feature in your life. If you see the same prime factors appearing with great frequency or marked exponential strength (and it is likely that you will), that suggests that these particular numbers are very influential in your life.

For example, without revealing my telephone number, passport number, etc., I can tell you that the most commonly occurring factors in the numbers in my life are 2, 3^2 or 9 (much more frequent than any other), 3^3 or 27, 5, 13 and 37. However, the process for finding prime factors can be difficult and time-consuming. One of the factors of my telephone number is 1,714,411, which is prime – but it takes a lot of trial division by consecutive primes to discover that fact!

The many thousands of different Barry Knights (Barries Knight?) in the real world no doubt have very different characters and personal histories. There will be a Barry A. Knight and a Barry G. Knight, and Barry G. Knight may stand for Barry Geoffrey or Barry George. Mrs Esmerelda Knight may have started out as Ms Esmerelda Smith, so what does the number significance of Knight have to do with her? We will examine these questions in detail later. However, the simple point to be made is this: despite all the diversity and divergence, numerology says that common to every Barry Knight will be at least some events, experiences, attitudes and attributes which resonate within the broad frameworks of meaning attributed particularly to the numbers 2, 3, 5, 17 and 510.

It might just happen that these correspondences manifest themselves quite dramatically and overtly. It is just possible that at least one Barry Knight will read this and leap from his chair saying, 'My God! My phone number is 235 1751!' or, 'My birthday is the 23rd of May and I'm seventeen!' More likely, however, that the numerological correspondences will be far less obvious, because correspondences which are based merely on digit order are probably more or less fortuitous – I do not state categorically that they are impossible, but there is no logical reason to make them the basis for all subsequent interpretations, as most numerologists do. All the evidence from traditional numerology suggests that the essential key to understanding is analysis of the sums of sequences, and factors of totals, and the relationships between sums and factors.

It is quite likely, however, that Barry Knight (any one of him) thinks of 2, 3, 5 or 17 as his 'lucky' number. Some day I shall persuade some distinguished university to give me a large enough grant to conduct a large-scale quantitative study correlating people's ideas of their personal lucky numbers with the numbers generated by gematria interpretation of their names, but in the mean time, the reader will have to accept my unsupported observation that lucky numbers and gematria factors do, in fact, quite frequently appear to correspond.

We shall look at interpretive, diagnostic and analytical numerology in much more detail in Chapter Nine, but we can round off this first example, in which our subject has been the mythical Barry Knight, with a few more comments:

The equal presence of the 2 and 3 suggests sexual stability. I'm sure there are some Barry Knights who are perverts and sexual deviants, but the numerology of the name suggests a healthy sexuality. (It may be homosexual or heterosexual – the 2 is feminine, the 3 masculine.) The combination of 2, 3 and 5 is also very balanced and stable. The 2 suggests a quieter, more introverted type, the 3 a more outgoing type, but the presence of both helps to stabilize the 5, which represents impulsivity, even recklessness. The 17 represents some unusual or distinguishing feature – whenever a comparatively high prime number crops up in interpretation, it suggests something very individual or unusual – a particular gift, talent or interest. The name Barry reads as: family – wealth – identity – identity – hand (of God), or as: bloodline – cattle – face – face – hand, depending on how each letter is interpreted. These may appear fairly meaningless to you and me, but the sequences may generate some meaningful resonances and correspondences for any Barry who happens to be reading. The name Knight reads as: palm of the hand – support – hand (of God) – sign of the cross; or as: fate – need – hand – serpent or sky god. The factors of the total 510 suggest stability, equanimity, a sociable nature, some impulsivity and some individual unusual interest or quirk of character. On the strength of nothing better than numerological intuition, I would be willing to bet that a majority of the thousands of Barry Knights in the world do work in the following occupations: manual, semi-manual, clerical, sales, insurance, teaching, administration, social service, the armed forces; but do not work in the following: higher academics, city financial, professional sport, entertainment, music. I'm sure I will hear from those Barry Knights who want to tell me I've got it wrong.

But gematria interpretation of a person's name is merely the beginning of the story. Each one of us has a unique combination of numbers which relate directly to us or impinge directly on our lives. The sceptic says that these numbers are entirely fortuitous and random, and that there can be no possible relationship between the numbers and the individual to whom they relate. The numerologist says that there will be a discernible relationship or connection between the numbers (although it may be very difficult to find); moreover, that awareness of the significance of the numbers and their impact is empowering, if for no better reason than that the more we know about ourselves, the more likely we are to feel in control of our own lives and contented to be who we are.

Let us begin with a list, by no means exhaustive, of the ways in which numbers relate to us individually:

Date of birth
Time of birth
Place of birth (coordinates of latitude and longitude)
Father's date, time and place of birth
Mother's date, time and place of birth
Street address of place of birth
Telephone number of place of birth
Current address
Current telephone numbers, home and work, fax numbers
Social security or welfare reference numbers
Payroll reference
Bank accounts and credit cards, PIN numbers
Keys, combination locks, security codes
Vehicle registration numbers
Insurance policy numbers
Driving licence
Passport
Regular bus and train route numbers
Club membership numbers
Clothing sizes, shoe sizes
Height and weight
Heart rate, blood pressure, cholesterol count, body temperature

In Chapter Nine, we shall look in more detail at how all these numbers can be interpreted and analysed. For the moment, however, it is important to note how thick and fast the numbers pile around us –there are swarms of them!

So, the first practical question in numerology – where do we find the numbers? – is to some extent already answered: we are all surrounded by numbers. Even if you were marooned alone and naked on a desert island, you would still have height, weight, a pulse, a level of blood pressure, a birth date, a latitude and longitude, and so on.

But most numerologists (myself included) believe that beyond the overt numbers which surround us all as individuals, there are numbers which influence our lives deeply, but which may remain hidden to us. Sometimes we find or recognize these numbers simply by intuition – we call them 'lucky' numbers, and have a special fondness for them which has no logical or practical basis. Lucky numbers are very common in almost all cultures. Some numbers – for example, the number 3 – have a religious or cultural tradition behind them which makes them more common or frequent. Others are less obvious, more personal and individualistic. The number 37 (which is prime) is a common factor of many of the numbers in my life. It was the number of the house in which I grew up. 37 is a factor of my daughter's name by gematria. I was 37 when my son was born. I have learnt to take it for granted that 37 will keep appearing, sometimes significantly, sometimes trivially, in my life. Maybe there will be 37 people at my funeral.

Since these influential numbers are not always obvious, the second part of practical numerology involves the finding of numbers. There are many traditional ways of doing this. The classical Chinese divinatory text, the *I Ching*, is consulted by the casting of straws or coins – the combinations produce figures called hexagrams, which could just as easily be represented by numbers, especially by numbers in binary notation. Indian numerologists traditionally consulted random number charts, with certain numbers attributed to different gods in the vast Hindu pantheon. The abacus has been used as a practical counting machine for centuries, but it can also be used for divinatory purposes.

The rest of this chapter, then, is devoted to the simple practicalities of these two aspects of numerology – dealing with numbers which we already have to hand, and finding numbers which may be influential.

Every serious numerologist ought really to keep his or her own Book of Numbers. (The Biblical Book of Numbers, or the Fourth Book of Moses, is, incidentally, of great interest to numerologists because of its very frequent and precise attributions of numbers to families, events, offerings, armies, laws, and so on.) The numerologist's Book of Numbers is a work book. From practical experience, I suggest that the loose-leaf format is the most convenient. Once you start working seriously with numerology, you will be astonished at how quickly material accumulates, and it is useful to be able to re-organize your material fairly easily. Your Book of Numbers will probably begin with your own notes on the numbers 1 to 10 – leave space for additional material here, because new ideas will come to you as you learn more. For numbers above 10, if you are using a loose-leaf system, you can add pages as numbers present themselves, or further information appears for a number you already have.

Your Book of Numbers should probably contain the following (some of which you could copy from this book): a table of the prime numbers, say up to 1,000; a list of random numbers; a logarithm table (although most people prefer to use calculators for logarithms and antilogarithms these days); a binary conversion table. However, the most important contents of the book will be your tables of correspondences and attributes, and remember that these need to be reversible. You need two gematria lists: one to convert letters to numbers, the other to convert numbers to letters. If you want to do this really seriously and thoroughly, be prepared for some long lists. For example, the letter A has a numerological value of 1 in these alphabet systems: Arabic, Irish (Celtic), Coptic, serial English, Enochian, Fadic, Georgian, Homeric

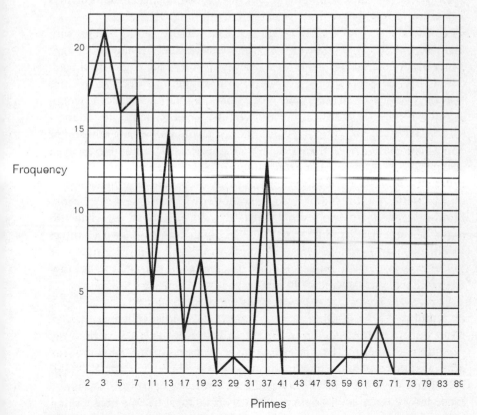

Figure 38 Frequency of primes

Greek, classical Greek, Hebrew, Latin and Aryabhata Sanskrit, but in Crowley's esoteric alphabet its value is 9, in the Hebrew Tree of Life it is 11, in Ogham it is 16, in the Elder Futhark it is 4, in the Younger Futhark it is 10, in Anglo-Saxon runes it is 25 or 26, in the KaTaPaYaDhi system of Sanskrit it has no value, and in Pali Sanskrit it is 2. When we start the reverse table, we find that 1 represents A in most alphabets, but it is B in Ogham, F in the runic Futharks, K, T or V in Sanskrit (depending on the system), and so on. For practical purposes, it might be as well to keep a simplified short list (as I have done in Appendices One and Two) and store the variants separately.

Include some graph paper in your book. Graphing can be fun, and can produce some interesting and unexpected results. There is not space here to discuss the mathematics of graphing equations, but you can experiment on your own. There are many software programs now available which will construct graphs for you – all you have to do is feed your computer with numbers to crunch and it will throw up bar charts, pie graphs, and lots of other fancy and impressive stuff. Graphing is best used for indicating the relationship between two or more sets of information: speed and distance, cost and volume, and so on. Figure 38, for example, is a graph showing the frequency with which various primes (or their powers) below 100 appear in my own life numbers.

The abacus is still used in many parts of the world, often with bewildering speed and dexterity. The most ancient type was a board covered with dust, later with wax, on which numerals could be traced. Later this was replaced by a stone or wood table on which fixed lines were permanently marked, and loose coins or markers made of wood, metal or bone were slid up and down the lines. Finally, the counter abacus emerged, in which the counters, usually hollow beads of wood or glass, rest on rods held in a frame. The Chinese used bamboo rods, even using them to represent algebraic values. This system came into Japan in about 600 AD, where it was known as *sangi* or *sanchu*, and the abacus is still a common sight in the East. The modern Chinese abacus or *suan-pan*, and the Japanese *soroban*, which dates from about the sixteenth century, both use 5 rather than 10 as the counting base. Two counters above each row of five are used to indicate each completion of five counter movements. It looks more complicated than a ten-counter system, but for rapid calculation it is actually easier and quicker – mistakes are more likely with ten counters (see figure 39).

A different type of abacus developed by the Turks, called the *coulba*, or the *choreb* by the Armenians, found its way eventually throughout the Middle East and into Russia, where it was known as the *schoty*; it is still used in some isolated Russian communities to this day. Pope Sylvester II, who lived about 1000 AD, has the unfortunate historical distinction of inventing the arc abacus, one of the world's most useless inventions – it had no way of representing zero, and it was invented just as the Arabs

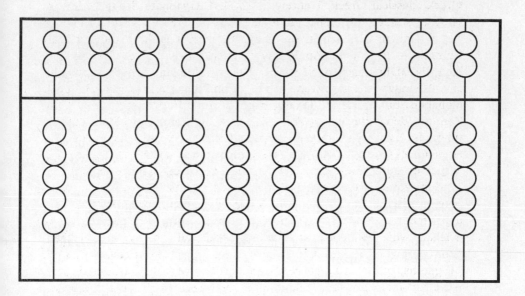

Figure 39 The suan-pan

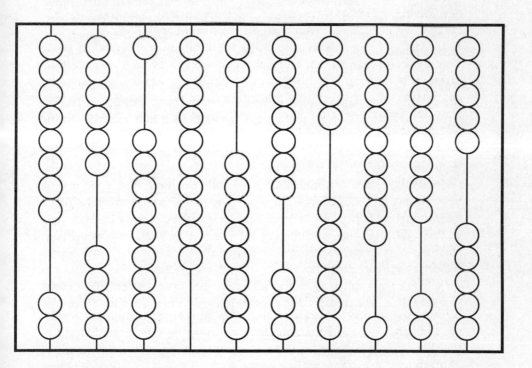

Figure 40 The number 2,490,835,125 on a base-10 abacus

were introducing zero to the West, so nobody used it. The Egyptians (who used pebbles on lines, rather than a fixed abacus) moved the counters from right to left, while the Greeks moved their counters from left to right. The Russian *schoty*, the classical Roman abacus and most Chinese and Japanese abacuses are orientated up and down, with counters being brought down to come into the reckoning. The phrases 'borrow one', 'carry two', and so on, which we still use in basic arithmetic, probably had their origin in the use of the abacus. It is quite easy to buy a children's counting frame or to make an abacus of your own, using dowel rods, drilled wooden beads and a simple wooden frame. Figure 40 shows how the number 2,490,835,125 would be represented on a vertical base-10 abacus.

How is the abacus used for numerology? Traditionally, it has been used in many cultures for the computation involved in interpretation, particularly for finding factors, and so it has come to have connotations of mystic or divinatory power by association – the tool has become associated with the magic worked by the tool. But it can also be used as a device for generating numbers more or less randomly. (Numerologists are very fond of numbers which are generated by a combination of chance and conscious or unconscious will; dice, playing cards and darts will be discussed shortly.) Hold the abacus horizontally and shake it gently up and down, or from side to side, so that the counters move apart as randomly as possible. Friction will naturally tend to create gaps between the counters. Try to let the numbers 'find themselves' by relaxing and letting subconscious rather than conscious decisions affect the movement. When you are done, take the widest gap in each set of counters to create a number, which may be read as one whole number or as a series of separate digits. Read the number, or digits for interpretation, then carefully turn the abacus through 180° and see what numbers or digits are created by reading the pattern upside-down. Just doing sums can be fun with an abacus, but finding number patterns and trying to interpret them is even more fun.

Playing dice are also useful for generating numbers. You need two of them, however, because the numbers of greatest interest are 1 to 10. It seems a trivial point, but the dice should ideally be of the same size and colour. The numbers generated should be read as totals, not as digits; a 1 and a 6, for example, is always 7, not 16. Dice are very convenient, because they can easily be carried around in a pocket.

A single dodecahedral die is actually much more effective than two six-spot dice. The disadvantage of ordinary playing dice (and it's quite a big disadvantage) is that the lowest number obtainable is 2. The dodecahedral die has twelve faces: 0, 1, 2, 3, 4, 5, 6, 7, 8, 9, 10 and ∞, which represents infinity. You'll have to make your own – I have never seen one for sale anywhere. A template for a card or paper dodecahedral die is given in figure 41.

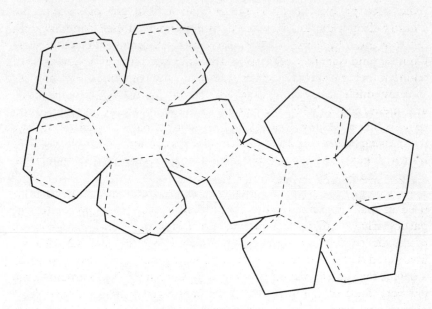

Figure 41 The template for a dodecahedral die

There are other advantages to the dodecahedral die. Each of its faces is a regular pentagon, and therefore contains the implied infinity of nested pentagons and pentagrams (see page 41), which is so beautiful and sacred. Each face also contains within it an undrawn representation of the Divine Proportion. As a numerological tool, especially for magical purposes, the dodecahedral die is literally 'infinitely' more suitable than plain playing dice. As with the cubic die, the number read is the number which lies uppermost after the casting. It is important to make the die as evenly balanced as possible. If you decide to make one out of wood, choose balsa wood rather than anything heavier, to avoid imbalance or constant bias.

Some numerologists use dominoes, just picking them randomly from a face-down pack, then laying them out for a 'reading', rather like Tarot cards. I have never tried this method myself, so I can't comment on its effectiveness. In theory, all the numbers from 0 to 12 are available, so it should be potentially quite useful. I imagine the dominoes would be laid out in a similar fashion to that of a Tarot reading.

Ordinary playing cards are extremely useful in numerology. To begin with, simple and common as playing cards are, they have a long and fascinating history packed with rich associations with esoteric and magical lore. Originally from Asia, playing cards appear to have come into the West during the twelfth and thirteenth centuries. The Council of Worcester in 1240 condemned the playing of games *de rege et regina* (king and queen), which is assumed to refer to playing cards, although there may be some confusion with chess. Cards were universally condemned and attacked by medieval Christian clergy. They were banned in Paris by an edict of the provost in 1397. In 1423, St Bernardino of Siena preached a famous sermon in Bologna against the evils of card-playing. In the seventeenth century, special packs began to appear, used to teach logic, grammar, even geography and heraldry, and these were generically known as 'scientall' cards. Spanish soldiers brought playing cards with them to the New World, where the Aztecs were the first to be fascinated by them. The emblematic or divinatory cards called *tarocchi* in medieval Italian became the modern Tarot – they seem to be at least as old as numeral playing cards, if not older. The four suits have varied throughout history. The earliest German packs had suits of hearts, bells, leaves and acorns. Italian and Spanish cards of the fifteenth century have swords, batons, cups and coins. The modern suits are Hearts (derived from the German); Clubs (known as *trèfle* in French, probably derived from the suit of acorns); Spades (derived from the German suit of leaves, called *pique* in French, although the name 'spade' is not the English digging implement, but rather the Italian word *spade*, meaning 'swords'); and Diamonds, known in French as *carreaux*. Originally, the court cards were King, Chevalier and Knave (*Koenig, Knecht* and *Knabe* in German). It was probably the Italians who first replaced the Chevalier with a Queen, some time during the seventeenth century. In English-speaking countries, the Knave is also popularly known as the Jack. The modern Tarot has four face cards: King, Queen, Knight and Page.

Unlike the Tarot, numerology uses playing cards simply as generators of number. The Ace represents 1, the Knave 11, the Queen 12 and the King 13 (which is a propitious number). The number cards have their face value. The value of the suits was established centuries ago, and survives in the games of Whist and Bridge: in descending order from strongest to weakest, the suits are: Spades, Hearts, Diamonds, Clubs. The most valuable and potent card in the 52-card pack, therefore, is the Ace of Spades, followed by the Ace of Hearts, Ace of Diamonds, Ace of Clubs, King of Spades, King of Hearts, and so on.

There are enough ways of using playing cards esoterically to fill a book. I have only enough space here to mention briefly two of my favourite methods.

The first is for solitary enquiry or divination. In a suitably receptive state of mind (more will be said about magic in Chapter Ten), shuffle a single pack of 52 cards loosely, and then deal nine cards face up on the table, left to right, top to bottom, in three rows of three. Why nine cards? Because 9 is the number of incompleteness, transformation and magical working, the dragon's number, the number of the restless green ocean,

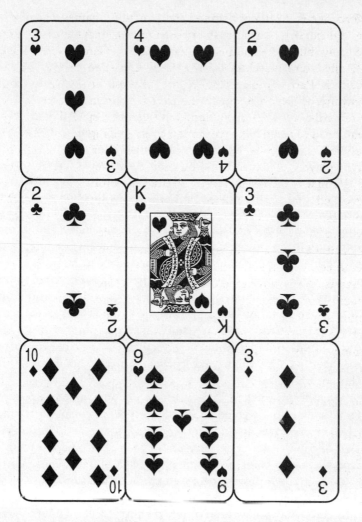

Figure 42 A nine-card reading

Merlin's number. The nine cards create a square. Each card can be read for its numerical face value. The significance of each card is increased or decreased by its standing in the suit-potency sequence – a five of spades is more influential than a five of clubs. The suits represent the following: Spades – power, influence, science; the transcendent; Hearts – love, generosity, spirituality, compassion; Diamonds – wealth, fame, material success; Clubs – practicality, handiness, action, the physical world. If the same number appears twice, pay special attention to it; if it appears three or four times, it is very, very important; if it appears five times, you've mixed up two different packs of cards! The card in the centre of the square will dominate the reading: whatever number it represents is the presiding influence over all the others. The numbers can be read in

159

sequences of three, horizontally, vertically and diagonally. There are horizontal, vertical and diagonal totals, as well as a grand total for the reading. Figure 42 shows a square which I dealt immediately after writing this paragraph, asking the cards the questions: How am I doing on this book? What are its chances of success? The following is my analysis of what the cards said.

The most striking aspects are the central dominance of the King (13) of Hearts, and the presence of three 3s, the 3 of Hearts, 3 of Clubs and 3 of Diamonds, which find their counterpart in the powerful 9 of Spades. These are all highly favourable and auspicious indications. The dominance of the Heart suit indicates satisfaction rather than wealth, although the two Diamond cards add up to the favourable 13 (you did pay for the copy you're reading, didn't you?) and the 9 of Spades indicates a small but significant measure of influence. The number 3 and its multiples or powers absolutely dominate this reading. The top horizontal line (which is an integer sequence in the same suit) adds up to 9, and the central horizontal line adds up to 18. The central vertical triplet sums to 26, which has prime factors of 2 and 13 – and there are two 2s and one 13 in the cards. The whole square totals to 49, which is 7 times 7. Traditionally, 7 represents material possessions, religious authority, intuition and a global perspective. In brief, the reading says: You're doing fine; this will work very well and give you and others great satisfaction. I hope so!

The second card method I use is for two people, and uses two packs; it's rather similar to the game of Snap. Each person deals a card face up from his or her own pack, after shuffling them and deciding what question or topic is under enquiry. As in Snap, the object is to spot the moment when two cards of identical value fall in sequence. With two packs, there are two possibilities: two cards of the same number value may fall in sequence, say the 5 of Hearts and the 5 of Clubs, or two identical cards may follow each other, say the Queen of Clubs from one pack followed by the Queen of Clubs from the other. All the pairs which are generated during the laying-down sequence are set to one side until the whole pack has been turned up. The pairs are then interpreted. If two identical cards are paired, the significance of that pairing is much greater than the others. If a large number of pairs is generated, the reading can be rather complicated and confusing, but usually only a small number of pairs emerges, so that there is usually a very small and clear number sequence to interpret. As with the first method, the numbers and suits can be dealt with singly and in sequence, paying particular attention to the numerical total. It is also possible to use the two-pack method alone, turning a pack with each hand.

Finally, a brief mention of darts. The use of darts in numerology is by no means traditional – in fact, I don't know of anyone else who uses them. I love to play darts, and I have my own board at home, but I am a sufficiently bad player not to be able to guarantee that the number which I aim at is the number which I actually hit, so the dartboard, for me, is a fun tool for generating semi-random numbers – it has a very appealing mixture of conscious (even determined) volition and random chance. I throw for a 19 and hit a treble 7, so I have to deal with 21 now instead. I have no way of proving it, but I always get the feeling that my subconscious mind somehow influences my miss-throws. The dartboard is a very useful tool for plugging away at a diagnostic problem; it generates a constant stream of numbers, usually not exactly the numbers intended, and it provides a little exercise into the bargain.

We shall look at interpretive, diagnostic, analytical, predictive and magical practical numerology in more detail in Chapters Nine and Ten, but first we need to add one last ingredient before we start baking the cake – we need to see how some topics in modern mathematics might be applied to the ancient numerological tradition.

eight

MODERN MATHEMATICS AND NUMEROLOGY

x=+−√÷x=+−√÷x=+−√÷x=+−√÷x=+−√÷x=+−√÷x=+−√÷x=+−√÷x=+−√÷x=+−√÷x=+−√÷

This chapter looks at binary notation and logarithms, although consideration of logarithms will also lead us a little further into investigation of e, the extraordinary number discussed briefly on pages 93 to 95.

There is an entire system of number notation based on 2. It is called the binary system. It first appears in Europe in the writings of Gottfried Wilhem Leibnitz (1646–1716), although the Chinese may have used binary notation as early as 3000 BC. In binary notation, there are only two digits: 0 and 1. For Leibnitz, these represented nothingness (0) and God (1). At the highest esoteric or spiritual level, therefore, the binary system allows for all of creation to be expressed in terms of the presence or absence of God. It is a very simple, beautiful and profound concept. Leibnitz used the ancient Greek term for 1, the *monad*, to represent the simple, self-active beings which are the constituent elements of all things – a similar theory in some ways to modern atomic theory, except that for Leibnitz each atom or monad, eternal, indivisible, was the paradigm of God, the prime cause and final end of the universe. Although it is quite different in style and origin, Leibnitz's philosophy has obvious similarities to ancient numerological notions of the meaning of 1, in particular to the Kabbalistic notions of the Ain Soph. Leibnitz's philosophy has long been superseded by more sophisticated ideas, but his philosophical and mathematical writings are still widely studied for their simplicity and elegance.

As well as having a deep philosophical background, binary notation also has a history of useful practical application. All modern computers operate using some form of the binary system, for example. The obvious and immediate value of this system for electronic computing is that 0 can represent 'off' and 1 can represent 'on'. Even in mechanical systems, the same principle can be applied – think of player-piano rolls with holes punched in them (hole = 1, no hole = 0). In fact, Charles Babbage's Analytical Engine, a forerunner of the modern computer, used punched cards instead of magnetic tapes or disks. As early as 1725, Bouchon had invented a device which used a roll of perforated paper to feed instructions to a mechanical loom.

In the decimal system, we represent numbers by place as well as digit value, and each place identifies a power of 10:

10^6	10^5	10^4	10^3	10^2	10^1	10^0
1,000,000	100,000	10,000	1,000	100	10	1

The number 4,786,523 means $(4 \times 1,000,000) + (7 \times 100,000) + (8 \times 10,000) + (6 \times 1,000) + (5 \times 100) + (2 \times 10) + (3 \times 1)$. We do exactly the same in the binary system, except that each place value represents a power of 2 instead of a power of 10:

2^{10}	2^9	2^8	2^7	2^6	2^5	2^4	2^3	2^2	2^1	2^0
1024	512	256	128	64	32	16	8	4	2	1

The number 110100101 means $(1 \times 2^8) + (1 \times 2^7) + (1 \times 2^5) + (1 \times 2^2) + (1 \times 2^0)$. In decimal numbers, that is the same as $(1 \times 256) + (1 \times 128) + (1 \times 32) + (1 \times 4) + (1 \times 1) = 421$. To convert a binary number to a decimal number, imagine (or write) each 1 or 0 under a column according to its position. Add up the values of the columns with a 1 in. Example: What is 10101 in decimal notation?

Binary columns	2^4	2^3	2^2	2^1	2^0
Decimal equivalent	16	8	4	2	1
Number	1	0	1	0	1
Decimal equivalents	16		4		1

Answer: 10101 binary equals 21 decimal.

To convert a number from decimal notation to binary notation, find the highest power of 2 within the number. Subtract it, leaving a remainder. Find the highest power of 2 within that remainder. Subtract it, leaving another remainder. Repeat until you have the entire decimal number broken down into the sum of powers of 2. Imagine (or write) each power under the appropriate column as a 1. Example: What is 48,793 in binary notation?

Find the highest power of 2.
$2^0 = 1$ $2^1 = 2$ $2^2 = 4$ $2^3 = 8$ $2^4 = 16$ $2^5 = 32$ $2^6 = 64$ $2^7 = 128$ $2^8 = 256$
$2^9 = 512$ $2^{10} = 1,024$ $2^{11} = 2,048$ $2^{12} = 4,096$ $2^{13} = 8,192$ $2^{14} = 16,384$ $2^{15} = 32,768$ $2^{16} = 65,536$ $2^{17} = 131,072$ $2^{18} = 262,144$ $2^{19} = 524,288$

The highest power of 2 within 48,793 is 2^{15}, which equals 32,768. So we have one 'unit' of 2^{15}. Subtract this from the original number: $48,793 - 32,768 = 6,025$. Now we look for the highest power of 2 within this remainder. The highest power of 2 within 16,025 is 2^{13}, which equals

163

8,192. So we have one 'unit' of 2^{13}. Subtract this from the remainder, as follows: $16,025 - 8,192 = 7,833$. Now we look for the highest power of 2 within this remainder. The highest power of 2 within 7833 is 2^{12}, which equals 4,096. So we have one 'unit' of 2^{12}. Subtract this from the remainder: $7,833 - 4,096 = 3,737$.

Continue this process and you should reach remainder 9. The highest power of 2 within 9 is 2^3, which equals 8. So we have one 'unit' of 2^3. Subtract this from the remainder: $9 - 8 = 1$. Now we look for the highest power of 2 within this remainder. The highest power of 2 within 1 is 2^0, which equals 1 exactly with no remainder.

Now we list all our 'units' by writing a 1 in the appropriate column for each power of 2 we have found, putting in a 0 where there was no power of 2:

2^{15} 2^{14} 2^{13} 2^{12} 2^{11} 2^{10} 2^9 2^8 2^7 2^6 2^5 2^4 2^3 2^2 2^1 2^0

1   0   1   1   1   1   1   0   1   0   0   1   1   0   0   1

Answer: 48,793 decimal is 1011111010011001 binary.

Since binary notation was devised by Leibnitz only at the beginning of the eighteenth century, and even then remained the fairly exclusive province of mathematicians and philosophers, it does not appear in traditional numerology. However, binary notation is potentially very useful in numerological interpretation. The essential idea is simplicity itself: 1 means on, present, active, alive, positive, go; while 0 means off, absent, inert, dead, negative, stop. Every number (at least every positive integer – let's keep it simple for the moment) – can be expressed in this simple on–off, go–stop, pattern. Each of the most potent numbers, the numbers from 1 to 10, has a binary form which has a visual pattern of its own:

Decimal:	Binary:
1	1
2	10
3	11
4	100
5	101
6	110
7	111
8	1000
9	1001
10	1010

If you find it hard to 'read' binary numbers, think of the 'units' column as representing 1, the 'tens' column' 2, the 'hundreds' column 4, the 'thousands' column 8, and so on.

If you begin to think in binary terms, there is suddenly an extraordinary number of events which can be interpreted as expressing or revealing number. For example, the British telephone system has a rhythmical pattern in its ringing tone which consists of two rings followed by a pause, the length of the pause being equivalent to the time which would be required for three rings. In other words, every British telephone rings 11000, which is the binary notation for decimal 24. The prime factors of 24 are 2 and 3 ($2^3 \times 3$). The American system has a longer, two-second ring followed by a four-second pause, which could be represented as 110000, decimal 48, whose only factors are 2 and 3 ($2^4 \times 3$).

Wherever nature produces intermittent rhythms, she produces numbers in binary form – waves, gusts of wind, rays of sunshine between scudding clouds. Human activity, wittingly or unwittingly, generates a vast range of binary sequences. A rock song on the radio is belting out the basic off-beat rhythm, tap-BAM-tap-BAM, which is 101 in binary (actually 0101, but binary numbers never begin with 0), the equivalent of 5, the number of radicalism, recklessness and impulsivity – highly appropriate. The waltz is LA-da-da, or 100, or 4 in decimal notation, the number of homeliness, the practical, stability. Every lighthouse is flashing not just its beacon light, but also a binary number, repeated over and over, its value depending on the lengths of the on–off sequences. If you're reading this on a bus ride, count every stop at which the bus stops as a 1, every stop which it passes without stopping as a 0 – there you have a binary number.

It can sometimes be interesting to see how the numbers which are significant in your life appear when they are converted to binary notation. The 37 which figures in my life, for example, is 100101. I could write a piece of music in 6/8 time with the rhythmic accents on the first, fourth and sixth beats, or a poem with the same rhythmic pattern, or I could paint a visual sequence of light-dark-dark-light-dark-light, to express that number. The possibilities are endless.

Deliberately generating random binary numbers can be done in a variety of ways. The simplest is to use coins. Seven coins would allow you to generate any number from 1 to 127 decimal. Call every head a 1, every tail a 0. Toss or shake the coins in a bag, then let them drop in a line and read from left to right: Head-head-tail-tail-tail-head-tail, for example, would be 1100010, or decimal 98. Another way, similar to the method used with the *I Ching*, would be to cast long and short straws, the long representing 1, the short 0.

Logarithms are often described as the 'invention' of John Napier, who was born in 1550 near Edinburgh, Scotland, but it might be better to call his work a discovery rather than an invention. What Napier did was to observe a consistent relationship between numbers, using as his starting point the patterns generated by correspondences between numbers in an arithmetic series (a series with a common difference, such as 2, 4, 6, 8, 10...) and in a geometric series (a series with a common ratio of multiplication, such as 2, 4, 8, 16...). Logarithms have subsequently had a huge influence on pure mathematics, but they are also of practical significance, as will be explained in more detail shortly. Napier was widely talented – he was a published theologian and inventor of weapons as well as a mathematician. His first description of logarithms, *Canonis Descriptio*, appeared in 1614. In 1617 he published *Rabdologia*, which described the use of certain rods for multiplication and division tasks – these became popularly known as 'Napier's bones'. He liked practical systems – he also devised methods of calculation involving small metal plates in a box and other methods involving a chessboard. He was probably the first Western mathematician to make extensive use of the decimal point. Logarithms as we now know them were developed from Napier's work by Henry Briggs, Professor of Geometry at Gresham College in London, who continued Napier's work after his death in 1617, publishing the first table of logarithms as we would now recognize them.

So what are logarithms? They are closely related to exponents, or powers of numbers, which were mentioned earlier. If we multiply 3 by itself, we write that as 3^2, spoken as 'three to the power of two' or 'three squared' – the number 3 is called the base of the power and the small number 2 written to the right and a little above the 3 is called the exponent of the power. So far, we have only considered positive integer (whole number) exponents: 5^4 means 5 times 5 times 5 times 5, which equals 625. However, we can also use negative numbers and fractions as exponents: 5^4 is 625; 5^3 is 125; 5^2 is 25. 5^1 is just 5; any number to the power of 1 is just itself. 5^0 is 1; any number to the power of 0 is 1. If we keep moving down the integers, the next exponent is -1. What is 5 to the power of -1? The answer is: it is 1 divided by 5, or $\frac{1}{5}$, which can be written as 0.2 in decimal notation. 5^{-1} is $\frac{1}{5}$, 5^{-2} is $\frac{1}{25}$, 5^{-3} is $\frac{1}{125}$, and so on. If we use fractions as exponents, we obtain roots: $5^{\frac{1}{2}}$ is the square root of 5, or $\sqrt{5}$. $5^{\frac{1}{3}}$ is the cube root of 5, or $\sqrt[3]{5}$, and so on.

Logarithms can be based on any number, but logarithms to base 10 are called common logarithms. Consider the number 500 for a moment. It is higher than 100, which is 10^2, but lower than 1,000, which is 10^3. If we write exponents as fractions or decimals, we can come close to an expression for 500 as a power of 10. $10^{2.1}$ is 125.8925412..., $10^{2.2}$ is 158.4893192, and so on. We need to go higher. If we try $10^{2.9}$ we get 794.3282347..., too high this time. By trial and error, we could arrive at this approximation: $500 = 10^{2.698970004}$. That exponent, namely 2.698970004, is the common or base-10 logarithm of the number 500. The decimal part of the number is called the mantissa. The number before the decimal point, in this case a 2, is called the characteristic; it tells us where the value of the number must lie – in this case, the answer must lie between 10^2 and 10^3 (i.e., between 100 and 1,000). Tables of common logarithms (usually just called 'log tables') give only the mantissa, usually just to four decimal places – the user has to supply the characteristic on the basis of where the number lies in the range of powers of 10. For example, 503,000 has a characteristic of 5, since it lies between 10^5, or 100,000 and 10^6, or 1,000,000, whereas 50.3, which has the same significant digits, has a characteristic of 1, because it lies between 10^1, or 10, and 10^2, or 100. Most modern calculators give logarithms to eight or nine decimal places – just enter the number followed by LOG. To reverse the process, enter the logarithm and press the antilogarithm key (often Shift-LOG or 2nd-LOG, usually marked 10^x). Calculators can only give estimates. My Texas Instruments TI-30X, a very good and relatively inexpensive calculator, gives 2.698970004 as the logarithm of 500, but gives the antilogarithm of 2.698970004 as 499.9999996.

Why do logarithms matter, in mathematics or in numerology? In mathematics, logarithms have many practical applications. They are closely related to functions and to the elements of calculus. They are used to simplify and accelerate complex calculations, because they have certain invariable laws. For example, $\log_b MN = \log_b M + \log_b N$ can be read as 'the logarithm to base b of M times N equals the logarithm to base b of M plus the logarithm to base b of N'; if M and N are very large or complex numbers, adding their logarithms and then finding the antilogarithm of the sum can be much simpler and quicker than multiplying them directly.

Logarithms are especially useful in exponential growth or decay problems. Financiers use this compound interest formula: if an amount P (the Principal) is invested at an annual interest rate r compounded n times a year, then in t years the investment will grow to an amount A given by $A = P(1 + r/n)^{nt}$. Scientists use a time–growth formula to measure increases in populations, say bacteria in a test sample, using this formula: if a population of size N_0 doubles every d hours (or any other time unit), then the number N in the population at time t is given by $N = N_0 \times 2^{t/d}$. Half-life decay is well known; it is used in radiocarbon testing to determine how old archaeological finds and other ancient objects actually are. The half-life decay formula is: if an amount N_0 has a half-life h, then the amount remaining at time t is given by $N = N_0(\frac{1}{2})^{t/h}$. Even without fully understanding these formulae, the reader can appreciate that they are of great practical significance, and they are very commonly used in industry, in science, in commerce, in research, and so on. In most cases, the fact that the formulae include complex exponents means that the quickest and simplest way to work the equations is by converting the numbers to logarithms first.

In advanced science and mathematics, the most important logarithm function is the natural logarithm function. This brings us back to e, the number described briefly on page 94. e is an extremely important number in the differential and integral calculus. It was named by

167

Leonhard Euler, the eighteenth-century Swiss mathematician whose work underpins a great deal of modern science and mathematical theory. Euler was an extraordinarily gifted man. Towards the end of his life, almost blind, he completed a book on lunar motions, *Theoria motuum lunae*, after a fire had burnt many of the papers in his house, by carrying all the elaborate computations involved in his head. Euler took a simple expression with one variable, $(1 + \frac{1}{x})^x$, and then observed what values were generated as he increased the value of the variable. When x equals 100, the expression as a whole equals 2.70481. When x equals 1,000, the expression equals 2.71692. Increasing the value of x tenfold each time brings us closer and closer to this number, which Euler called e: 2.7182818284590452353602874713526624977757247093699....The decimal never ends, because e is irrational.

The natural logarithm of a number is the logarithm of that number to the base e, rather than to the base 10, or any other number. It is sometimes written as $\log_e x$, but more often simply as ln x. On a scientific calculator, it is found by entering a number and pressing the natural logarithm key, usually marked LN. For example, the natural log of 500, or ln 500, is 6.214608098.... As with common or base-10 logarithms, it is possible to find the antilogarithm to base e, and, again, calculators will sometimes give approximations, simply because they are working to a limited number of decimal places. My calculator gives the natural antilogarithm (e^x) of 6.214608098 as 499.99999998.

The numerological significance of e is that it is the value which is generated as the x of Euler's original expression approaches infinity. In the same way that the Divine Proportion or Golden Ratio interests us because of its intimate relationship with the infinite Fibonacci series (see page 40), so also the number e is of especial significance, because it too is intimately related to the infinite.

The reciprocal of e, or $\frac{1}{e}$, which can also be written as e^{-1}, is 0.36787944117144232159552377016146086744658.... This number crops up frequently in probability theory. For example, if you shuffle two packs of cards separately, then turn over the top card from each pack simultaneously, repeating the exercise until all possible pairs are exhausted, the probability that there will be no matching pair turned up simultaneously is approximately e^{-1}. I mentioned in the last chapter the 'reading' method in which two packs of cards are turned over simultaneously, looking for pairs, especially identical pairs. The reciprocal of e represents precisely the probability that not a single pair will occur during the sequence.

In the same way that converting a number to binary notation can sometimes give us a fresh insight into its significance, even reveal a completely new pattern or sequence, so also finding the common or natural logarithm of a particularly important number can be revealing. My favourite 37, for example, already mentioned a few times, has a natural or base-e logarithm of 3.610917913..., in which my most personal number, 3, and its multiples 6 and magic 9, appear significantly. I can give you the logarithm of my home telephone number in the confidence of knowing that calculator limitations will prevent you from working it out – the antilog of the number given is *not* my telephone number! – and the same abundance of 3 and its multiples is immediately apparent: 9.308931385.... The common log of my birth date is 6.330808923..., the natural log of my house number is 3.737669618..., and so on.

Binary notation and common and natural logarithms do not appear anywhere in traditional numerology, but, with a little application and calculator work, they are very easily applied to traditional techniques and they can generate some very interesting and unexpected patterns.

Lastly, a few thoughts about i, the imaginary number first described on page 48. i is valuable in mathematics because it allows us to enter the realm of the impossible (that's precisely why it's called an imaginary number), and, once we are within that realm, to proceed with systems of reckoning which are entirely logical and self-consistent. Without such imaginary numbers, much that has been achieved in modern theoretical physics would have been impossible. But what does i represent to the numerologist? It does not appear in traditional numerology at all, so the following suggestions, right or wrong, are simply my own. I think of i as a powerful tool for extracting a difficult negative. In plain mathematical terms, an example would be wanting to find the square root of negative nine, written -9. There is no such number, because no number times itself can ever give a negative product. However, I can write $\sqrt{-9}$ a different way, by factoring out i. I now write $\sqrt{-9}$ as $\sqrt{9} \times \sqrt{-1}$ (root positive nine times the root of negative one). The other name for $\sqrt{-1}$ is i, so $\sqrt{-9}$ equals $3i$. Esoterically, then, perhaps we should think of i as a propitious number, in that it extracts difficult negatives. It is the number which takes us into the impossible, since it is itself an impossible number. It is closely related to 1, the source of all numbers. I visualize i as the impossible white shadow of a blinding radiance. If your bank balance is overdrawn by £121, or $121, or whatever other currency you're in debt in, think of it not as -121, with no square root, but as -1 times 121, which has the square root $11i$. Then look to see whether the positive 11 has any suggestions to make to you.

Now that our tool box is fairly well stocked, we can spend the final two chapters looking in more detail at some examples of practical numerology.

nine

INTERPRETIVE NUMEROLOGY

0123456789876543210123456789876543210123456789876543210

We invented a hypothetical Barry Knight earlier. Now let's flesh him out with some more numerical details. The names and numbers given below are fictitious – the numbers were mostly generated from a random number list (the longitude and latitude are genuine, the post codes and telephone area codes genuine but slightly scrambled).

> Name: Barry Knight
> Date of birth: 27 February 1947
> Time of birth: 5.22 a.m.
> Place of birth: Frome, Somerset, England (51°10'N, 2°20'W)
> Present address: 47 Abbey Close, Hillingdon, Middlesex, UB7 9EX, England
> Home telephone: 0895 445264
> Work address: Bryant Electronics, 222 Strand, London WC2R 0BB
> Work telephone: 071 463 3216
> National Insurance no.: YF 05 73 62 D
> National Health Service no.: MBFD 509
> Driving Licence no.: KNIG9 204128 BG9LT
> Vehicle registration no.: 523 MOR T

We could add a lot more detail if we wanted to – car-insurance policy number, life-insurance policy number, and so on. However, we already have plenty to work with. The objective here is to see whether any numbers stand out as significant factors. Since the numbers have been generated semi-randomly, it may well be that no clear pattern emerges, but let's wait and see.

We already interpreted the name briefly in Chapter Seven, but let's review:

B A R R R Y K N I GH T
$2 + 1 + 200 + 200 + 10 + 20 + 50 + 10 + 8 + 9 = 510$, prime factors 2, 3, 5 and 17. The 2 and 3 suggest harmony, stability, the 5 suggests energy, and the 17 represents something quirky or idiosyncratic – an unusual interest or character trait, perhaps (in Pythagoreanism, 17 is an unlucky number, a something-not-quite-right number).

If we do a simple frequency count of each digit as it appears in Barry's personal numbers, we see that 2 appears much more frequently than any other digit: 2 appears sixteen times, 1 nine times, 5 eight times, 4 seven times, 7 seven times, 9 five times, 6 four times, 8 three times and 3 only twice. This would indicate that 2 is the dominant number.

However, there are several letters included in and among the numbers, and to obtain a more accurate interpretation, we need to convert these to numbers, including the number equivalents of the name letters, and obtain the full numerical sequence:

Name: $2+1+200+200+10+20+50+10+8+9=510$, factors $2\times3\times5\times17$

Date of birth: $27 + 2 + 1947 = 2005$, factors 5×41 (The American convention is to write the month first and the day second (i.e., 2/27/47 instead of 27/2/47), but the total remains the same.)

Time of birth: 322, factors $2 \times 7 \times 23$ (This needs some explanation. There are 60 minutes in an hour, and I prefer to work all in the same units, so for me five o'clock in the morning is 300, three o'clock in the afternoon is 900, and so on. Other numerologists use different systems.)

Place of birth: $3070 + 140 = 3210$, factors $2 \times 3 \times 5 \times 107$ (Latitude and longitude are expressed in degrees, minutes and seconds – as with time, the counting base is 60, and I have converted these to minutes.)

Address: 47 and $6 + 2 + 7 + 9 + 5 + 60 = 89$, which is prime. (I don't attempt to convert the street or town names. The two dominant numbers are the house number, and the postal code, or zip code in America, which I reckon separately.)

Home telephone: 895,445,264, factors $2^9 \times 3^2 \times 7 \times 17 \times 23 \times 71$ (The area code and individual number could be dealt with separately, or the digits could be dealt with separately and added to give a total, but I prefer to use the whole number as it is most commonly used or as it might appear on a letterhead. In the modern age, the telephone number and, increasingly, the fax number have great numerological importance, because they impinge on our lives so frequently and significantly.)

Work address: 222 and $800 + 20 + 2 + 200 + 0 + 2 + 2 = 1,026$, factors $2 \times 3^3 \times 19$ (Same logic as for the home address.)

Work telephone: 714,633,216, factors $2^{12} \times 3 \times 11 \times 17 \times 311$

National Insurance: $12 + 500 + 5 + 73 + 62 + 4 = 656$, factors $2^4 \times 81$

NHS: $40 + 2 + 500 + 4 + 509 = 1055$, factors 5×211

Driving licence: $20 + 50 + 10 + 3 + 9 + 204 + 128 + 2 + 3 + 9 + 30 + 9 = 477$, factors $3^2 \times 53$

Vehicle registration: $523 + 40 + 70 + 200 + 9 = 842$, factors 2×421

Note, incidentally, that I leave digits grouped as a number if that is how they are presented. For example, I read the first part of the vehicle registration as 523, not as 5 + 2 + 3.

Once the personal information has all been converted to numerals, we begin by drawing up a simple frequency chart, including every number which appears either as a number in its own right or as a significant factor. The digits 1 to 9, which are the most influential, are recorded each time they appear within other numbers, as well as numbers in themselves. If a number appears as a factor and it is raised to a power, we count it once for each power in the chart – for example, 5^3 counts as three entries in the 5 column. For the fictitious Barry Knight, we end up with this frequency:

Number	1	2	3	4	5	6	7	8	9
Frequency	21	62	21	16	19	9	17	7	11

Number	10	11	12	17	19	20	23	27	30	40
Frequency	3	1	1	3	1	3	2	1	1	2

Number	41	47	50	53	60	62	70	71	73	81
Frequency	1	1	2	1	1	1	1	1	1	1

Number	89	107	128	140	200	204	211	222	311
Frequency	1	1	1	1	4	1	1	1	1

Number	322	421	477	500	509	510	523	656	800
Frequency	1	1	1	2	1	1	1	1	1

Number	842	1,026	1,055	1,947	2,005	3,070	3,210
Frequency	1	1	1	1	1	1	1

Number	714,633,216	895,445,264
Frequency	1	1

It is this frequency count which provides the first and most important raw data for interpretation. The most significant distribution is that of the nine digits, 1 to 9. In this example, there is a very striking frequency of the number 2 , which means that the influence of 2 for this particular Barry Knight is very marked. 2 represents beginnings, birth, family line, but it also represents the female, sexual attractiveness, sensitivity, secrecy, tact and diplomacy. This Barry Knight seems to have a very strong feminine side to his character. He is far more likely to be an introvert than an extrovert. At work, he may be involved in a lot of coding, or work with jargon or symbols which would be cryptic or unintelligible to the layman. The relatively moderate frequency of the odd numbers, 1, 3, 5 and 7, suggests that his work does involve some independent thinking and creativity, but not a great deal.

Low frequencies can be as informative as high frequencies. The frequencies of 6 and 8 are comparatively low. This tells us that this Barry

Knight's life may not be as harmonious as the name alone suggests. Six is the marriage number, and this Barry Knight is probably not married or in a stable relationship, and there is probably very little public service in his life – commercial and work interests tend to predominate, although the 5 and 7 do suggest a certain measure of creativity and spirituality. The low 8 suggests that he has limited prosperity, and his discrimination is also limited – he can perhaps be small-minded about large issues, with a tendency to narrow and prejudiced political opinions.

The unusual 17 appears as a factor in his name, as a factor in his home telephone number, and as a factor in his work telephone number, so it appears to be a peculiarity or trait or special characteristic which appears most frequently or is most active during telephone conversations. It may be something simple, like a lisp or some other peculiarity of speech, or it may be a particular talent such as a very effective telephone sales technique, or it may be something far more sophisticated and abstruse, but, whatever it is, it seems to be related to telephone use. The feminine 2 is a very dominant factor in both the work address and the work telephone number, which could either mean that Barry's occupational position involves a great deal of tact, diplomacy or secrecy, or that there is discord and disharmony for him at work.

The vehicle registration and driving licence numbers are generally much more even and propitious than the other numbers. It appears that Barry enjoys driving, and derives some pleasure from his car ownership – he probably thinks of his car as a prized possession, rather than as a plain utility vehicle. He has the letter R, numerological value 200, twice in his name, and once in his vehicle registration – 200 is 2 times divine 10 times divine 10, and so is a number of high contentment. It may be that Barry drives a Frog–eye Sprite or an MG, or some other similar vehicle associated with a high level of pride of ownership.

Some things are definitely going right in Barry's life. He is fairly independent, as the frequency of 1 suggests, and he is fairly successful at his work, as the frequency of 3 suggests, even if he is not particularly happy there. The dominant influence, however, is the secretive, tactful, feminine 2. This Barry Knight appears likely to be a rather quiet and withdrawn character, with a not particularly rich inner life, stable in character but not living entirely harmoniously either at home or at work, yet probably able to conceal his small discontentments.

Now, let us suppose that Barry Knight has a specific problem, and instead of general interpretation, we want to try a specific diagnosis. Barry's problem – this is fictitious again, of course – is that his firm is moving out of London, but is heading east, while he lives to the west of London. If he stays with the firm, he is going to have a grim commute around the M25 motorway. If he leaves, he has to start looking around for another job. He has seen a managerial position in a business machines retail outlet, where his computer experience would be of little use, but it is just down the road in Uxbridge. The salary would be slightly less than he is earning now, but his daily commute would be ten minutes by car instead of the hour he spends on the train every Monday to Friday getting to central London at present. Where do his best interests lie?

We begin by looking at some of the material we have already gathered from the general interpretation. In particular, we note the strong presence of the 2 in his present work environment, and the moderate frequency of the harmonious 6. The retail firm is Uxbridge Business Machines, 72 High Street, Uxbridge, UB1 1AB, telephone 0895 429600. We run the letters through the gematria mill, factor out the composites, and obtain the following:

U X B R I D G E B U S I N E S S
$6 + 60 + 2 + 200 + 10 + 4 + 3 + 5 + 2 + 6 + 60 + 10 + 50 + 5 + 7 + 7 +$
M ACH I N E S
$40 + 1 + 8 + 10 + 50 + 5 + 7 = 558$, factors $2 \times 3^2 \times 31$

Address: 72 and $6 + 2 + 1 + 1 + 1 + 2 = 13$, which is prime.

Telephone: 895,429,600, factors $2^5 \times 5^2 \times 13^2 \times 37 \times 179$

Now we run up a frequency chart for the potential new workplace:

Number	1	2	3	4	5	6	7	8	9	10
Frequency	15	20	10	4	14	9	9	4	3	3

Number	13	31	37	40	50	60	72	179	200	558
Frequency	3	1	1	1	2	2	1	1	1	1

Number	895,429,600
Frequency	1

This is a much more balanced picture. The 1 and 2 are more closely balanced, suggesting that Barry would have a greater measure of independence if he were to take the retail manager job. The 6 is more obviously present, suggesting greater harmony. The street number is 72, which is Barry's dominant 2 times 36, or 6^2, which again suggests a harmonious relationship. The postal code totals to 13, which is an auspicious number, and the work telephone also contains 13^2 as a factor, which is very auspicious. The number 17 does not appear anywhere in the prospective workplace, either as a factor or in its own right. That might suggest that Barry's particular talent would not be useful in the new job, or it might suggest that a particular characteristic, for example a slight lisp or speech impediment (remember that the 17 seems to be related directly to use of the telphone), would not matter or would not be significant in the new job. There are two fairly high primes present, 31 and 179, which suggests some interest or novelty in the position.

Taken all together, this reading would tend to suggest that Barry might be happier in business machines retail in Uxbridge High Street than commuting across London to continue his present job with the electronics company. He could think about moving house, of course, but then that would lead us into another set of interpretations ....

Names are very important starting points for numerological interpretation, particularly the forenames or nicknames by which we are most commonly addressed throughout the day. Remember that the tradition of numerology says that *sound* generates number. Most numerology texts concentrate on the full formal name, which misplaces the emphasis. My full name is John Robert King, which is $12 + 70 + 8 + 50 + 200 + 70 + 2 + 5 + 200 + 9 + 20 + 10 + 50 + 3 = 709$, which is prime, but I am only John Robert King on official forms – most of the time, I'm just John, which is $12 + 70 + 8 + 50 = 140$, factors $2^2 \times 5 \times 7$. If you're an Edward, but everyone calls you Ted all the time, the Ted number correspondences ($9 + 5 + 4 = 18$, factors 2×3^2) are far more influential than the number correspondences of your full name. My wife is Mary Jane ($40 + 1 + 200 + 10 + 12 + 1 + 50 + 5 = 319$, factors 11×29), but in her family she was always known as Janie ($12 + 1 + 50 + 10 + 5 = 78$, factors $2 \times 3 \times 13$), and now, while most people at work call her Mary Jane, at home she is usually just MJ ($40 + 12 = 52$, factors $2^2 \times 13$, the divine feminine to the power of 2, multiplied by auspicious and happy 13).

Here is a short list of some common forenames, with some brief additional notes on derivations, and with their number correspondences according to my system:

Adam a Hebrew name which also means 'humankind' and 'red' $= 1 + 4 + 1 + 40 = 46$, factors 2×23

Agnes from Greek Αγνος (AGNOS), meaning 'pure' $= 1 + 3 + 50 + 5 + 60 = 119$, factors 7×17

Alan an ancient Celtic forename $= 1 + 30 + 1 + 50 = 82$, factors 2×41

Albert a Teutonic name meaning 'noble-bright' $= 1 + 30 + 2 + 5 + 200 + 9 = 247$, factors 13×19 (BERT $= 2 + 5 + 200 + 9 = 216$, factors $2^3 \times 3^3$)

Alexander from Greek roots *alex-*, meaning 'defend' and *ander*, meaning 'man' $= 1 + 30 + 5 + 60 + 1 + 50 + 4 + 5 + 200 = 356$, factors $2^2 \times 89$ (Alex $= 1 + 30 + 5 + 60 = 96$, factors $2^5 \times 3$)

Alfred from Old English, literally 'one who receives counsel from spirits' $= 1 + 30 + 500 + 200 + 5 + 4 = 740$, factors $2^2 \times 5 \times 37$ (Alf $= 1 + 30 + 500 = 531$, factors $3^2 \times 59$)

175

Alice derived like Adela and Adele from Teutonic *athal*, 'noble' = $1 + 30 + 10 + 60 + 5 = 106$, factors 2×53

Andrew from Greek Ανδρειος (ANDREIOS), meaning 'manly' = $1 + 50 + 4 + 200 + 5 + 800 = 1060$, factors $2^2 \times 5 \times 53$ (Alices and Andrews should have a lot in common)

Ann the Greek form of Hebrew Hannah = $1 + 50 + 50 = 101$, which is prime (Anne = $1 + 50 + 50 + 5 = 106$, factors 2×53, Anna = $1 + 50 + 50 + 1 = 102$, factors $2 \times 3 \times 17$, Annie = $1 + 50 + 50 + 10 + 5 = 116$, factors $2^2 \times 29$)

Anthony an ancient Roman family name = $1 + 50 + 9 + 70 + 50 + 10 = 190$, factors $2 \times 5 \times 19$ (the alternate spelling Antony makes no difference, since T and TH both equal 9; Tony or Toni = $9 + 800 + 50 + 10 = 869$, factors 11×79)

Arnold from Teutonic *arin* , 'eagle', and *vald*, 'power' = $1 + 200 + 50 + 70 + 30 + 4 = 355$, factors 5×71 (Arnie = $1 + 200 + 50 + 10 + 5 = 266$, factors $2 \times 7 \times 19$)

Audrey from Old English Etheldreda, meaning 'noble strength'= $800 + 4 + 200 + 5 + 10 = 1,019$, which is prime (Au = long O)

Barbara the feminine form of Greek *barbaros* or Latin *barbarus*, 'stranger' = $2 + 1 + 200 + 2 + 1 + 200 + 1 = 407$, factors 11×37

Barry from the Irish Gaelic for 'spearman' = $2 + 1 + 200 + 200 + 10 = 413$, factors 7×59

Basil from the Greek for 'kingly' = $2 + 1 + 7 + 10 + 30 = 50$, factors 2×5^2

Benjamin the son of Rachel and Jacob in Genesis, originally named Benoni ('son of pain') by his mother, but renamed Benjamin ('son of my right hand') by his father = $2 + 5 + 50 + 12 + 1 + 40 + 10 + 50 = 170$, factors $2 \times 5 \times 17$ (Ben = $2 + 5 + 50 = 57$, factors 3×19)

Carol from the same Germanic root as Charles and Carl = $20 + 1 + 200 + 70 + 30 = 321$, factors 3×107

Charles from Germanic root meaning 'common man' = $8 + 1 + 200 + 30 + 5 + 60 = 304$, factors $2^4 \times 19$ (Charlie or Charley = $8 + 1 + 200 + 30 + 10 + 5 = 254$, factors 2×127)

Christine from the Greek for 'Christian' = $20 + 200 + 10 + 60 + 9 + 10 + 50 + 5 = 364$, factors $2^2 \times 7 \times 13$

Christopher   from Greek, meaning 'Christ-bearer' = 20 + 200 + 10 + 60 + 9 + 70 + 500 + 5 + 200 = 1,074, factors $2 \times 3 \times 179$ (Chris= 20 + 200 + 10 + 60 = 290, factors $2 \times 5 \times 29$)

Colin   possibly Celtic for 'young dog', possibly Norman French derived from Nic(h)olas = 20 + 70 + 30 + 10 + 50 = 180, factors $2^2 \times 3^2 \times 5$

Daniel   meaning 'God the judge' in Hebrew = 4 + 1 + 50 + 10 + 5 + 30 = 100, factors $2^2 \text{x } 5^2$ (Dan = 4 + 1 + 50 = 55, factors 5×11)

David   Hebrew in origin, probably meaning 'beloved one' = 4 + 1 + 6 + 10 + 4 = 25, the perfect square of 5 (Dave = 4 + 1 + 6 + 5 = 16, the perfect square of 4, or 2^4)

Derek   a Dutch variant of German Theodoric, 'ruler of the people' = 4 + 5 + 200 + 5 + 20 = 234, factors $2 \times 3^3 \times 13$

Donald   Scots Gaelic meaning 'strong' = 4 + 70 + 50 + 1 + 30 + 4 = 159, factors 3×53

Edward   from Old English *ead* , 'fortunate', and *weard*, ' guardian' = 5 + 4 + 800 + 1 + 200 + 4 = 1,014, factors $2 \times 3 \times 13^2$, a very auspicious combination (Eddie = 5 + 4 + 4 + 10 + 5 = 28, factors $2^2 \times 7$, and Ted = 9 + 5 + 4 = 18, factors 2×3^2)

Elizabeth or Elisabeth   Hebrew meaning 'God has promised' = 5 + 30 + 10 + 7 + 1 + 2 + 5 + 9 = 69, factors 3×23

Emily   from the Roman family name Aemilius, which is also the root of Emil, Amelia and other names = 5 + 40 + 10 + 30 + 10 = 95, factors 5×19

Emmeline   early Celtic and Norman French, probably from an Indo-European root *amal*, meaning 'worker' = 5 + 40 + 40 + 5 + 30 + 10 + 50 + 5 = 185, factors 5×37

Eric   from Old Norse, the *ric* element, common to all Teutonic languages, meaning 'powerful' = 5 + 200 + 10 + 20 = 235, factors 5×47

Francis   from Latin Franciscus = 500 + 200 + 1 + 50 + 60 + 10 + 60 = 881, which is prime (Frank = 500 + 200 + 1 + 50 + 20 = 771, factors 3×257)

Frederick   from Teutonic *frithu*, 'peace', and *ric*, 'powerful' = 500 + 200 + 5 + 4 + 5 + 200 + 10 + 20 = 944, factors $2^4 \times 59$ (Fred = 500 + 200 + 5 + 4 = 709, which is prime, and Freddie = 500 + 200 + 5 + 4 + 4 + 10 + 5 = 728, factors $2^3 \times 7 \times 13$)

George   from the Greek for 'earth–man' or 'farmer' = 12 + 70 + 200 + 12 (J + O + R + J) = 294, factors $2 \times 3 \times 7^2$

Harold   from Old English *hereweold*, 'battle leader' = 5 + 1 + 200 + 70 + 30 + 4 = 310, factors $2 \times 5 \times 31$

Harry   derived from Henry via Hal = 5 + 1 + 200 + 200 + 10 = 416, factors $2^5 \times 13$

Helen   derivation possibly from early Greek, meaning 'bright', but uncertain = 5 + 5 + 30 + 5 + 50 = 95, factors 5×19

Henry   from a Teutonic root meaning 'home–ruler' = 5 + 5 + 50 + 200 + 10 = 270, factors $2 \times 3^3 \times 5$

Irene   Greek for 'peace' = 10 + 200 + 5 + 50 + 5 = 270, factors $2 \times 3^3 \times 5$, just like Henry – any Henry and Irene married to each other should be a very happy couple

Jack   derived from John = 12 + 1 + 20 = 33, factors 3×11

James   derived like Jacob from Hebrew, via Greek Jakobos, Latin Iacobus, later Iacomus = 12 + 1 + 40 + 5 + 60 = 118, factors 2×59 (Jim = 12 + 10 + 40 = 62, factors 2×31)

Jane   a feminization of John, variants are Jean, Joan, Johanna and Jeanne = 12 + 1 + 50 + 5 = 68, factors $2^2 \times 17$

Jennifer an Anglicized variant of Welsh Gwenhwyfer or Guenevere = 12 + 5 + 50 + 50 + 10 + 500 + 5 + 200 = 832, factors $2^6 \times 13$

John   found as Johanan in the Old Testament, Graecized as Ioannes in the Septuagint, original meaning 'God is gracious' or 'beloved of God' = 12 + 70 + 8 + 50 = 140, factors $2^2 \times 5 \times 7$ (Johnnie = 12 + 70 + 8 + 50 + 50 + 10 + 5 = 205, factors 5×41)

Jonathan related to Nathan, Nathaniel, Nat, etc., from Hebrew meaning 'gift of God' = 12 + 70 + 50 + 1 + 9 + 1 + 50 = 193, which is prime (Jon = 12 + 70 + 50 = 132, factors $2^2 \times 3 \times 11$)

Joseph   probably from Hebrew, meaning 'increaser' = 12 + 800 + 7 + 5 + 500 = 1,324, factors $2^2 \times 331$ (Joe = 12 + 800 + 5 = 817, factors 19×43)

Katherine from a Greek name Aikaterine, meaning unknown,
or   perhaps related to *katharos*, meaning 'clean, pure'
Catherine = 20 + 1 + 9 + 5 + 200 + 10 + 50 + 5 = 300, factors $2^2 \times 3 \times 5^2$ (Kate = 20 + 1 + 9 + 5 = 35, factors 5×7)

Kenneth   from Scots Gaelic, meaning 'fair–head' or 'handsome' = $20 + 5 + 50 + 50 + 5 + 9 = 139$, which is prime (Ken = $20 + 5 + 50 = 75$, factors 3×5^2)

Linda   probably from the Spanish for 'beautiful' = $30 + 10 + 50 + 4 + 1 = 95$, factors 5×19

Margaret   from the Greek *margarites*, meaning 'pearl', often familiarized to Maggie, also to Meg, Peg and Peggy = $40 + 1 + 200 + 3 + 1 + 200 + 5 + 9 = 459$, factors $3^3 \times 17$ (Maggie = $40 + 1 + 3 + 3 + 10 + 5 = 62$, factors 2×31; Peg = $80 + 5 + 3 = 88$, factors $2^3 \times 11$; and Peggy = $80 + 5 + 3 + 3 + 10 = 101$, which is prime)

Maria   the Latin form of Mary = $40 + 1 + 200 + 10 + 1 = 252$, factors $2^2 \times 3^2 \times 7$

Mary   originally Miriam in Hebrew (Mrym), mistakenly rendered as Mariam in the Septuagint, which Latin speakers took to be the accusative form of Maria = $40 + 1 + 200 + 10 = 251$, which is prime

Matthew   probably a Greek variant of an earlier Hebrew name, meaning uncertain = $40 + 1 + 9 + 5 + 800 = 855$, factors $3^2 \times 5 \times 19$ (Matt = $40 + 1 + 9 + 9 = 59$, which is prime)

Michael   from the Hebrew, meaning 'he who is like the Lord' = $40 + 10 + 20 + 1 + 5 + 30 = 106$, factors 2×53

Nicholas   from Greek roots meaning 'victory' and 'people' = $50 + 10 + 20 + 70 + 30 + 1 + 60 = 241$, which is prime (Nick = $50 + 10 + 20 = 80$, factors $2^4 \times 5$)

Paul   from Latin *paulus*, meaning 'small' = $80 + 800 + 30 = 910$, factors $2 \times 5 \times 7 \times 13$

Peter   from Greek Πετρος (Petros), meaning 'stone, rock' = $80 + 5 + 9 + 5 + 200 = 299$, factors 13×23, a very powerful combination of auspicious 13 and the high prime 23 (Pete = $80 + 5 + 9 + 5 = 99$, factors $3^2 \times 11$)

Rachel   which means 'lamb' in Hebrew, but may be older in origin = $200 + 1 + 8 + 5 + 30 = 244$, factors $2^2 \times 61$

Richard   from Teutonic roots *ric* , 'powerful' and *heard*, 'hard' = $200 + 10 + 8 + 1 + 200 + 4 = 423$, factors $3^2 \times 47$ (Rich = $200 + 10 + 8 = 218$, factors 2×109; Rick = $200 + 10 + 20 = 230$, factors $2 \times 5 \times 23$; Dick = $4 + 10 + 20 = 34$, factors 2×17)

Robert   found in Old English as Hreodbeorht, meaning 'fame-bright', popularized by the Norman French in its present form $= 200 + 70 + 2 + 5 + 200 + 9 = 486$, factors 2×3^5 (Bob $= 2 + 70 + 2 = 74$, factors 2×37)

Samuel	from Hebrew, meaning 'heard by God' $= 60 + 1 + 40 + 6 + 5 + 30 = 142$, factors 2×71
Sarah	explained in Genesis as a replacement for Sarai, sometimes translated as meaning 'princess' $= 60 + 1 + 200 + 1 + 8 = 270$, factors $2 \times 3^3 \times 5$ (Sally $= 60 + 1 + 30 + 30 + 10 = 131$, which is prime)
Simon	a variant of the tribal name Simeon found in Genesis $= 60 + 10 + 40 + 70 + 50 = 220$, factors $2^2 \times 5 \times 11$
Stephen	from the Greek for 'crown' $= 60 + 9 + 5 + 500 + 5 + 50 = 629$, factors 17×37, another unusually powerful combination (Steven $= 60 + 9 + 5 + 6 + 5 + 50 = 135$, factors $3^3 \times 5$ – the spelling does make a difference! Steve $= 60 + 9 + 5 + 6 + 5 = 85$, factors 5×17)
Susan	from the Hebrew for 'lily' $= 60 + 6 + 7 + 1 + 50 = 124$, factors $2^2 \times 31$
Thomas	from Aramaic (the language spoken by Jesus), meaning 'twin' $= 9 + 70 + 40 + 1 + 60 = 180$, factors $2^2 \times 3^2 \times 5$ (Tom $= 9 + 70 + 40 = 119$, factors 7×17)
Timothy	from Greek roots meaning 'honour' and 'God' $= 9 + 10 + 40 + 70 + 9 + 10 = 148$, factors $2^2 \times 37$ (Tim $= 9 + 10 + 40 = 59$, which is prime)
Walter	from Teutonic, meaning 'ruler of the people' $= 800 + 1 + 30 + 9 + 5 + 200 = 1,045$, factors $5 \times 11 \times 19$ (Walt $= 800 + 1 + 30 + 9 = 840$, factors $2^3 \times 3 \times 5 \times 7$)
William	from Teutonic *vilja*, 'will' and *helm*, 'helmet' $= 800 + 10 + 30 + 30 + 10 + 1 + 40 = 921$, factors 3×307 (Bill $= 2 + 10 + 30 + 30 = 72$, factors $2^3 \times 3^2$; Will $= 800 + 10 + 30 + 30 = 870$, factors $2 \times 3 \times 5 \times 29$)

There is not space to give detailed analyses of each of these names, but there is a wealth of information here, which you can work out for yourself by using the tables of attributes and correspondences on pages 204 to 213. (You can use the same tables to work out the number value of your own name, if it is missing from the list above.) The name Edward, for example, has 2, 3 and 13^2 as its factors, a particularly harmonious and happy combination. Similarly, the name George has factors of 2, 3 and 7^2, and you may recall (see page 71) that the colour of 7 is royal purple and 7 is strongly associated with monarchy, which perhaps accounts for the popularity of George as a king's name. Note that some names have similar, or even identical, lists of factors. The names Emily, Helen and Linda, for example, all have 5 and 19 as their sole factors, so sisters or friends named Emily, Helen and Linda should be particularly close and sisterly. Harry has factors of 2^5 times 13, and Jennifer has factors of 2^6 times 13, so Harry and Jennifer should make a good couple.

Some names are intractably difficult, depending on what correspondence system is used. In my system, the name Jesus, for example, should be $12 + 5 + 7 + 6 + 7 = 37$, which is prime, and, because 37 is a special personal number to me, I like that correspondence. However, historically, the first sound of the name has often been a consonantal [Y] sound, usually spelled with the letter I – variants are Iesus and Iesu. In my system, [J] and [Y] both correspond to 12, so my system still works for Iesus, but not for Iesu or Jesu, which becomes $12 + 5 + 7 + 6 = 30$, factors 2, 3 and 5.

Looking at the list of names, it becomes immediately obvious that certain factors appear more frequently than others. Across the whole range of positive integers, 2 is logically bound to be the most common prime factor – every other number is even, of course. Next most common is 3, then 5, and so on. In fact, the probabilities of each of the primes being present as a factor in any given number can be precisely described, using mathematics which is too complicated to include here. For that reason, when we interpret names and personal numbers numerologically, we should be aware that there are simple mathematical reasons why 2 should appear more frequently than, say, 997. On the other hand, the range of numbers within which we normally work, at least by comparison with the literally infinite range of positive integers, is extremely small, so we should not exaggerate unduly the weighting in favour of 2, 3, 5 and the other low primes. As a general rule, any high prime number which appears as a factor in a name, or in any other object for interpretation, is considered significant. It is especially significant if it is the only factor of the value of the name. It strongly implies the presence of 1 (which is, of course, a factor of every real number, but is not usually counted as such), and 1 signifies an uncommon strength of identity, uniqueness and individuality.

Some of the connections will be purely personal. For example, the prime 37, the number of the house in which I was raised, and my age when my son was born, and a number which recurs with great frequency as a factor in all the personal numbers pertaining to my life, also appears as a factor in my grandfather's name (Alfred, 740, factors $2^2 \times 5 \times 37$), as well as in my daughter's name (Emmeline, 185, factors 5×37). My father's full name is Frederick Ypres King. (He was born in 1918, and my grandfather gave him the unusual middle name to commemorate all of his comrades who died in the two great battles at Ypres in World War 1.) My father's official full name, therefore, tallies to 1,384, factors

$2^3 \times 173$, but to most of the people in his life he has always been just Fred, which totals 709, which is prime. My mother's forenames were Margaret Minnie, but she was always known as Peggy, value 101, which is prime. They were both very strong–willed, independent characters with a great sense of their own identity.

Some of the information about a particular prime factor is of interest because the factor has unusual mathematical characteristics or belongs to an unusual sequence or pattern. The sequences of special numerological significance, as explained in Chapter Four, are the Fibonacci series, the Mersenne primes, Pythagorean triples, amicable numbers, sociable numbers and weird numbers. Appendix Four may give you further information on a particular number. For example, 89 is a prime factor of the name Alexander. 89 is the eleventh Fibonacci number (see page 38), and so it is part of that famous sequence from which the Divine Proportion is derived. 89 is a factor of the name Napoleon $(50 + 1 + 80 + 70 + 30 + 5 + 70 + 50 = 356$, factors $2^2 \times 89)$, which might be interpreted as representing material gain (2^2 is 4, the number of the real world, the mundane, the practical, material possessions) on a prodigious scale (89 representing prodigious increase), which, of course, correlates well with the known events of Napoleon's personal history.

When we look at historical names, we are beset by choices. Is John F. Kennedy best characterized as John Kennedy, John F. Kennedy, JFK or just Kennedy? Should we describe Mohandas K. Gandhi as Mohandas K. Gandhi, or Bapu ('father') or Mahatma ('great soul'), or just Gandhi? If we return to plain Barry Knight – who is not famous for anything apart from being the unwitting hero of this book – it seems reasonable to argue that the number value of Barry is likely to be the most influential numerological correspondence in his personal life, that of his full name Barry Knight most influential in his professional and public life, and that of his family name Knight probably least influential of all. For the great and famous, it is probably the other way about. Shakespeare is more widely known and mentioned by that name alone than by the name William Shakespeare, or Will Shakespeare (or Shaksper, and all the other variant spellings). So, generally speaking, for the great and famous we use the most commonly known and articulated name; we use Brahms (311, which is prime), for example, rather than Johannes Brahms. John F. Kennedy in that form totals to 784, factors $2^4 \times 7^2$, while JFK is $12 + 500 + 20 = 532$, factors $2^2 \times 7 \times 19$: the common factor of 7, as mentioned earlier, is often associated with royalty, which is not too fanciful a connection in Kennedy's case; the strong presence of 4 (2^4 is 4^2, or 16, in the first variant) again indicates wordly power or significant influence in worldly matters, and is common to both variants.

The skill in interpreting these gematria correspondences lies in, firstly, finding where the significant numbers 1 to 10 are present, and then, secondly, relating their attributes to each other and to whatever larger primes are also present. In other words, the interpretations flow from the combination of attributes of the separate factors; a name with factors of, say, 2, 5 and 17, should indicate some measure of the attributes of each of those numbers, working in combination. There are infinitely many possible combinations, but some are listed below, with illustrations of how the sequences or correspondences might be interpreted.

Prime

Uniqueness, individuality, strength of character, leadership, exceptional originality, and isolation are all suggested. Examples: Beethoven = 157; Einstein = 199; Michelangelo = 1583; Shakespeare = 677; Gandhi = 67, which is not only prime, but the digits 6 and 7 also indicate harmony and spirituality.

Prime × prime

An unusual pattern, in which enterprise and originality in two separate fields is suggested. An example is Geoffrey Chaucer (1073, factors 29×37), who was an accomplished senior diplomat before he achieved immortal fame as a poet.

2 × prime

The attributes and associations of the number 2 include bloodline, ancestry, family, sexual attractiveness, secrecy, diplomacy and political skill. Example: Winston Churchill = 262, factors 2×131.

2^2 × prime

2^2 is 4, the number of flesh as opposed to spirit, the mundane, the real world, stability, dedication and patriotism. Coupled with a high prime, the product suggests prodigious success in the material world – in commerce, for example, or in miltary affairs. We saw above that Napoleon = 56, factors $2^2 \times 89$, and the other name by which he was commonly known, Buonaparte (the original spelling) yields 212, which is $2^2 \times 53$. Another example is Washington = 1,252, factors $2^2 \times 313$.

3 × prime

Three is the number of all nature, fertility and creativity, regeneration, success and enlightenment. It is especially associated with artistic creativity and originality. Examples: Dante Allighieri = 363, factors 3×121; Milton = 219, factors 3×73; Mozart = 327, factors 3×109; Salvador Dali = 417, factors 3×139.

3^2 × prime

3^2 or 9 is the number of transformations, particularly magical transformations. It is associated with energy, especially sexual energy,

183

restlessness, healing, prayer and spiritual passion. Bach totals to 603, which is $3^2 \times 67$. The original Welsh name of the magician Merlin is Myrddyn (the *dd* is pronounced like voiced *th*), and Myrddyn = 711, factors $3^2 \times 79$.

5 × prime

5 is another restless number, closely associated with fertility and procreation in the natural world, spirit within flesh, the quintessence. In terms of human character it is often associated with intuitiveness, impulsivity, curiosity and radicalism. Examples: Keats = 95, factors 5 × 19; Lenin = 145, factors 5 × 29.

7 × prime

Seven is the number of spirituality, religious authority, global perspectives and ambitions, the colour purple, royalty, transcendentalism and aloofness. It is common to the name Caesar, which was originally pronounced like Kaiser, Caesar = 287, factors 7 × 41, and to Hitler = 259, factors 7 × 37. There is nothing 'evil' about the number 7 – it simply represents a global perspective or an unusual degree of vision. Leonardo da Vinci, for example, totals to 469, which is 7 × 67.

2^5 × prime

2^5, or 32, is the essence of the female, the hidden and secretive, the seductive, raised by the power of 5, the number of Venus, sexual attractiveness and impulsivity, but by extension the number of lust, either sexual, commercial or political. Examples: Cleopatra = 208, factors $2^5 \times 13$; Stalin = 160, factors $2^5 \times 5$.

These few illustrative examples reveal, I hope, the method employed here. In each case, we look for the interaction of factors, using all the traditional attributes and associations of the principal numbers 1 to 10 as our guidelines. A combination of 2, 3 and 5 suggests stability. A combination of 3 and 7 might suggest an unusual level of spiritual or religious achievement. A combination of 3^2 and 5, or 9 and 5, might suggest unusual restiveness, a life full of rapid transformations and new experiences, and so on.

If we use the ' prime factor' test to isolate true greatness and individuality among modern politicians, we find Margaret Thatcher amounting to 691, which is prime, but John Major, whom many dismiss as greatly inferior in strength of character to his predecessor, amounts to 463, which may be a lesser prime, but it is still prime, nonetheless. Bill Clinton, with the prime 311 as his total, easily outclasses Ronald Reagan (615, factors 3 × 5 × 41), in terms of originality, but Reagan's 3 indicates higher popularity. Hillary Rodham Clinton totals to 848, factors $2^4 \times 53$, the 2^4 indicating success in financial matters, as well as a very high level of feminine intuition and political wisdom, despite her apparent unpopularity and lack of success with the review of the American health system.

Interpreting and analysing all these names of people and places can be endlessly entertaining, but it could have practical utility as well. If your numerology is up to par, you think very carefully before naming your house, or your boat, or even your company. In India, where numerology is still widely used and respected, no one would dream of starting a major enterprise without first consulting an astrologer for appropriate dates, and then a numerologist for appropriate names, dimensions, quantities, and so on.

In traditional numerology, especially in the Kabbalah, the most felicitous correspondences were between words which came to the same numerical total. There are countless examples of these correspondences. For example, the first word of the Mosaic Pentateuch is *Berashith* (see page 105) which, by gematria, has the numerical value of 913. The Hebrew phrase for 'He created the Law' also totals to 913. This system was adapted to Greek, first by the pagan Greeks, later by Christians. For example, the number value of the word Σταυρος (STAUROS or STAVROS), meaning 'cross', is 1271 in the Greek system, and 1271 is also the value of the phrase Ἡ Γνοσις ('E GNOSIS), meaning the Gnosis, the wisdom or knowledge of God. I recently visited the catacombs or burial caves of St Sebastian, which lie underground beside the ancient Appian Way in Rome. The early Christians who met secretly in the catacombs often left graffiti in Greek letters. One such is Ζησης (ZESES), which means, 'May you live!', but is also, by gematria, the number 420, the number of the Egyptian mother-goddess Isis. These numerological correspondences, first in the Kabbalah, then in early Christianity, were often jealously guarded secrets passed on only to the initiated. They were gradually unravelled by hermeneutic scholars, pagan and Christian, in the early Middle Ages. Unfortunately, a very great deal of this esoteric lore has been lost or garbled since then.

Nevertheless, the art of numerological interpretation still flourishes, albeit in a sadly weakened state. The truth is that interpreting the deep significance of numbers and their attributes and correspondences is often long, hard and painstaking work. It requires a commitment of time and energy, and often a good deal of patience and reliance on intuition, when the patterns seem stubborn and reluctant to emerge. When they do emerge, however, they can be wonderfully revealing and illuminating.

ten

APPLIED NUMEROLOGY – NUMBER MAGIC

5713571357135713571357135713571357135713571357135713571357135713571357135713

Many serious modern neopagans, occultists and magicians prefer to spell magic as magick, to distinguish between conjuring tricks and the serious craft of change and invocation. Magic has also been tainted by its associations with so-called 'black magic' and diabolism. These associations are offensive and distressing to modern pagans, who do not even conceive of a universal god of evil like the Devil, let alone worship one. I have never read a more simple, sensible description of the essentials of serious modern magic than that written by the late Scott Cunningham:

> Contrary to what you may have heard, *magic is a natural process*. It is not the stuff of demons and unsavory creatures, and no 'fallen archangel' lends us the ability to practice magic. These are the ideas of a religious philosophy which abhors individualism .... Is magic 'supernatural'? No. The supernatural doesn't exist. Think about it for a moment. *Super*, meaning extra, outside of, differing from, and *natural*. Outside of nature? Different from nature? No way! Magic is as natural as stone, as real as our breath, as potent as the Sun .... The power is neutral. It cannot be divided into positive and negative energies. *Power* is *power*. It is our responsibility as Magicians (wielders of the powers) to work with it toward beneficial ends (see note 1).

So, our first question is: To what ends or purposes do we intend to direct our number magic? We turn to Scott Cunningham again for what he describes as the three essential prerequisites of magic: need, emotion and knowledge. Cunningham describes a need as 'an empty space in your life or a critical condition ... which must be worked on immediately.' A desire (for a new car, a better-looking partner) is not a need; the need must be real. Real magic simply does not work for trivial or recreational purposes, or for vague dissatisfactions. The need has to be clearly recognized, acknowledged and defined. Secondly, the need must generate emotion. As Cunningham puts it: 'If you aren't emotionally involved in your need, you will be unable to raise sufficient power from any source and direct it to your need. In other words, your magic won't work.' Finally, we need the knowledge of techniques like visualization, invocation and ritual, in order to make the magic work: 'If we have the need and the emotion but not the knowledge of how to utilize these things, we would be like a Neanderthal human contemplating a can opener or a computer. We wouldn't know how to use the tools.' And Cunningham has one last comment to make about the morality of magic: 'Magic isn't (or shouldn't be) an instrument of selfishness, domination, pain, fear, manipulation, ego-gratification or control. On the contrary, it is life-affirming, infused with love, joy, contentment, pleasure and growth' (see note 2).

There is no separate religion or esoteric school of numerology, with fixed ritual practices and liturgies. Nevertheless, there are many established religions, including Judaism, Christianity and Islam, and many semi–mystical movements, such as Freemasonry, in which certain numbers have ritual or liturgical significance. Although it is not a religion, numerology flourishes in India as a popular means of spiritual investigation and expression. Common to all of these, and to the ancient traditions of the Chinese, the Chaldeans, the Babylonians, the Egyptians, the followers of Pythagoras, the Hebrew Kabbalists, the Christian numerologists and the medieval hermeneutic scholars, is a literal reverence for number as the representation of eternal truth, of verities beyond time and space and beyond the limited understanding of humankind. When, therefore, we consider the purposes to which number magic may be put, we should remember that the power we are trying to invoke and deal with is widely considered to be a sacred power, even though it is not confined to any specific religion.

The basest purpose is a material purpose. As I said in the Foreword, this book is not intended to help you win lotteries. Nevertheless, some material needs are real. There are many kinds of magic dedicated to increasing prosperity. The key thought, or word, here is *need*, as defined by Scott Cunningham. Many Christians would find nothing immoral or objectionable about a congregation praying for the funds necessary to repair a church or to save an orphanage from closure. In the same way, there is no reason why you cannot invoke the power of number to achieve a financial objective, if the need is genuine and the purpose valid. Working number magic to secure your property, to house and protect your family, to attain or maintain useful employment, to protect your vehicles and their occupants, to make your flowers and vegetables flourish, and so on, are all valid material purposes.

Most purposes, however, are not material: they are either emotional or spiritual. Securing good health, which might be considered physical, emotional and spiritual all in one, is one of the most frequently intended purposes of magic, including number magic. In all magical traditions, healing has played an important role. Number magic may be used for sleep disorders, digestive disorders, sexual dysfunction, infertility, irregular sleep patterns, and so on. Other emotional purposes include seeking inner tranquillity, becoming more courageous or outgoing, learning to be more eloquent and articulate, understanding and interpreting dreams or nightmares, or making friends more easily. Spiritual purposes include self-projection, exorcism in the Judaic and Christian traditions, strengthening psychic powers and clairvoyance, and so on.

If the need is real, the second requirement is emotion. This does not mean that every act of number magic has to be committed in a state of morbid passion. It simply means that there must be a genuine, motivating emotional basis for the working. The scientific community uses the term 'validity' in research to represent the concepts of seriousness and suitability. Research may be reliable – i.e., conducted along recognized lines of procedure, with appropriate recording and analysis of data, and so on – but it also has to be valid; in other words it has to address a real question and propose a real and appropriate solution. Exactly the same holds true of magic.

Probably the most useful starting place for number magic is for the would-be practitioner to become thoroughly familiar with the numbers already influencing his or her life. We cannot escape numbers. We are surrounded by them. If you would like to gain a greater understanding of the numbers which affect you most strongly, you will need to spend some time on self-analysis. Write down every number you can think of which impinges on your life. Do a frequency count of all the digits. Factorize every important number, and take note of which numbers emerge as the most common factors. Use gematria to analyse your name, in all its variant forms, the names of your family, your school, your town, your company, your work place, and so on. For the most common and familiar names (which therefore have the most powerful influence), try to connect the meaning of each and every letter into a coherent personal statement about yourself. There is plenty of room for flexibility and personalization here. My name is John, which is $12 + 70 + 8 + 50 = 140$, factors $2^2 \times 5 \times 7$, which already tells me a lot. For me, the 2^2 represents a strongly feminine side to my character, and a firm rooting in the mundane, the real world, discipline and stability, practical skill with tools and machines, and a domestic nature, all of which are signified by the number 4, which is 2^2. The 5 represents an abundance of spirit, of quintessential vitality, of energy and creativity, and also indicates a radical nature, politically and socially. The 7 represents a deep spirituality, which has always been with me, and a sense of global perspective.

The letters themselves have ancient meanings and associations. J is Jera in the Futhark, meaning the year, the pattern of the seasons, all cyclical movements and events, the great clockwork of the cosmos. O is Ayin in Hebrew, the eye, especially the eye of illumination and intuition – I have been blessed with a life full of guesses, most of them right, including some wild life decisions based entirely on intuition which turned out to be wonderfully correct, and I have learnt to place enormous trust in my intuition as a result. The silent H is a mystery – it was once the aspirate H of Iohannes, the Huath or hawthorn of the Celts, but now it is silent, with the number value of Greek Eta, the long E, the 5 of quintessence, of spirit within flesh. The N is Greek Nu, and Hebrew Nun, my support, and Nion, the Celtic ash, and its 50 contains the restlessness and fertility and creativity of the 5 coupled with the perfection of the 10. So, when someone speaks my name, as happens perhaps dozens of times every day, my ear hears 'John', but my soul hears a constantly self-enriching expression of my self in the contained magic of letters and numbers: Through changes, through the great cosmic cycles, as moons wax and wane, as the years inexorably turn, there comes illumination, the eye opens, the inner mind perceives and rejoices, and there is blessed and mysterious silence, in which all restlessness, fertility, creativity and spiritual energy is brought to perfect fruition. All that, and much more, is contained in the simplest and most common of names. Other Johns will probably have different inter-pretations for their own names, each as subtle and complex as the indi-vidual to whom it belongs.

Your name has a whole story to tell, too, a story unique to you, even if your name is as common as mine. Your best starting place is with yourself, studying long and hard until you feel truly confident that you are aware of the numbers exerting a powerful influence in your life and of the story they tell. If you already have a 'lucky' number, don't be at all surprised if it emerges as a significant factor in your life numbers – that happens very frequently, because people choose lucky numbers by intuition, and their intuition is often correct. But you should also expect to find that more than just one number is influential for you; it is far more likely that a group or sequence of numbers emerges, and usually it will be quite apparent which numbers are significant in your life and which numbers are not – the frequency count alone should give you a strong indication.

The materials with which you surround yourself will either reinforce the number correspondences in your life, or detract from them. Certain woods and metals and precious stones are particularly associated with certain numbers, and have been so for thousands of years in some instances, so you should check the alignments and misalignments of attributions in table 6 to see whether your material possessions reinforce or detract from the influence of your significant numbers.

Table 6

Number	Wood	Metal	Stone
1, all primes	silver fir, ash	–	diamond
2	birch, aspen	–	sapphire
3	yew, elm	lead	jet, obsidian
4	oak, gorse	tin	amethyst
5	birch, hawthorn	iron	garnet, ruby
6	heather, vine	gold	topaz, amber
7	water-elder, maple	copper	coral, emerald, jade
8	alder, beech	mercury	agate
9	hazel, holly	silver	moonstone, pearl
10	ivy, chestnut	uranium	amber
11	holly, walnut	caesium	mother-of-pearl
12	oak, reed	plutonium	tourmalated quartz

Table 6 is simplified from correspondences which were described more fully in earlier chapters. They may not appear fully appropriate to you. You probably shouldn't start trying to wear lead and tin jewellery, or mercury, uranium, caesium and plutonium about your person. Or you may have a beautiful sapphire ring which is absolutely 'you', but 2 hardly figures in your personal numbers. These correspondences are the traditional ones (apart from the 'modern' metals), that's all. The tree correspondences come largely from the Celtic and Northern traditions. The metals and stones come mostly from Greek, Roman and medieval traditions. Silver has always been the metal of the Moon, whose number is 9. Silver and copper together combines Luna and Venus – the Romans wore such rings as love tokens. If 5 is one of your influential numbers, you may not wear rings of iron, but iron may figure largely in your life in some other way – in the form of steel, perhaps. There is an ancient Northern tradition of burying iron objects like scissors or nails, or hanging iron objects, like horseshoes, for good luck and protection. Tin is the national metal of Cornwall and of St Piran, her patron saint; it streams suddenly white from black ore, and so figuratively represents sudden transformations. Amber has been associated with luck and protection for countless ages – it was traded even in neolithic times. If these correspondences 'work' for you, good. If you can't see any obvious connection, don't dismiss them out of hand. There may be some rather more obscure characteristic of the particular wood or stone or precious metal which does relate to your life, but which is not immediately apparent.

As well as overt personal numbers, like house and telephone numbers, the name correspondences generated by gematria, and so on, and the numbers associated with possessions, we are also surrounded by all the numbers which relate to time and space. The Romans used to count hours from dawn – the sixth hour, or *sexta hora*, became eventually the *siesta* of modern Spanish. If we count the day's hours in the same way, we may find correspondences between certain numbers and the way we feel each day at a particular time. Every day also has a calendar date, which is a number, of course. In the Northern tradition, certain calendar dates are considered very unlucky, days on which one should not undertake an arduous journey, start a new job, get married, and so on (see note 3):

January 1, 2, 4, 5, 10, 15, 17, 29
February 8, 10, 17, 26, 27, 28
March 16, 17, 20
April 7, 8, 10, 16, 20, 21
May 3, 6, 7, 15, 20
June 4, 8, 10, 22
July 15, 21
August 1, 19, 20, 29, 30
September 2, 4, 6, 7, 21, 23
October 4, 6, 16, 24
November 5, 6, 15, 20, 29, 30
December 6, 7, 9, 15, 22, 28

But there is another calendar to which some of us may be more attuned – I certainly am, by nature, not by conscious choice or skill. A very ancient figurine of a female figure holds up a crescent horn which clearly symbolizes the Moon. On the crescent are marked 13 notches, assumed by many to represent the 13 lunar months of the year. The fingers of her other hand are touching her abdomen, perhaps representing the cycle of menstruation and reproduction. The Moon takes about 27 days to circle the Earth, but, because the Earth herself is moving around the Sun, the period between similar phases of the Moon, the so-called lunar month or synodic period, is approximately 29.5 days. Every solar calendar day, therefore, is also a day in the lunar month, which is usually reckoned from new Moon to new Moon. The synodic period is very deeply embedded in our culture: it was the original month used by early Christians, which is why a religious convocation in Christianity is still called a Synod. Indeed, the lunar month was not legally replaced by the solar calendar month as the official legal definition of a month until as late as 1926. If we count 'Moon days' towards the full Moon from the first appearance of the sliver of the new Moon, the Moon approaches the full on or shortly after the thirteenth day, staying at her highest power through to about the seventeenth day, with the full coming usually on the fifteenth day. A slight complication is that many religions, including Islam, Judaism and Druidism, count a day as the period from dusk to dusk, which therefore straddles the numbers of the solar calendar. There are 13 lunar months in a year, which may also partly explain why the number 13 long ago acquired connotations of propitiousness and good fortune in traditional paganism, directly in contrast to its more recent reputation as an unlucky number. The number of the Moon day constantly changes from 1 to 29, and only occasionally will it happen to coincide exactly with the number of the solar date. If certain numbers are especially propitious or influential in your life, their influence may be felt to be greater on those days. Since childhood, I have been very conscious of the lunar cycle and have always felt greatly affected by it, with the period around the full of the Moon always a busy, happy and propitious time for me and the dark of the Moon frequently a time of difficulty, obstruction and frustration. You might like to try keeping closer track yourself of the phases of the Moon, and seeing whether you notice any correspondences between how you feel and perform in daily life and how the Moon stands.

But not only are we surrounded by numbers which impinge constantly on our daily lives whether we want them to or not, we can also generate or manipulate numbers for deliberate effects or towards specific ends, and this, simple as it is, is a kind of number magic. If we want to introduce more harmony in a love relationship, for example, we flood it with the number 6 – we arrange dinner on the sixth of the month, or the sixth Moon day, we meet at six o'clock for drinks before dinner, perhaps we invite four good friends so that we are six at table.

In this 'everyday' magic, the ancient and well-documented numerological attributes of the first numbers give us a very useful indication of the areas for which they are most appropriate, to promote or enhance the qualities or attributes with which they have long been associated:

1 authority, leadership, independence, material wealth, seclusion, and isolation

2 femininity, sexual attractiveness, fertility, secrecy, sensitivity, tact, tolerance and stillness

3 harmony, fruition, pregnancy and childbirth, family, equilibrium, enlightenment and resurrection

4 discipline, stability, practical skill, domesticity and community service

5 creativity, intuition, radicalism, innovation and spiritual energy

6 harmony, marriage, devotion, orderliness, fidelity, emotional warmth and seaworthiness

7 physical or military strength, self-discipline, sexual attractiveness, global perspective, majesty, spirituality, skill in meditation, and spiritual leadership

8 good fortune, justice, regeneration, motherhood, sense of proportion and equity

9 change, transformation, skill in magic, sexual energy and healing

10 perfection, completion, perseverance, and closure

We can deliberately seek to enhance or promote these qualities in different aspects of our lives by consciously favouring, using, displaying, noticing or otherwise emphasizing the number associated with the attribute we wish to promote. For example, if your life is emotionally chaotic and untidy, with too much time spent in the clouds and not enough on the ground, and with others constantly taking the lead in your relationships with them, you could try actively seeking out the disciplining and tidying influence of 4, and the self–reliance and independence of 1. Consciously create four spaces in which to start tidying your belongings, or divide your chaotic lists of tasks into four headings, or buy four notebooks to separate your confused accounts, and so on. Reduce your sentences, spoken and written, to one idea. Complete tasks one at a time, without exception. Dress in one colour only for any particular day, and so on. To the sceptic, these may seem fairly childish approaches, but, in my experience, if they are undertaken from real need, with a real emotional commitment in good faith, they are often surprisingly successful. This is very simple number magic, but it works.

We cannot actually invoke the numbers by name, as we might invoke gods or spirits: they are too remote and somehow austere, although, as we shall see shortly, it is possible to use visualization very effectively to 'draw down' the power of a number, no matter how abstract. Nevertheless, although the numbers themselves are not thought of as personal intervening deities, they have been associated with certain gods and goddesses in many religious traditions and mythologies. The best known associations are shown in table 7. This, for reasons of space, is only a partial list of associations; angels, archangels, demons and archdemons have been omitted.

Although numbers are not usually called or invoked by name, the gods or goddesses associated with them frequently are. Most religions share similar practices for invoking a deity: singing, sometimes dancing, words or songs of prayer and supplication, hymns of praise, devotional images or icons and ritual liturgies are common to most. The rituals for number magic need not be elaborate; in fact, the simpler they are, the better, generally speaking. One of the great appeals of numerology is that the power of number is very pure, very abstract. A number is at once a very simple thing, something a small child would recognize in many instances, yet, at the same time, it represents an extremely profound and complex concept. The simpler and clearer we can keep whatever liturgical or ritual devices we use to approach the mystery of number, the greater the likelihood that we will achieve success.

Table 7

	Greek	Roman	Celtic	Norse	Other
1	Apollo Hephaestus	Apollo Vesta	Apollo-Belenus	Frey	Pangu (Chinese) Neter (Egyptian) Ptah (Egyptian) Con Ticci (Inca) Jehovah (Judaism) God the Father (Christianity) Allah (Islam)
2	Aphrodite Rhea Ceres	Venus Diana	Rhiannon Branwen	Frigga Loki	Lucifer or Satan (Christianity)
3	Cronos Hecate	Saturn Pluto	Bendigeidfran Brigit Cerridwen	Tyr or Tiw	The Holy Trinity (Christianity)
4	Zeus	Jupiter	Llyr	Odin	
5	Dionysus Cythereia	Mars	Bel or Belinus	Thor	Ishtar (Babylonian)
6	Amphitrite	Sol (the Sun) Bacchus	Medb	Freya	
7	Athena	Minerva	Cu Chulainn Ferghus Fionn	Frigga Iduna	Mithras (Babylonian)
8	Hermes Gaea Hera Cybele	Mercury Cybele or Magna Mater	Oisin Pryderi	Heimdal	
9	Hecate Proserpine Terpsichore	Luna (the Moon) Juno	Gwydion Midhir Merlin	Odin Hella	
10	Uranus Atlas	Coelus	Blodeuwedd	Skuld	
11	Poseidon	Neptune	Manannan mac Lir	Niord	
12	Boreas	Janus	Matholwch	Baldur	
13	Hades	Pluto	Arawn	Uller	

Devotional space, or just thinking space, is an essential prerequisite. If this is a literal geographical place, it can be cleansed and prepared with an offering of flowers, the lighting of a candle, and so on. If it is part of a room, try to keep it as a space apart, however small, which can be kept clear of mundane to and fro traffic. The most amenable outside places are quiet, isolated ones, as most people know by common experience, even if they do not deem themselves to be religious-minded. It is much easier to commune with great powers on a bare hilltop, or by a quiet stream, or at a holy well, or deep within the wild wood, or on a moonlit seashore. It is perfectly possible to maintain prayerful concentration in a crowded train carriage on the 7.29 from Slough to Paddington, but it's just much harder to do.

Fire and water are common to many rituals, pagan and non-pagan, because they have such a wealth of meaning and ancient resonances for humans. They are also very important symbolically for numerologists, since fire represents 1, and water represents 2, and from them come air (3), earth (4), spirit (5), and all the other elements and numbers, all things animal, vegetable, mineral and spiritual, which make up the cosmos. The fire can be a plain candle, and the water just tapwater in a dish (although fresh rain or dew are even better). Exactly how you use the fire and water is up to you. At the very simplest level, you can just put them down somewhere and think about them. Many pagan groups have quite elaborate rituals with fire, including a cleansing incense of smoke from sage and other herbs. It is common to sprinkle water on the ground in offering to the gods or spirits of the chosen place, along with other offerings, perhaps of cornmeal, flower petals or fruit. The native American tradition is to scatter small amounts of tobacco, which is pleasing to the ancestral spirits.

As important as cleansing and preparing your outside space is the cleansing and preparation of your inner space. There are countless traditional ways of doing this in various religions, but some practices are common to many of them. The first is to adopt a particular posture. It may be kneeling on a cassock with the palms of the hand held together, or sitting cross-legged, or kneeling with the forehead touching the ground, or sitting on top of a pole. Whatever it is for you, it ought to be a posture which you associate with contemplative thought or meditation, and not with anything else. It should preferably be comfortable – you may be thinking for a long time. The second common feature is the regulation of breathing, which is actually far more common in the East than in the West, where it is best known through yoga. Quiet, deep and regular breathing promotes a contemplative and meditative state of mind. The third practice is hardly even recognized in the orthodox religions of the West, or at least not in their liturgies, yet it is very common in most other religious traditions: it is the deliberate emptying of the mind of all intruding conscious thoughts or distractions. Most of us in the West are not very skilled at this.

Assuming all preparations have been completed, the simplest way of drawing on the power of a particular number is to attempt to visualize it in the inner mind's eye. We may conjure an image of the number itself, or of the number contained in a set of objects. For example, I always envisage the number 5 as five red apples, the biggest, brightest and crunchiest apples there ever were. It is very common for a colour to present itself along with the number. Associated colours may vary from individual to individual, although some numbers have very strong traditional associations, too – for example, 1 is strongly associated with white in the Kabbalah, where it is sometimes called Risha Havura, 'the White Head'; 7 is traditionally associated with royalty and royal purple; 6 is the colour of the Sun, 9 the colour of the Moon, and so on. Here are my colour associations, most of which are from traditional sources:

1 white or crystal clear, white-hot fire
2 water blue, dark blue
3 living green, plant green
4 earth brown
5 blood red
6 golden, the colour of the Sun
7 royal purple
8 tawny orange
9 silver, the colour of pearls, the colour of the Moon
10 pale blue, the blue of the sky
11 aquamarine, the green-blue of oceans
12 pale yellow
13 black

You may find it helpful to speak the number, perhaps using a letter equivalent, or one of the mystic titles from the sephiroth of the Kabbalah, or a word with the gematria value of the number on which you are calling. If you feel self-conscious trying to make a mantra-like utterance out of a ridiculously commonplace word like 'three' or 'eight', find some other way to express it which feels 'nobler' to you. If you are preoccupied with how mundane what you are saying sounds, you can't be working very effective magic. If in doubt, say nothing at all out loud, but let your relaxed, cleansed and attuned mind do the speaking for you. Personally, I have no difficulty in finding a powerful charge in speaking the ordinary names of numbers, even though I rattle through vast amounts of numbers every day. I vividly remember the hypnotic effect of the repeated, 'Number nine, number nine, number nine ...' when I first heard it on the Beatles' 'White Album' (I think it was) many years ago.

If you are seeking to direct a particular number attribute towards a particular need, try to visualize the two together. For example, if you are seeking creative inspiration for a project, and your number is 5, you should try to visualize the number in the terms of whatever the project is: five shining pens, if you are writing something, five dancing coins for a new commercial idea, five golden staves for a musical composition, five lines or five colours for a painting, and so on. Or, as a second example, suppose you have been wronged by someone and still feel aggrieved and unsettled, to the extent that it is interfering with your contentment. Your number is 8, the number of justice, of proportion and equity. Visualize any object or concept relating to your grievance in a pattern of eight, or in groups of eight, whatever your imagination can handle: eight clean new anchors if someone smashed into your boat, yourself skipping through eight empty and carefree meadows if your ex-husband won't leave you alone, eight bouncing labrador puppies if your boss unreasonably criticizes your lack of productivity – or whatever works in your own imagination to restore a sense of calm, equilibrium and justice within you. This idea sounds extraordinarily simple on paper, and it is, but I know from personal experience that it is also remarkably effective.

Sacred names are important in many traditions, and numerology is predicated on a belief in the power of spoken utterance. Ancient Druids believed that a spoken satire or lampoon could raise real blisters on an enemy, even kill him. The Kabbalah is endlessly rich in variations and permutations through the gematria of sacred names. Your own name has a corresponding number, with factors. Find other names or words with the same total, and see where they lead you. Alternatively, if you are already active in a religion, look at the number correspondences of the names which are sacred to your beliefs. That is exactly what the early Christian hermeneutic scholars did, using numerological attributes which came from the Jews and the pagan Greeks originally.

It sometimes happens that a number presents itself with unusual frequency or persistence. This is particularly true if you are using some of the numerological tools and techniques described in the last chapter, in other words if you are actively pursuing mystic information from number investigation. The ever-present danger of divination is that it can become a terrible crutch for the weak-willed and emotionally vulnerable. Such persons cannot make a move without consulting the oracle, reading the tea-leaves, casting the dodecahedral die. They won't walk down to the corner to buy a newspaper without consulting the magic square first. This is patently silly. If a serious-minded search reveals a particularly strong influence from a certain number, it may well be that we can expect that number to continue to exert a powerful influence, and it would be sensible to be alert to the possibilities implied in that knowledge. But, as in all things, it is important to maintain a proper sense of proportion. The fact that 11 has come up five times in a row on the die doesn't necessarily mean that you will be run down by the first number 11 bus in the street. By the same token, it does not mean that the greyhound in the fourth race at odds of eleven to one is bound to win and make your fortune. Assuming the die is working properly (hand-made dodecahedral dice can sometimes be unbalanced), it certainly looks as though the 11 means something significant, but precisely what the meaning is may take some unravelling. Very often, the meaning becomes clear after the event. You roll 11 five times. A month later you suddenly have to take an unexpected business trip which involves a sea crossing, and you realize that all those elevens were revealing Poseidon or Neptune, although at the time they made no sense.

197

Figure 43 The triskel or trefot

Numbers are used as talismans in many religious traditions, either as numbers in their own right, or in some kind of geometrical representation. The *valknut* is a Norse talisman, comprised of three interlaced triangles. It is dedicated to Odin, and represents sacred 3 times sacred 3, yielding 9, the number of magical transformation. The *triskel* or *trefot* is a variant form, well known as the heraldic device of the Isle of Man (see figure 43).

The Mogen David or Star of David, also based on triangles but effectively representing 6 rather than 3 or 9, was mentioned earlier (see page 66).

One of the most powerful and ancient talismans of 4, the sun-wheel or swastika, also known in the northern tradition as the *fylfot*, has been irretrievably tainted by Hitler's appropriation of it as a symbol of Nazism. There many different versions of four-point crosses, both vertical-horizontal and diagonal. The cross of the Crucifixion is now almost universally depicted as a four-point, vertical-horizontal cross, but the actual historical cross was probably T-shaped, exactly like the letters Tav in Hebrew and Tau in Greek, both of which mean 'cross'.

5 and 7 are rare as the number base of talismans, but 8 – a double cross – is quite common. 7 is the base number of a very ancient talisman and symbol of fertility and regeneration, the classical labyrinth. (There is also a version based on 11.) I first saw this pattern carved in the rocks of Rocky Valley near Tintagel in Cornwall. It may be more than 3,000 years old, and it is found not only in Cornwall, but in Ireland and all across Europe.

Both the swastika, which is a figure of 4, and the labyrinth, which is a figure of 7 or 11, begin with a pattern of 9, the most powerful number of magical transformation. It is sometimes said that the swastika or fylfot represents the Sun, the male, while the labyrinth represents the Moon, the female. Each figure can be drawn beginning with 9 dots. The swastika connects the dots in the most obvious, immediate way, using straight lines; the labyrinth connects the dots in the most indirect way, using spaces and curves (see figure 44).

By tradition, particularly in the North, talismans should be drawn or constructed during the waxing of the Moon, and the power of the number in them should be formally invoked and asked for protection. The Northern tradition is for the talisman to be actually or symbolically buried – wrapped in black cloth or put in a box, for example – and for the deity or number power to be invoked before the talisman is brought

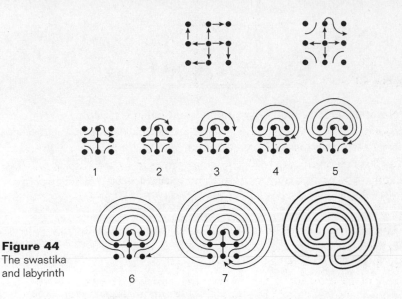

Figure 44
The swastika
and labyrinth

back into the light of day (see note 4). Tools and talismans are often given sacred names to personalize and centralize their power – Arthur's sword Excalibur, the name of which is derived from Celtic Kalespolgh, meaning 'Hard Handle', is a famous example. The talisman should be passed through or over a candle flame or brazier three times, invoking the eponymous powers or deities, then sprinkled with water as the name itself is given. Sacred places are also cleansed with fire or smoke and with water, and salt is also frequently used. Number talismans can be placed directly on to buildings, usually above or beside the main entrance way. 6, the number of harmony, is very commonly used as the basis for protective talismans for homes and farm buildings, most notably in the hexagonal talismans in the Germanic tradition which are frequently to be seen in rural communities, especially in New England and in Pennsylvania. In classical times, magic squares (see pages 87 to 92) were commonly used to protect buildings and their occupants.

The greatest number magic anyone can perform is simply to remain in awe of the true meaning of every number, no matter how plain or commonplace it may be. I hope that sceptics who have completed the journey from beginning to end of this book have enjoyed the scenery on the way, and I repeat that I have no wish to proselytize or convert anybody to my way of thinking. But numerology has a long and honourable tradition – sadly ignored by many modern numerologists – and, for me, what is revealed in that tradition is a glorious reassurance: there is a divine will at work in the universe, metaphysical and metatemporal, ineffable, whose sacred names are many, but whose presence and influence is eternally observable in the austere purity and beauty of numbers.

CHAPTER NOTES

Chapter One
1 Needham, J. *Science and Civilization in China.*
2 *National Geographic*, vol. 186, no. 4, October 1994, pp. 80–103.
3 McLeish, John *Number*, p.10.
4 ibid., p. 247.
5 Russell, Bertrand *History of Western Philosophy.*
6 ibid.
7 Wells, David *The Penguin Dictionary of Curious and Interesting Numbers.*
8 ibid.

Chapter Two
1 Gagliardo, A. and Divac, I. 'Effects of ablation of the presumed equivalent of the mammalian prefontal cortex on pigeon homing' in *Behavioral-Neuroscience*, April 1993, vol. 107, part 2, pp. 280–8.
2 Bingman, V.P., Ioale, P., Casini, G. and Bagnoli, P. 'The avian hippocampus Evidence for a role in the development of the homing pigeon navigational map' in *Behavioral-Neuroscience*, December 1990, vol. 104, part 6, pp. 906–11.
3 Collett, T.S. and Baron, J. 'Biological compasses and the co-ordinate frame of landmark memories in honey-bees' in *Nature*, March 1994, vol. 368 (6467), pp. 137–140.
4 Dyer, F.C. 'Nocturnal orientation by the Asian honey-bee, *Apis dorsata*' in *Animal Behaviour*, August 1985, vol, 33, part 3, pp. 769–74.
5 Pontecorvo, C. 'Figure, parole, numeri: un problem di simbolizzazione' (Pictures, words, and numbers a problem of symbolization) in *Eta Evolutiva*, October 1985, no. 22 pp. 5–33.
6 Heller, M.A., Rogers, G.J. and Perry, C.L. 'Tactile pattern recognition with the Optacon Superior performance with active touch and the left hand' in *Neuropsychologia*, 1990, vol. 28, part 9, pp. 1003–6.
7 By Oliver Sacks, 9 January 1995.
8 Menninger, K. *Number Words and Number Symbols.*
9 Dixon, R. M.W. *The Languages of Australia.*
10 Crump, Thomas *The Anthropology of Numbers.*
11 e-mail address is: superseeker@research.att.com, reported in *Newsweek*, 9 January 1995.
12 Wells, David *The Penguin Dictionary of Curious and Interesting Numbers*, pp. 65–6.
13 Rosten, Leo *The Joys of Yiddish.*
14 In particular, Cunningham, Scott *Cunningham's Encyclopedia of Crystal, Gem & Metal Magic.*
15 In Adams, D. *The Hitchhiker's Guide to the Galaxy.*
16 The fractal fern in figure 16 was drawn using a Macintosh program called Fractal Attraction, by Kevin D. Lee and Yosef Cohen.
17 Keith Devlin, *Mathematics: The New Golden Age*, pp. 36–48.

Chapter Three
1 Schimmel, Anne-Marie *The Mystery of Numbers*, p. 7.
2 Quoted in Wells, David *The Penguin Dictionary of Curious and Interesting Numbers*, p. 30.
3 Radford, Tim report in the *Guardian Weekly*, 15 November 1994.
4 Tyson, Donald (ed.) and Freake, James (trans.) *Three Books of Occult Philosophy by Henry Cornelius Agrippa of Nettesheim* – a very thorough edition, highly recommended.
5 ibid.
6 ibid.
7 Schimmel op. cit., p. 94.
8 Wells op. cit., p. 60.
9 Rosenberg, Donna *World Mythology*, pp. 488–94.
10 Tyson and Freake op. cit., p. 265.
11 See the author's *The Celtic Druids' Year*, p. 186.
12 ibid., pp. 193–224.
13 Wells op. cit., p. 71.
14 Tyson and Freake op. cit., p. 268.
15 Schimmel op. cit., p. 174.

Chapter Four

1 Ulam, Stanislaw *Adventures of a Mathematician*.
2 Hulse, David Allen *The Key of It All*, pp. liv–viii.
3 *The Penguin Dictionary of Curious and Interesting Numbers*, p. 24.

Chapter Five

1 Waite, A. E. *The Holy Kabbalah*, p. 5.
2 Scholem, Gershom G. *On the Kabbalah and Its Symbolism*, p. 1.
3 Gonzalez-Wippler, Migene *A Kabbalah for the Modern World*, p. 1.
4 Scholem op. cit., p. 30.
5 Pennick, Nigel *Magical Alphabets*, p. 16.
6 ibid., p. 17.
7 *The Penguin Dictionary of Curious and Interesting Numbers*, p. 82.
8 Gonzalez-Wippler op. cit., p. 50.
9 Henry Cornelius Agrippa of Nettesheim, *Three Books of Occult Philosophy*, ed. Donald Tyson. Tyson takes these attributions in turn from S.L. MacGregor Mathers's translation of Knorr von Rosenroth's *Kabbalah Unveiled*, 1887 and 1962.
10 *The Key of It All*, pp. 321–34.

Chapter Six

1 Graves, Robert *The White Goddess*, p. 345, footnote.
2 *The Key of It All*, Book 2, p. 19.
3 *Magical Alphabets*, p. 57.
4 For the Nordic runes, I particularly recommend Nigel Pennick's *Practical Magic in the Northern Tradition* and *Runic Astrology*; Freya Aswynn's *Leaves of Yggdrasil*; and Edred Thorsson's *Northern Magic*. For Ogham and various related British topics, I recommend Robert Graves's *The White Goddess*; Caitlin Matthews's *Mabon and the Mysteries of Britain*; and John Matthews's *Taliesin*.
5 *Magical Alphabets*, p. 93.
6 *Northern Magic*, p. 59.
7 *The Key of It All*, Book 2, pp. 86–7.
8 These reconstructions are included in a fascinating and very thorough description of all the English systems in *The Key of It All*, Book 2, pp. 461–538.

Chapter Seven

1 I intend no general disparagement of astrology. Of the astrology books I have read, the most impressive, in my view, is Linda Goodman's very popular *Sun Signs*.

Chapter Ten

1 The first part of the quotation is from *Cunningham's Encyclopedia of Crystal, Gem & Metal Magic*, p. 5. The second part is from *Cunningham's Encyclopedia of Magical Herbs*, p. 4.
2 These quotations are all taken from *Cunningham's Encyclopedia of Crystal, Gem & Metal Magic*, p. 7.
3 Adapted from Nigel Pennick's *Practical Magic in the Northern Tradition*, p. 53.
4 ibid., pp. 211–27.

Appendix One

ENGLISH ALPHABET
GEMATRIA
(The Author's System)

A = 1
B = 2
C, CH = 20 (as in castle or character)
C = 60 (as in cement or police)
CH = 8 (as in church)
CH = 600 (as in Scottish loch, or German Bach)
D = 4
E = 5
F = 500
G = 3 (as in garden)
G, GE = 12 (as in Giovanni or George)
GH = 8 (silent, as in night)
H = 5 (as in hat)
H = 8 (silent)
I = 10
ING = 22
J = 12
K = 20
L = 30
M = 40
N = 50

O = 70 (as in hot)
O, OO = 800 (as in rose or good)
P = 80
PH = 500
Q, QU = 100
R = 200
S = 60 (as in snake)
S = 7 (as in rose)
SH = 300
S = 15 (as in pleasure)
T = 9
TH = 9 (as in thin)
TH = 400 (as in this)
TION = 350
U = V = 6
W = 800
X = 80
X = 600 (in some foreign words)
Y = 10 (as in happy or dysentery)
Y = 12 (as in yellow)
Z = 7

Appendix Two

ENGLISH ALPHABET
GEMATRIA REVERSED
(The Author's System)

1 = A

2 = B

3 = G as in *g*arden

4 = D

5 = E as in m*e*n, silent E as in bon*e*, aspirate H as in *h*at

6 = U, V

7 = Z, voiced S as in ro*s*e

8 = CH as in *ch*urch, silent H as in o*h*m, silent GH as in ni*gh*t

9 = T, unvoiced TH as in *th*in

10 = I, final Y as in happ*y*, Y as a vowel

12 = J, Y as in *y*ellow

15 = S as in plea*s*ure

20 = K, C as in *c*at, CH as in *ch*aracter

22 = -ING

30 = L

40 = M

50 = N

60 = S, C as in *c*ement

70 = O as in h*o*t

80 = P

90 = (TZ not found in English)

100 = Q, QU

200 = R

300 = SH

350 = -TION

400 = TH as in *th*is

500 = F, PH

600 = CH as in lo*ch*

800 = O as in r*o*se, OO as in w*oo*d, OU as in c*ou*ld, W as in *w*et

Appendix Three

BRIEF SUMMARY OF
NUMBER ATTRIBUTES 1 TO 10

Number Attributes

1 Gematria A; Hebrew *Aleph* means ox, cattle, wealth; *Kether*, the Crown, the head, in the Tree of Life; Greek *Alpha* means cattle, wealth; Celtic or Ogham is *Ailm*, meaning silver fir, tree of birth; ego; F_1 and F_2 in the Fibonacci series; the monad; the prime cause or *primum mobile*; the point of one dimension; now; fire, Vesta, the great White Flame, the burning bush which Moses saw; Kronos; Apollo; Atlas; the one God; the first Being; the egg of creation, the world egg; Neter; Lord Con Ticci Viracocha; Azoth; the philosopher's stone; independence; creativity; androgyny and hermaphroditism; authority; leadership; material wealth; seclusion.

2 Gematria B; Hebrew *Beth* means house, family, bloodline; *Chokmah* or Wisdom in the Tree of Life; Greek *Beta*; F_3 in the Fibonacci series; Ceres; Diana; Rhea; Aphrodite; Venus, sexual attractiveness and arousal; natural opposites; *yin* and *yang*; discord, disharmony; the anti-Christ; the female; sensitivity; tact, diplomacy; tolerance; the descent of spirit into matter; the silent and secret; the sleeping princess.

3 Gematria G; Hebrew *Gimel* means camel, all nature, living creatures; *Binah* or Intelligence in the Tree of Life; Greek *Gamma*; F_4 in the Fibonacci series; the first Pythagorean number (male); first of Pythagorean triple 3-4-5; Saturn; lead; Pluto; Gaea, the Earth; Hecate; Cerridwen, Brigid, Rhiannon; the Triple Goddess; Isis, Osiris and Horus; Brahma, Shiva and Vishnu; the three Moiras of Greece, three Norns; fate; the Christian Trinity; the primary colours; fertility, creativity; generation and regeneration; pregnancy; youth; completeness; fulfilment, success; resurrection from death; enlightenment.

4 Gematria D; Hebrew *Daleth* means tent-flap or door, figuratively authority; *Chesed* or Love in the Tree of Life;

Greek *Delta* also means triangle; Jupiter; tin; four elements, earth, air, fire and water; Bacchus; Mercury; order: four winds, four compass points, watchtowers; Michael, Raphael, Gabriel and Uriel; the guardian beasts; a blue star; four rivers in paradise; stability; discipline; practicality, homeliness; the real world, the mundane; directness; patriotism; community service; loving protection; dedication.

5   Gematria E, H; *Geburah* or Strength in the Tree of Life; Greek *Epsilon;* F_5 in the Fibonacci series; the Pythagorean number of marriage; first of Pythagorean triple 5-12-13; Venus, or Ishtar, and Mars; iron; the pentagram; the Platonic solids; the Celtic life-cycle of vowels; the five worlds of the Navaho; five senses; the five Sikh holy possessions; the quintessence; spirit resurrected from the flesh; Christ before Thomas and at the Ascension; Venus rising from the waves; curiosity, impulsivity, restlessness; radicalism; spiritual energy.

6   Gematria U, V; the first perfect number; Hebrew *Vau* means peg or nail, figuratively associated with the sea and fertility; *Tiphareth* or Beauty in the Tree of Life; the Mogen David; marriage in Pythagorean system; the Sun; gold; Zeus, Jupiter; Amphitrite, the ocean; the day of man's creation and Christ's suffering; red flowers; wine and intoxication; the Eucharist; marriage, harmony; devotion; orderliness; tolerance; public service; seaworthiness and protection from storm.

7   Gematria Z, S; Hebrew *Zayin* means spear or weapon, figuratively material possessions, religious authority; *Netzach* or Victory in the Tree of Life; Greek *Zeta* means offering; first of Pythagorean triple 7-24-25; Venus; copper; the Celtic demigod or warrior-hero; military or physical prowess; Apollo and Athena, wisdom, sexual attractiveness, charisma; royalty; the seven gates of Mithras; seven levels of Purgatory; end of sequence, cusp, time for change; seven ages of human life; spirituality, meditation, spiritual leadership; intuition; global persepective, transcendentalism; aloofness.

8   Gematria CH, H (silent); Hebrew *Cheth* means enclosure, figuratively barrier of discrimination; *Hod* or Splendour in the Tree of Life; F_6 in the Fibonacci series; eight regions of three-dimensional space; Gaea, the Earth, as Great Mother; Cybele; the Magna Mater; Mercury; quicksilver; paradise;

fecundity, motherhood; prosperity, good fortune; proportion; divine and secular law, divine and secular justice; great trees, forests; crystal.

9   Gematria T, TH; Hebrew *Teth* means serpent, figuratively energy, particularly sexual energy; *Yesod* or Foundation in the Tree of Life; first of Pythagorean triple 9-40-41; the Square of Saturn; the Moon; silver; the energy of the universe, the divine will; high magic, invocation, making and loosening barriers, magical change; Myrddyn (Merlin); prayer; healing; incompleteness, long waiting; patience, compassion, selflessness; melancholia; the green of the ocean; dragons.

10   Gematria I; Hebrew *Yod* means hand, frequently hand of God, destiny; *Malkuth* or Kingdom in the Tree of Life; Greek *Iota;* Pythagorean number of perfection; the tetraktys; Uranus; uranium; completion, fulfilment; the entire creation; salvation; eternity; saintliness; perfection; closure.

Appendix Four

BRIEF SUMMARY OF NUMBER ATTRIBUTES, SELECTED NON-INTEGERS AND NUMBERS ABOVE 10

$\sqrt{-1}$	i
1.41421...	The square root of 2, the bane of the Pythagoreans.
1.61803...	ϕ, the Divine Proportion or Golden Ratio
2.71828...	e
3.141592....	π

11 Poseidon or Neptune, the sea; the first repunit; the number of dimensions in current number theory; begins the Pythagorean triple 11-60-61; the Fool in the Tarot; holly.

12 J, Y; used as a counting system base, still used for time; 12 months in a year; 12 tribes of Israel in the Old Testament; 12 Apostles in the New Testament; begins the Pythagorean triple 12-35-37; the Magician in the Tarot; oak.

13 F_7 in the Fibonacci series; the second emirp; begins the Pythagorean triple 13-84-85; considered unlucky in the West, associated with Hades and Pluto in classical mythology, and with Judas Iscariot in Christianity; a lucky and propitious number in the Hebrew Kabbalah; considered powerful and propitious by many modern numerologists; Richard Wagner's dominant personal number; the High Priestess in the Tarot; the ash tree; fear of 13 is triskaidekaphobia.

14 The Empress in the Tarot; rowan or mountain-ash.

15 S (ZH); the Emperor in the Tarot; elder.

16 Begins the Pythagorean triple 16-63-65; one of only two numbers which can simultaneously represent the perimeter and area of a rectangle, the other is 18; the Hierophant in the Tarot.

17 The third emirp; considered unlucky by the Pythagoreans; the Lovers in the Tarot.

18 The Chariot in the Tarot.

19 The number of the Great Year which reconciles solar and lunar calendars; Strength in the Tarot.

20 K, hard C; Hebrew Caph; the palm of the hand; healing energy; life and death; the base of many counting systems; begins the Pythagorean triple 20-21-29; the Hermit in the Tarot.

21 F_8 in the Fibonacci series; the Wheel of Fortune in the Tarot.

22 -ING; goddess and god of hearth and home; Justice in the Tarot.

23 The Hanged Man in the Tarot.

24 Factorial 4; the number of hours in a day; Death in the Tarot.

25 Temperance in the Tarot.

26 The Devil in the Tarot.

27 The Tower in the Tarot.

28 The second perfect number; begins the Pythagorean triple 28-45-53; the number of days in a month in a 13-month year; the length of the menstrual cycle; Tolstoy's dominant personal number; the Star in the Tarot.

29 Twin prime with 31; the Moon in the Tarot.

29.5 Approximately the number of days in the lunar synodic period or lunar month.

30 L; Hebrew Lamed; ox-goad; progress; self-sacrifice; work; the Sun in the Tarot.

31 Twin prime with 29; the fourth emirp; the fourth Mersenne prime; El, the Mighty One; Judgment in the Tarot.

32 The World in the Tarot.

33 The age to which Christ lived; the age of the mahatma or spiritual leader; begins the Pythagorean triple 33-56-65.

36 Eloh, the Almighty; the magical number of protection at sea, since it is 6 times 6; begins the Pythagorean triple 36-77-85.

37 The fifth emirp.

39 Highly propitious, being the 3 or completion of potent 13; begins the Pythagorean triple 39-80-89.

40 M; Hebrew Mem; water; in Christianity, the number of days in the Flood, of years spent by the Israelites in the wilderness and of Christ's days and nights in the wilderness.

41 Twin prime with 43; the first number in Ulam's Big Doodle.

43 Twin prime with 41.

45 The second Kaprekar number; the sum of the square of Saturn.

46 Shakespeare's name revealed in the forty-sixth words, counting first forwards from the beginning, then backwards from the end, of Psalm 46.

48   Begins the Pythagorean triple 48-55-73.

50   N; hebrew Nun; fish; movement; new beginnings.

55   The third Kaprekar number.

59   Twin prime with 61.

60   S, soft C, X; Hebrew Samekh; prop, support; charity; anger; used as a counting system base, especially for time and degrees.

61   Twin prime with 59.

65   Adonai, Lord; begins the Pythagorean triple 65-72-97.

67   Ghandi.

70   O (short); Hebrew Ayin; eye; vision; merriment; the first weird number.

71   Twin prime with 73; the sixth emirp.

73   Twin prime with 71; the seventh emirp.

79   The eighth emirp.

80   P; Hebrew Pe; mouth; immortality; power and servitude.

86   Elohim, the Lord.

90   (TZ); Hebrew Tzaddi; fish hook; necessary opposites; imagination; womanhood.

97   The ninth emirp.

99   The fourth Kaprekar number.

100   Q, QU; Hebrew Qoph; the back of the head; intuition; inspiration; sleep; the perfection of perfection.

101   Twin prime with 103; the tenth emirp.

103   Twin prime with 101.

107   Twin prime with 109.

109   Twin prime with 107.

111   Klax, a key; home; bloodline.

127   The fifth Mersenne prime.

136   The sum of the square of Jupiter.

137   Twin prime with 139.

139   Twin prime with 137.

149   Twin prime with 151.

151   Twin prime with 149.

153   The number of fish caught in Simon Peter's net, revered by St Augustine.

157   Beethoven.

170   Amen, let it be so.

179   Twin prime with 181.

181   Twin prime with 179.

191   Twin prime with 193.

193   Twin prime with 191.

197   Twin prime with 199.

199   Einstein; twin prime with 197.

200   R; Hebrew Resh; head; the persona; identity; peace and war.

216 The smallest cube which is the sum of three cubes ($3^3 + 4^3 + 5^3$); Plato's 'number of a human creature'.

220 The amicable pair of 284.

222 Nazarene, Jesus of Nazareth.

227 Twin prime with 229.

229 Twin prime with 227.

239 Twin prime with 241.

241 Twin prime with 239.

259 Hitler.

269 Twin prime with 271.

271 Twin prime with 269.

281 Twin prime with 283.

283 Twin prime with 281.

284 The amicable pair of 220.

287 Caesar.

297 Elohim Gabor, the Lord of Battles; the fifth Kaprekar number.

300 SH; Hebrew Shin; tooth; transformation, great change.

311 Twin prime with 313.

313 Twin prime with 311.

314 Shaddai, the Almighty.

325 The sum of the square of Mars.

333 Kaisara, Caesar.

347 Twin prime with 349.

349 Twin prime with 347.

350 -TION

354 The original number of days in the Babylonian calendar.

356 Napoleon.

358 Iba Shilh, until Shiloh come; Mshich, the Messiah; Nachash, the brazen serpent of Moses.

360 The original number of days in the Egyptian solar year; the number of degrees in a circle, seconds in an hour.

361 Adonai He-Aretz, Lord of Earth.

365.25 An approximation to the number of days in a year.

400 TH (voiced); Hebrew Tav; the phallus; the sign of the cross; the Egyptian ankh; eternal life; riches and poverty.

419 Twin prime with 421.

420 Zeses, may you live; Isis.

421 Twin prime with 419.

431 Twin prime with 433.

433 Twin prime with 431.

444 Sarx Kai Aima, flesh and blood; the material world.

454 Eloah Va-Daath, God Manifest.

461 Twin prime with 463.

463 Twin prime with 461.

496 The third perfect number.

500 F, PH

521 Twin prime with 523.

523 Twin prime with 521.

525 Jehovah Sabaoth, God of Hosts.

555 Drakonti, the Dragon; Satan.

569 Twin prime with 571.

571 Twin prime with 569.

585 Elohim Sabaoth, Lord of Hosts.

599 Twin prime with 601.

600 CH (guttural); the perfect perfection of harmony.

601 Twin prime with 599.

610 Kosmos, the Cosmos; Ho Theotes, the Godhead.

617 Twin prime with 619.

619 Twin prime with 617.

641 Twin prime with 643.

643 Twin prime with 641.

659 Twin prime with 661.

661 Twin prime with 659.

666 The infamous number of the Beast; the sum of the square
     of the Sun; Logos Agapes, the Word of Love.

677 Shakespeare.

700 Pneuma Agion, Holy Spirit.

703 The sixth Kaprekar number.

711 Myrddyn (Merlin).

729 Plato's number for how much happier a king is than a
     tyrant: the sum of 364 and 365.

777 Stavros, the Holy Cross.

784 John F. Kennedy.

800 O (long), W

808 Iesou Rabbi, Rabbi Jesus.

809 Twin prime with 811.

811 Twin prime with 809.

821 Twin prime with 823.

823 Twin prime with 821.

827 Twin prime with 829.

829 Twin prime with 827.

836 The second weird number.

849 Kyrios, Lord.

857 Twin prime with 859.

859 Twin prime with 857.

881 Twin prime with 883.

883 Twin prime with 881.

888 Iesous, Jesus.

911 The telephone emergency number in the United States.

913 Berashith, In the beginning.

999 The seventh Kaprekar number; the telephone emergency number in the United Kingdom; Theos Aneklaltos, the ineffable God.

1,184 The amicable pair of 1,210.

1,201 The amicable pair of 1,184.

1,225 The sum of the square of Venus.

1,271 Stavros (in the Greek system), the Cross; 'E Gnosis, the knowledge of God.

1,480 Xristos, Christ.

1,583 Michelangelo.

2,080 The sum of the square of Mercury.

2,223 The eighth Kaprekar number.

2,368 Iesous Xristos, Jesus Christ.

2,620 The amicable pair of 2,924.

2,728 The ninth Kaprekar number.

2,924 The amicable pair of 2,620.

3,321 The sum of the square of the Moon.

3,999 The sum of the whole person in the Soma Sophia.

4,030 The third weird number.

5,020 The amicable pair of 5,564.

5,040 Plato's ideal number of inhabitants in a city, since it can be divided by any number from 1 to 10.

5,564 The amicable pair of 5,020.

5,830 The fourth weird number.

6,232 The amicable pair of 6,368.

6,368 The amicable pair of 6,232.

7,192 The fifth weird number.

7,272 The tenth Kaprekar number.

7,777 The eleventh Kaprekar number.

8,128 The fourth perfect number.

10,744 The amicable pair of 10,856.

10,856 The amicable pair of 10,744.

12,285 The amicable pair of 14,595.

14,595 The amicable pair of 12,285.

17,296 The amicable pair of 18,416.

18,416 The amicable pair of 17,296.

63,020 The amicable pair of 76,084.

76,084 The amicable pair of 63,020.

66,928 The amicable pair of 66,992.

66,992 The amicable pair of 66,928.

142,857 A famous puzzle number, since multiplying by 2, 3, 4, 5 and 6 merely rearranges the digits.

12,960,000	A Platonic number, the product of 216 and 60,000, perhaps representing a Great Year.
33,550,336	The fifth perfect number.
1,234,567,891	Prime.
8,589,869,056	The sixth perfect number.
137,438,691,328	The seventh perfect number.
2,305,843,008,139,952,128	The eighth perfect number.
12,345,678,901,234,567,891	Prime.
18,446,744,073,709,551,615	The number of grains on the sixty-fourth square of a chessboard if you begin by placing one grain on the first square, two on the second, four on the third, and so on.
1,234,567,891,234,567,891,234,567,891	Prime.
2,235,197,406,895,366,368,301,560,000	The odds against 1 that all four Bridge players will receive a complete suit of cards in a single deal.
$2^{756,839} - 1$	The highest prime yet discovered.
1 googol	10^{100}
1 googolplex	10^{googol}

Appendix Five

PRIME NUMBERS 2 TO 997

2	3	5	7	11	13	17	19	23	29	31	37
41	43	47	53	59	61	67	71	73	79	83	89
97	101	103	107	109	113	127	131	137	139	149	151
157	163	167	173	179	181	191	193	197	199	211	223
227	229	233	239	241	251	257	263	269	271	277	281
283	293	307	311	313	317	331	337	347	349	353	359
367	373	379	383	389	397	401	409	419	421	431	433
439	443	449	457	461	463	467	479	487	491	499	503
509	521	523	541	547	557	563	569	571	577	587	593
599	601	607	613	617	619	631	641	643	647	653	659
661	673	677	683	691	701	709	719	727	733	739	743
751	757	761	769	773	787	797	809	811	821	823	827
829	839	853	857	859	863	877	881	883	887	907	911
919	929	937	941	947	953	967	971	977	983	991	997

Appendix Six

EUCLID'S
GEOMETRIC DEMONSTRATION
OF IRRATIONALS

The demonstration, found in Book X of Euclid, runs:

Suppose each of the equal sides of a right-angled isosceles triangle to be 1 unit long.

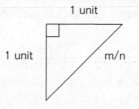

Let the fraction representing the length of the hypotenuse be expressed as m/n.

By Pythagoras's Theorem, $m^2/n^2 = 2$. If m and n have a common factor, divide it out, then either m or n must be odd. But $m^2 = 2n^2$, meaning that m must be even, which means that n must be odd. However, suppose $m = 2p$. Then $4p^2 = 2n^2$, therefore $n^2 = 2p^2$, therefore n must be even, *contra hyp*. Therefore, there is no fraction m/n, for which m and n are both integers, which will measure the hypotenuse. Russell assumes that this proof was known to Plato.

Appendix Seven

THE BINOMIAL THEOREM

The binomial theorem, discovered by Newton when he was still in his twenties, reveals the expansion of $(x + y)^n$, where n is a whole number and x and y are two unknown numbers.

If $n = 2$, the expansion is $x^2 + 2xy + y^2$ (the product of $(x + y)$ multiplied by itself). If $n = 3$, the expansion is $x^3 + 3x^2y + 3xy^2 + y^3$ (the product of $(x + y)(x + y)(x + y)$.

Newton's observation was that a pattern is revealed in the coefficients of successive terms. Suppose, for example, we begin the expansion of $(x + y)^{10}$. The first term will be x^{10}, which has a coefficient of 1. (The term coefficient refers to the constant qualifying the variable: for example, the coefficient of $5x$ is 5, the coefficient of $13y$ is 13, and so on.) The second term, x^9y, has a coefficient of 10. The third term, x^8y^2, has a coefficient of 45. The full expansion of $(x + y)^{10}$, therefore, would begin $x^{10} + 10x^9y + 45x^8y^2$ ....

The pattern of the coefficients can be explained as follows:

The coefficient of x^{10} is given by:

$$\frac{10 \times 9 \times 8 \times 7 \times 6 \times 5 \times 4 \times 3 \times 2 \times 1}{1 \times 2 \times 3 \times 4 \times 5 \times 6 \times 7 \times 8 \times 9 \times 10} = 1 \text{ (by cancelling)}$$

If we repeat the fraction, but leave off the two numbers at the end, we arrive at the coefiicient of the second term:

$$\frac{10 \times 9 \times 8 \times 7 \times 6 \times 5 \times 4 \times 3 \times 2}{1 \times 2 \times 3 \times 4 \times 5 \times 6 \times 7 \times 8 \times 9} = 10$$

If we repeat this fraction, and again leave off the two numbers at the end, we arrive at the coefiicient of the third term:

$$\frac{10 \times 9 \times 8 \times 7 \times 6 \times 5 \times 4 \times 3}{1 \times 2 \times 3 \times 4 \times 5 \times 6 \times 7 \times 8} = 45$$

The number of terms in the denominator (the bottom line of the division) is the same as the exponent of x. So, if we want to know the coefficient of the term x^6y^4, we write the division as:

$$\frac{10 \times 9 \times 8 \times 7 \times 6 \times 5}{1 \times 2 \times 3 \times 4 \times 5 \times 6} = 210$$

Using this method, we can rapidly arrive at the full expansion of $(x + y)^{10}$:-

$(x + y)^{10} = x^{10} + 10x^9y + 45x^8y^2 + 120x^7y^3 + 210x^6y^4 + 252x^5y^5 + 210x^4y^6 + 120x^3y^7 + 45x^2y^8 + 10xy^9 + y^{10}$

Appendix Eight

DIFFERENTIAL AND INTEGRAL CALCULUS

Calculus is the branch of mathematics which deals with problems involving variable quantities, hence Newton's original name of 'fluxions'. Such problems arise frequently in the sciences. A typical example of the kind of problem involving calculus would be that of water being supplied at a constant rate filling an inverted cone. At first, the level of the water would rise very rapidly, but, as the cone grows wider, so the rate of rise in the water level slows down. Calculus is used to describe the relationship between the two rates, the constant rate of the water flow and the varying rate of the rise in water level in the cone.

The essential concept, as described in the text, is the idea of a *function*, in which a consistent relationship between two sets is described. Functions can be graphed, and their graphs may be straight or curved, *linear* or *non-linear*.

A simple example of a linear equation would be the graph of $f(x) = x + 2$, which produces a straight line rather like this:

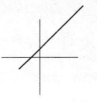

A simple example of a non-linear equation would be the graph of $f(x) = x^?$, which produces a curve rather like this:

The *differential calculus* deals with the relationships between straight lines (specifically tangents) and curves. It allows us to draw a straight line as a tangent to any given curve. This is related to problems concerning rates of change in quantities.

The *integral calculus* deals with areas enclosed by curves, with the lengths of curves, or with volumes contained within curved surfaces. It is used for determining variable quantities when rates of change are known. The most obvious practical example is the behaviour of objects subject to gravity, for example, a ball dropped from a high window. We need to use integral calculus to fully describe the gravitational effects exerted by celestial bodies on each other. Newton's work on the laws of gravity and his work on calculus are, therefore, closely related to each other.

Appendix Nine

VERHULST'S FORMULA

Let the maximum possible population be X, and the constant growth rate r. As the population approaches X, r approaches 0.

Let the variable growth rate be represented as $r - cx_n$, where c is some constant. When $x_n = X$, the population growth rate will be zero, and the value of the constant will have to be r/X. The process can thus be represented by the formula:

$$x_{n+1} = f(x_n) = (1 + r - cx_n)x_n = (1 + r)x_n - cx_n^2.$$

Once the maximum population has been reached, $f(X) = X$.

Appendix Ten

FIGURATE NUMBER FORMULAS

Shape	1st	2nd	3rd	4th	5th	nth
Triangular	1	3	6	10	15	$\dfrac{n^2 + n}{2}$
Square	1	4	9	16	25	n^2
Pentagonal	1	5	12	22	35	$\dfrac{3n^2 - n}{2}$
Hexagonal	1	6	15	28	45	$2n^2 - n$
Heptagonal	1	7	18	34	55	$\dfrac{5n^2 - 3n}{2}$
Octagonal	1	8	21	40	65	$3n^2 - 2n$
Nonagonal	1	9	24	46	75	$\dfrac{7n^2 - 5n}{2}$
Cubic	1	8	27	64	125	n^3
Tetrahedral	1	4	10	20	35	$\dfrac{n^3 + 3n^2 + 2n}{6}$

Appendix Eleven

BINARY CONVERSION TABLE

Decimal	Binary	Decimal	Binary
1	1	31	11111
2	10	32	100000
3	11	33	100001
4	100	34	100010
5	101	35	100011
6	110	36	100100
7	111	37	100101
8	1000	38	100110
9	1001	39	100111
10	1010	40	101000
11	1011	41	101001
12	1100	42	101010
13	1101	43	101011
14	1110	44	101100
15	1111	45	101101
16	10000	46	101110
17	10001	47	101111
18	10010	48	110000
19	10011	49	110001
20	10100	50	110010
21	10101	51	110011
22	10110	52	110100
23	10111	53	110101
24	11000	54	110110
25	11001	55	110111
26	11010	56	111000
27	11011	57	111001
28	11100	58	111010
29	11101	59	111011
30	11110	60	111100

BIBLIOGRAPHY

Mathematics and Numerology

Abbott, Edwin A. *Flatland: A Romance of Many Dimensions*, London and New York: Seeley & Co, 1884, and Dover, 1952 and 1992

Abdelnoor, R.E. Jason *A Mathematical Dictionary*, Leeds: E.J. Arnold & Son, 1979

Asimov, Isaac *Realm of Numbers*, Boston: Houghton Mifflin, 1959

Bell, Eric Temple *The Magic of Numbers*, New York: Dover, 1946, copyright renewed 1974

Crump, Thomas *The Anthropology of Numbers*, Cambridge: Cambridge University Press, 1990

Davis, Philip J. and Hersh, Reuben *The Mathematical Experience*, Boston: Houghton Mifflin, 1981

Devlin, Keith *Mathematics: The New Golden Age*, London: Penguin, 1988

Dunham, William *Journey Through Genius: the Great Theorems of Mathematics*, New York: John Wiley & Sons, 1990

Gardner, Martin *Mathematics, Magic and Mystery*, New York: Dover, 1956

Gauquelin, Miche *Birth Times: A Scientific Investigation of the Secrets of Astrology*, New York: Hill and Wang, 1983

Graubard, Mark *Astrology and Alchemy: Two Fossil Sciences*, New York: Philosophical Library, 1953

Hawking, Stephen W. *A Brief History of Time*, New York and London: Bantam, 1988

Helene, Corinne *Sacred Science of Numbers*, Marina del Rey, California: DeVorss, 1991

Hitchcock, Helyn *Helping Yourself With Numerology*, London: Wolfe, 1972

Hoffman, Paul *Archimedes' Revenge: The Joys and Perils of Mathematics*, New York: Fawcett Crest, 1988

Huntley, H.E. *The Divine Proportion: A Study in Mathematical Beauty*, New York: Dover, 1970

Julius, Edward H. *Rapid Math Tricks and Tips*, New York: Wiley, 1992

Karush, William *Webster's New World Dictionary of Mathematics*, New York: Seymour Publications, 1962, and Webster's New World, 1989

Macrone, Michael *Eureka! What Archimedes Really Meant*, New York: HarperCollins, 1994

McLeish, John *Number: The History of Numbers and How They Shape Our Lives*, (published in paperback as *The Story of Number*), New York: Fawcett Columbine, 1991

Menninger, K. *Number Words and Number Symbols*, Boston: MIT Press, 1969

Needham, J. *Science and Civilization in China*, Cambridge University Press, first four volumes published between 1952 and 1968

Peterson, Ivars *Islands of Truth: A Mathematical Mystery Cruise*, New York: W.H. Freeman, 1990

Schimmel, Anne-Marie *The Mystery of Numbers*, Oxford and New York: Oxford University Press, 1993

Smith, David Eugene *Number Stories of Long Ago*, London: Ginn, 1919

Wells, David *The Penguin Dictionary of Curious and Interesting Numbers*, London: Penguin, 1986

Religion, Mythology and Magic

Aldred, Cyril *Egypt to the End of the Old Kingdom*, New York, London: McGraw-Hill, Thames and Hudson 1965

anonymous ('seven pupils of E.G.') *The Mysteries of the Qabalah*, Chicago, Illinois: Yogi Publication Society, 1922

Aswynn, Freya *Leaves of Yggdrasil*, St Paul, Minnesota: Llewellyn, 1992

Cunningham, Scott *Cunningham's Encyclopedia of Crystal, Gem & Metal Magic*, St Paul, Minnesota: Llewellyn, 1988

Cunningham, Scott *Cunningham's Encyclopedia of Magical Herbs*, St Paul, Minnesota: Llewellyn, 1993

Gonzalez-Wippler, Migene *A Kabbalah for the Modern World*, New York: Bantam, 1977

Graves, Robert *The White Goddess*, London: Faber, 1948, revised 1961, and New York: Farrar, Straus and Giroux, 1966

Graves, Robert *The Greek Myths*, (two volumes), London: Penguin, 1955

Green, Miranda J. *Dictionary of Celtic Myth and Legend*, London: Thames and Hudson, 1992

Hulse, David Allen *The Key of It All*, St Paul, Minnesota: Llewellyn, 1994

King, John *The Celtic Druids' Year*, London: Blandford, 1994

LaCarriere, Jacques *The Gnostics*, New York: Dutton, 1977

Matthews, Caitlin *Mabon and the Mysteries of Britain*, London and New York: Arkana (Routledge & Kegan Paul), 1987

Matthews, John *Taliesin: Shamanism and the Bardic Mysteries in Britain and Ireland*, London: Aquarian Press, 1991

Mercatante, Anthony S. *The Facts on File Encyclopedia of World Mythology and Legend*, New York, Oxford: Facts on File, 1988

Nahm, Milton C. *Selections from Early Greek Philosophy*, New York: Appleton-Century-Crofts, 1964

Pennick, Nigel *Magical Alphabets*, York Beach, Maine: Samuel Weiser, 1993: published in the UK by Rider Books under the title *The Secret Lore of Runes and other Ancient Alphabets*

Pennick, Nigel *Practical Magic in the Northern Tradition*, Wellingborough: Aquarian Press, 1989

Pennick, Nigel *Runic Astrology*, London: Aquarian Press, 1990

Rosenberg, Donna *World Mythology: An Anthology of the Great Myths and Epics*, Lincolnwood, Illinois: National Textbook Company, 1986

Scott-Moncrieff, Philip D. *Paganism and Christianity in Egypt*, Cambridge: Cambridge University Press, 1913

Scholem, Gershom G. (ed.) *Zohar*, New York: Schocken Books, 1949

Scholem, Gershom G. *On the Kabbalah and Its Symbolism*, New York: Schocken Books, 1969

Silver, Daniel Jeremy *A History of Judaism*, (two volumes), New York: Basic Books, 1974

Suares, Carlo *The Cipher of Genesis*, Geneva and New York: Editions du Mont Blanc 1967, and Bantam 1973

Thierens, A.E. *Astrology & the Tarot*, Hollywood, California: Newcastle, 1975

Thorsson, Edred *Northern Magic: Mysteries of the Norse*, Germans and English, St Paul, Minnesota, Llewellyn, 1993

Tyson, Donald (ed.) and Freake, James (trans.) *Three Books of Occult Philosophy Written by Henry Cornelius Agrippa of Nettesheim*, St Paul, Minnesota: Llewellyn, 1993

Waite, A.E. *The Holy Kabbalah*, New York: University Books, 1960

Westcott, W. Wynn *An Introduction to the Kabbalah*, London: Neptune Press, 1910

Wilson, Colin and Grant, John *The Directory of Possibilities*, New York: Webb & Bower, 1981

General

Adams, Douglas *The Hitchhiker's Guide to the Galaxy*, Simon & Schuster, 1979

Barrett, John and Yonge, C.M. *Collins Pocket Guide to the Sea Shore*, London: Collins, 1958

Deutsch, Solomon *A New Practical Hebrew Grammar*, New York: Leypoldt & Holt, 1868

Dolan, J.R. *English Ancestral Names*, New York: Clarkson N. Potter, 1972

Dixon, R. M.W. *The Languages of Australia*, Cambridge University Press, 1980

Goodman, Linda *Sun Signs*, New York: Taplinger, 1968; New York: Bantam, 1971 and many reprints

Grieve, M. *A Modern Herbal*, New York: Harcourt, Brace & Co. 1931, Dover 1971

Lempriere, J. *A Classical Dictionary*, London: George Routledge & Sons, n.d.

Peterson, Roger Tory and McKenny, Margaret *A Field Guide to Wildflowers of Northeastern and North-central North America*, Boston: Houghton Mifflin, 1968

Rosten, Leo *The Joys of Yiddish*, London: Penguin, 1968

Russell, Bertrand *History of Western Philosophy*, London: Allen & Unwin, 1961

Ulam, Stanislaw *Adventures of a Mathematician*, New York: Scribners, 1976

INDEX

Page numbers in bold refer to illustrations.